Examining the Relationship Between the Russian Orthodox Church and Secular Authorities in the 19th and 20th Centuries

Bogdan Ershov
Voronezh State Technical University, Russia

Igor Ashmarov
Voronezh State Institute of Arts, Russia

A volume in the Advances in
Religious and Cultural Studies
(ARCS) Book Series

Published in the United States of America by
  IGI Global
  Information Science Reference (an imprint of IGI Global)
  701 E. Chocolate Avenue
  Hershey PA, USA 17033
  Tel: 717-533-8845
  Fax: 717-533-8661
  E-mail: cust@igi-global.com
  Web site: http://www.igi-global.com

Library of Congress Cataloging-in-Publication Data

Names: Ershov, Bogdan, 1982- author. | Ashmarov, Igor, 1975- author.
Title: Examining the relationship between the Russian Orthodox Church and
  secular authorities in the 19th and 20th centuries / by Bogdan
  Antolievich Ershov and Igor Anatolievich Ashmarov.
Description: Hershey, PA : Information Science Reference, [2022] | Includes
  bibliographical references and index. | Summary: "The monograph examines
  the relationship between the Russian Orthodox Church and the secular
  authorities in the provinces of the Central Black Earth region in the
  19th and early 20th centuries with special attention being paid to the
  system of spiritual education, the social and psychological
  characteristics of the clergy of the Russian Orthodox Church, and the
  tradition of Orthodox pilgrimage"-- Provided by publisher.
Identifiers: LCCN 2022012073 (print) | LCCN 2022012074 (ebook) | ISBN
  9781668449158 (hardcover) | ISBN 9781668449165 (paperback) | ISBN
  9781668449172 (ebook)
Subjects: LCSH: Russkaia︠ ︡pravoslavnaia︠ ︡tserkov′--Russia
  (Federation)--Central Chernozem Region--History--19th century. |
  Russkaia︠ ︡pravoslavnaia︠ ︡tserkov′--Russia (Federation)--Central
  Chernozem Region--History--20th century. | Church and state--Russia
  (Federation)--Central Chernozem Region--History--19th century. | Church
  and state--Russia (Federation)--Central Chernozem Region--History--20th
  century. | Central Chernozem Region (Russia)--Religious life and
  customs--History--19th century. | Central Chernozem Region
  (Russia)--Religious life and customs--History--20th century.
Classification: LCC BX494.C43 E77 2022 (print) | LCC BX494.C43 (ebook) |
  DDC 261.70947/09034--dc23/eng/20220429
LC record available at https://lccn.loc.gov/2022012073
LC ebook record available at https://lccn.loc.gov/2022012074

This book is published in the IGI Global book series Advances in Religious and Cultural Studies (ARCS) (ISSN: 2475-675X; eISSN: 2475-6768)

British Cataloguing in Publication Data
A Cataloguing in Publication record for this book is available from the British Library.

All work contributed to this book is new, previously-unpublished material.
The views expressed in this book are those of the authors, but not necessarily of the publisher.

For electronic access to this publication, please contact: eresources@igi-global.com.

Advances in Religious and Cultural Studies (ARCS) Book Series

ISSN:2475-675X
EISSN:2475-6768

Editor-in-Chief: Nancy Erbe, California State University-Dominguez Hills, USA

MISSION

In the era of globalization, the diversity of the world and various cultures becomes apparent as cross-cultural interactions turn into a daily occurrence for individuals in all professions. Understanding these differences is necessary in order to promote effective partnerships and interactions between those from different religious and cultural backgrounds.

The **Advances in Religious and Cultural Studies (ARCS)** book series brings together a collection of scholarly publications on topics pertaining to religious beliefs, culture, population studies, and sociology. Books published within this series are ideal for professionals, theorists, researchers, and students seeking the latest research on collective human behavior in terms of religion, social structure, and cultural identity and practice.

COVERAGE

- Social Stratification and Classes
- Group Behavior
- Stereotypes and Racism
- Globalization and Culture
- Sociology
- Gender
- Impact of Religion on Society
- Human Rights and Ethics
- Politics and Religion
- Cross-Cultural Interaction

IGI Global is currently accepting manuscripts for publication within this series. To submit a proposal for a volume in this series, please contact our Acquisition Editors at Acquisitions@igi-global.com or visit: http://www.igi-global.com/publish/.

Titles in this Series

For a list of additional titles in this series, please visit:
http://www.igi-global.com/book-series/advances-religious-cultural-studies/84269

Whole Person Promotion, Women, and the Post-Pandemic Era Impact and Future Outlooks
Michelle Crosby (Corvinus University, Hungary) and Julianna Faludi (Corvinus University, Hungary)
Information Science Reference • © 2022 • 300pp • H/C (ISBN: 9781668423646) • US $195.00

Evolution of Peace Leadership and Practical Implications
Erich Paul Schellhammer (International Leadership Association, Canada)
Information Science Reference • © 2022 • 382pp • H/C (ISBN: 9781799897361) • US $195.00

Impact of Women's Empowerment on SDGs in the Digital Era
Ingrid Vasiliu-Feltes (University of Miami, USA)
Information Science Reference • © 2022 • 325pp • H/C (ISBN: 9781668436370) • US $195.00

Autoethnographic Perspectives on Multilingual Life Stories
Eda Başak Hancı-Azizoglu (Mediterranean (Akdeniz) University, Turkey) Şehnaz Şahinkarakaş (Cağ University, Turkey) and Dan J. Tannacito (Indiana University of Pennsylvania, USA)
Information Science Reference • © 2022 • 335pp • H/C (ISBN: 9781668437384) • US $195.00

Women Community Leaders and Their Impact as Global Changemakers
Patricia Goodman Hayward (Northeastern University, USA) Sahar Rehman (Northeastern University, USA) and Zirui Yan (Tsinghua University, China)
Information Science Reference • © 2022 • 399pp • H/C (ISBN: 9781668424902) • US $195.00

For an entire list of titles in this series, please visit:
http://www.igi-global.com/book-series/advances-religious-cultural-studies/84269

701 East Chocolate Avenue, Hershey, PA 17033, USA
Tel: 717-533-8845 x100 • Fax: 717-533-8661
E-Mail: cust@igi-global.com • www.igi-global.com

Table of Contents

Detailed Table of Contents

Chapter 1

In this chapter, the authors examine the crisis in the relationship between the church and the authorities. The authors come to the conclusion that the strict constant control of the church by the state led to the fact that at that time the church began to advocate a change in its status. Therefore, the church ceased to be the guarantor of the stability of the autocracy. Historiography of the problem of the relationship of the Russian Orthodox Church and the state in the 19th-early 20th centuries can be divided into pre-revolutionary, Soviet, and post-Soviet periods. The importance of studying historiography is expressed in the fact that it represents the first attempt at a comprehensive review of the historiographic heritage created by Russian church historians. Proceeding from this, an attempt was made to personify the main representatives of the Russian church-historical school.

Chapter 2

It is shown that sources of research include several groups of documents from unpublished archival materials to memoirs, which only partially compensate for the ability to trace the development of state-church relations. This mainly relates to the field of church legislation, memoirs, and reference and statistical publications. At the same time, one should take into account, in general, a good knowledge of sources on the history of the orthodox church in the 19th-early 20th centuries. The peculiarities of the archival documents under study include the fact that they reflected issues of the economic life of monasteries and churches, prescriptions and orders received in monasteries, and churches from spiritual consistories.

Chapter 3

By the beginning of the 20th century, enormous changes had taken place in the state system of the Russian Empire. In addition to the emperor, the State Duma and the State Council, which included not only Orthodox people, became the supreme legislative bodies. But laws that related to the Orthodox Church, for example, on the finances of the Synod, were considered by the State Duma and the State Council. Until 1917, preparations were underway for the convocation of the Local Council. Documents related to this event are church-historical and church-legal monuments, as they show the spiritual consciousness of the episcopate, clergy, and parishioners.

Chapter 4

Spiritual awakening began in Russia in the 19th-early 20th centuries, the main meaning of which was to try to purify the spiritual image of Russia, return to the origins of Russian Orthodoxy, and comprehend the historical mission of the Russian people. Education in society was increasingly moving away from church foundations, and despite the awakening in Orthodoxy, the prejudice in society towards the clergy was already rooted historically, and overcoming the negative features of the perception of the clergy could not be overcome by a sharp jump, even with increased social activity of the clergy.

Chapter 5

The parish played a special role in the life of the peasant; he was an integral part of village life and life. The closure of the church in the village was perceived negatively, since it was believed that with the closure of the temple the village itself would disappear. All this stimulated the ardent desire of the peasants to have a temple in their village, which was most often built at the expense of peasant families and rural communities. Most of the temples and churches built in Russia in the 19th century were wooden: serfs could not afford to build a stone temple. (They were usually erected by landowners.)

Chapter 6

In the 19th-early 20th centuries, civil and church authorities, interacting with each other in the provinces of the Central Black Earth Region, had to take into account the opinions and the possibility of interference in decision-making by spiritual and secular authorities, while observing mutual interests. Deanery of the parish churches, personally appointed by the bishop from the most experienced and active clergy, and who had great oversight rights to various parties of the churches and clergy of their district, were the main business partners of the church organization with the county administration. In the county town, the deaneries were "status figures" in provincial life; they were among those "nomenclature" posts that had a great influence on decision-making in the county.

Chapter 7

Towards the end of the 19th century, Russian society began to change dramatically. Those who are only serving in the church are attracted to the clergy estate. Persons of other classes could join the ranks of the clergy if there were not enough persons of a clergy rank for the corresponding position, provided there was a leave certificate from peasant or city society. The clergy, awarded orders, acquire noble rights: the White clergy receive the hereditary nobility, and the Black clergy had the opportunity to transfer property by inheritance along with the order. Clerics compiled various kinds of statistical documents for secular and spiritual authorities and kept metric books and confessional sheets. An important characteristic of the clergy was the educational level.

Chapter 8

The process of transformation in the theological school began in the late 19th-early 20th centuries. New opportunities were opened up for the church in the field of enlightenment and missionary activity, which required the clergy to be prepared for the new realities of church life. The churching of Russian society before the revolution was due to the fact that children from an early age introduced themselves to church life and assimilated the fundamental truths of Christianity. In the 19th century, the clergy were not sufficiently educated, not all priests had a seminary education, and graduates of theological seminaries were appointed deans. It was enough for church servants to be literate.

Chapter 9

The position of the husband in the church ranks determined the legal status of a woman from the clergy, since after marriage the woman became a representative of the church department. Women from other classes, having married a priest, assumed the duties of "representative of the church department." The spouses of the archpriests and rectors of the parishes occupied the upper step in the church hierarchy, then the deacons and psalm-followers followed – they should not be confused with the priests. The rhythm of life of members of the spiritual family was different from the rhythm of the life of the parish priest, so it was very important to perform family prayers and services at home led by the father-priest.

Chapter 10

The Russian Orthodox Church before the revolution paid much attention to issues of mercy and social service in the 19th-early 20th centuries. Charity is reinforced by the charity of individuals, unions, the church, and the state through the charity of orphans, widows, poor, crippled. The concepts of morality and spirituality were rooted in the popular consciousness. The centuries-old traditions of Russian charity were being revived. The materials of the Code of Laws of the Russian Empire include reports that in imperial Russia there was a well-defined system of social assistance and public charity.

Chapter 11

The main thing in the work of charitable institutions was caring for the sick; therefore, professional medical workers were required, which was facilitated by the community of charity nurses. They contributed to the development of medical education, science, and healthcare in the Central Black Earth Region. Compassionate patients took turns caring for patients in hospitals and private homes. After 10 years of service, they received a pension, which, like the sign of compassion, remained with them until the end of their lives. High moral demands were placed on a woman who decided to devote herself to a charitable cause – to help the poor, defenseless, sick. Moral requirements were recorded in special documents – the oath, oath and instructions.

Chapter 12

The materials of the study show that the church in the 19th-early 20th centuries was an influential spiritual and moral force. The merit of the church consisted in the fact that it was actually the only institution conducting social work. In the 19th-early 20th centuries, the church was an ally of the autocracy, pursuing a pro-government policy to disseminate loyal ideas in Russian society, which was expressed in exercising control over the education system, as well as the all of public life. These scholars were of the opinion that a pilgrimage, even to a nearby monastery, is not rest and entertainment, but self-denial and bodily labor, which believers use to save the soul. The purpose of the pilgrims was not a cognitive goal (i.e., receiving information) although during the pilgrimage they acquired new knowledge.

Chapter 13

The practical life of monks has shown that their economic activity has a corrupting effect on the inner side of their lives. Only a few monasteries succeeded in organically incorporating agricultural and commercial activities into the routine of monastic life. The Orthodox Church in Russia owned three million hectares of land as property. A sign of the state's respect for millions of believing citizens and real material support for the Church was the transfer of land to the ownership of the temple. The land issue had a huge impact on the life of all the people of Russia and on its economy. In Russia, and in other countries of the world that are going through a time of change, the land issue is very important.

Chapter 14

In the provinces there were changes in the mentality and lifestyle of broad sections of society, which occurred under the influence of the "great reforms" and industrialization in Russia. The spread of education and the liberalization of social life created the conditions for spiritual emancipation and the destruction of traditional isolation, the spread of otkhodnichestvo, and the emergence of factories, and factories contributed to the spread of new religious ideas. Missionary work in the Russian Orthodox Church was internal and external: the internal carried out work directed against schismatics and sectarians, and the external was oriented towards foreigners inside Russia and outside it.

Chapter 15

In the 19th century, the financial position of the parish clergy in the countryside was not much higher than that of wealthy peasants, and in the city, it was comparable to the position of the lower part of the bureaucracy and the bulk of the townspeople (with the exception of the clergy of cathedrals and, of course, the court clergy). At this time, the practice (not formally legalized by any civil code or church canon) of the actual inheritance of church parishes was established, when the diocesan bishop, when the parish priest retired, secured, at the request of the latter, a place for his son or son-in-law.

Preface

The monograph examines the relationship between the Russian Orthodox Church and the secular authorities in the provinces of the Central Black Earth region in the 19th and early 20th centuries. Special attention is paid to the system of spiritual education, the social and psychological characteristics of the clergy of the Russian Orthodox Church, the tradition of Orthodox pilgrimage. The materials of the monograph can be used by professors to broaden their horizons on the history of the Russian Church. In modern Russia, the question is raised about the revival of the spirituality of the population, which increases interest in studying the history of the Church. In the pre-revolutionary period, the Orthodox Church in the Russian Empire had a significant impact on the formation of a national culture and statehood. Actively cooperating with the state, the Orthodox Church has accumulated vast experience in the field of education, missionary work, charity; this experience in today's Russia can be used to solve the most important tasks in moral education of young people who will contribute to the future of Russia.

The monograph from a conceptual point of view explores the key areas of charitable and educational activities of the Orthodox Church during the period of religious transformation in the XIX - early XX centuries. It was a time when the number of categories of miserable people («prizrevaemye») increased, the scale of assistance and the responsibilities of charitable organizations; control over the distribution of aid has improved, the role of the Church in the social protection of the population has increased. The monograph contributes to historical science in that it shows a complete picture of the activities of the Church to ensure the educational process in the parochial schools of the Central Black Earth region in the period under study. It is revealed that the specificity of the activity of the clergy, which was impossible without a proper level of education, put the clergy into the most competent category of the population. The clergy in the absence of a developed education system in Russia began to implement the initial public education. This work through historical perspectives helps to understand and comprehend the spiritual, moral and cultural heritage of Russia. The topic being researched is of particular importance, since this topic is regional in nature, which makes it possible to understand the general and the particular in the relationship between the institutions of the church and the state in Russia.

The book is intended for university professors, politicians, scientists interested in the history of the Russian Church in the XIX - XX centuries.

ORGANIZATION OF THE BOOK

In Chapter 1, "Historiography of the Problem," the authors examine the crisis in the relationship between the Church and the authorities. The authors come to the conclusion that the strict constant control of the church by the state led to the fact that at that time the church began to advocate a change in its status. Therefore, the Church ceased to be the guarantor of the stability of the autocracy. Historiography of the problem of the relationship of the Russian Orthodox Church and the state in the XIX - early XX centuries can be divided into pre-revolutionary, Soviet and post-Soviet periods. The importance of studying historiography is expressed in the fact that it represents the first attempt at a comprehensive review of the historiographic heritage created by Russian church historians. Proceeding from this, an attempt was made to personify the main representatives of the Russian church-historical school.

In Chapter 2, "Sources of the Study," it is shown that sources of research include several groups of documents from unpublished archival materials to memoirs, which only partially compensate for the ability to trace the development of state-church relations. This mainly relates to the field of church legislation, memoirs and reference and statistical publications. At the same time, one should take into account, in general, a good knowledge of sources on the history of the Orthodox Church in the 19th - early 20th centuries. The peculiarities of the archival documents under study include the fact that they reflected issues of the economic life of monasteries and churches, prescriptions and orders received in monasteries and churches from spiritual consistories.

Chapter 3 is "State and Legal Regulation of the Church's Activities." By the beginning of the 20th century, enormous changes had taken place in the state system of the Russian Empire. In addition to the emperor, the State Duma and the State Council, which included not only Orthodox people, became the supreme legislative bodies. But laws that related to the Orthodox

Church, for example, on the finances of the Synod, were considered by the State Duma and the State Council. Until 1917, preparations were underway for the convocation of the Local Council. Documents related to this event are church-historical and church-legal monuments, as they show the spiritual consciousness of the episcopate, clergy and parishioners.

Chapter 4 is "The Church as a Social and Spiritual Institution of Society." Spiritual awakening began in Russia in the 19th - early 20th centuries, the main meaning of which was to try to purify the spiritual image of Russia, return to the origins of Russian Orthodoxy, and comprehend the historical mission of the Russian people. Education in society was increasingly moving away from church foundations, and despite the awakening in Orthodoxy, the prejudice in society towards the clergy was already rooted historically, and overcoming the negative features of the perception of the clergy could not be overcome by a sharp jump, even with increased social activity of the clergy.

Chapter 5 is "The Role of the Church in the Life of Noblemen and Peasants." The parish played a special role in the life of the peasant; he was an integral part of village life and life. The closure of the church in the village was perceived negatively, since it was believed that with the closure of the temple the village itself would disappear. All this stimulated the ardent desire of the peasants to have a temple in their village, which was most often built at the expense of peasant families and rural communities. Most of the temples and churches built in Russia in the 19th century were wooden: serfs could not afford to build a stone temple (they were usually erected more often by landowners).

Chapter 6 is "Church and Secular Authority." In the XIX - early XX centuries civil and church authorities, interacting with each other in the provinces of the Central Black Earth Region, had to take into account the opinions and the possibility of interference in decision-making by spiritual and secular authorities, while observing mutual interests. Deanery of the parish churches, personally appointed by the bishop from the most experienced and active clergy, and who had great oversight rights to various parties of the Churches and clergy of their district, were the main business partners of the church organization with the county administration. In the county town, the deaneries were "status figures" in provincial life, they were among those "nomenclature" posts that had a great influence on decision-making in the county.

Chapter 7 is "White and Black Clergy." Towards the end of the 19th century, Russian society is beginning to change dramatically. Those who are only serving in the Church are attracted to the clergy estate. Persons of other classes could join the ranks of the clergy if there were not enough persons of a clergy rank for the corresponding position, provided there was a leave certificate from peasant or city society. The clergy, awarded orders, acquire noble rights: the white clergy receive the hereditary nobility, and the black clergy had the opportunity to transfer property by inheritance along with the order. Clerics compiled various kinds of statistical documents for secular and spiritual authorities, kept metric books and confessional sheets. An important characteristic of the clergy was the educational level.

Chapter 8 is "The System of Spiritual Education." The process of transformation in the theological school began in the late XIX - early XX centuries. New opportunities were opened up for the Church in the field of enlightenment and missionary activity, which required the clergy to be prepared for the new realities of church life. The churching of Russian society before the revolution was due to the fact that children from an early age introduced themselves to church life and assimilated the fundamental truths of Christianity. In the XIX century, the clergy were not sufficiently educated, not all priests had a seminary education, graduates of theological seminaries were appointed deans. It was enough for church servants to be literate.

Chapter 9 is "Family Basics of the Life of Clerics." The position of the husband in the church ranks determined the legal status of a woman from the clergy, since after marriage the woman became a representative of the church department. Women from other classes, having married a priest, assumed the duties of "representative of the church department". The spouses of the archpriests and rectors of the parishes occupied the upper step in the church hierarchy, then the deacons and psalm-followers followed - they should not be confused with the priests. The rhythm of life of members of the spiritual family was different from the rhythm of the life of the parish priest, so it was very important to perform family prayers and services at home, led by the father-priest.

Chapter 10 is "Church Charities and Institutions." So, the Russian Orthodox Church before the revolution paid much attention to issues of mercy and social service. In the XIX - early XX centuries. charity is reinforced by the charity of individuals, unions, the church and the state through the charity of orphans, widows, poor, crippled. The concepts of morality and spirituality were rooted in the popular consciousness. The centuries-old traditions of Russian charity were being revived. The materials of the Code of Laws of the Russian Empire include reports that in imperial Russia there was a well-defined system of social assistance and public charity.

Chapter 11 is "Communities of the Sisters of Mercy and the Orthodox Church." The main thing in the work of charitable institutions was caring for the sick; therefore, professional medical workers were required, which was facilitated by the community of charity nurses. They contributed to the development of medical education, science and healthcare in the Central Black Earth Region. Compassionate patients took turns caring for patients in hospitals and private homes. After ten years of service, they received a pension, which, like the sign of compassion, remained with them until the end of their lives. High moral demands were placed on a woman who decided to devote herself to a charitable cause - to help the poor, defenseless, sick. Moral requirements were recorded in special documents - the oath, oath and instructions.

Chapter 12 is "Folk Tradition of Orthodox Pilgrimage in the Sphere of Relations Between the Church and the State." The materials of our study show that the Church in the XIX - early XX centuries was an influential spiritual and moral force. The merit of the Church consisted in the fact that it was actually the only institution conducting social work. In the XIX - early XX centuries. The church was an ally of the autocracy, pursuing a pro-government policy to disseminate loyal ideas in Russian society, which was expressed in exercising control over the education system, as well as the entire public life. These scholars were of the opinion that a pilgrimage, even to a nearby monastery, is not rest and entertainment, but self-denial and bodily labor, which believers went to save the soul. The purpose of the pilgrims was not a cognitive goal, i.e. receiving information, although during the pilgrimage they acquired new knowledge.

Chapter 13 is "Church Land Tenure and Land Use." The practical life of monks has shown that their economic activity has a corrupting effect on the inner side of their lives. Only a few monasteries succeeded in organically incorporating agricultural and commercial activities into the routine of monastic life. The Orthodox Church in Russia owned 3 million hectares of land as property. A sign of the state's respect for millions of believing citizens and real material support for the Church was the transfer of land to the ownership of the temple. The land issue had a huge impact on the life of all the people of Russia and on its economy. In Russia, and in other countries of the world that are going through a time of change, the land issue is very important.

Chapter 14 is "Missionary Activity of the Church." In the provinces there were changes in the mentality and lifestyle of broad sections of society, which occurred under the influence of the "great reforms" and industrialization in Russia. The spread of education and the liberalization of social life created the conditions for spiritual emancipation ("emancipation"), and the destruction of traditional isolation, the spread of otkhodnichestvo, the emergence of factories and factories contributed to the spread of new religious ideas. Missionary work in the Russian Orthodox Church was internal and external: the internal carried out work directed against schismatics and sectarians; and the external was oriented towards foreigners inside Russia and outside it.

Chapter 15 is "Orthodox Posts in the Life of the Russian Province." In the XIX centuries the financial position of the parish clergy in the countryside was not much higher than that of wealthy peasants, and in the city it was comparable to the position of the lower part of the bureaucracy and the bulk of the townspeople (with the exception of the clergy of cathedrals and, of course, the court clergy). At this time, the practice (not formally legalized by any civil code or church canon) of the actual inheritance of church parishes was established, when the diocesan bishop, when the parish priest retired, secured, at the request of the latter, a place for his son or son-in-law.

Bogdan Ershov
Voronezh State Technical University, Russia

Igor Ashmarov
Voronezh State Institute of Arts, Russia

Chapter 1
Historiography of the Problem

ABSTRACT

In this chapter, the authors examine the crisis in the relationship between the church and the authorities. The authors come to the conclusion that the strict constant control of the church by the state led to the fact that at that time the church began to advocate a change in its status. Therefore, the church ceased to be the guarantor of the stability of the autocracy. Historiography of the problem of the relationship of the Russian Orthodox Church and the state in the 19th-early 20th centuries can be divided into pre-revolutionary, Soviet, and post-Soviet periods. The importance of studying historiography is expressed in the fact that it represents the first attempt at a comprehensive review of the historiographic heritage created by Russian church historians. Proceeding from this, an attempt was made to personify the main representatives of the Russian church-historical school.

INTRODUCTION

Based on the experience of all previous historiography on the topic, the contribution of Russian church historians to the development of national history and Russian historical thought was revealed, and the conceptual features of the construction of historical presentation in church historical works were shown. Given the fact that the development of historical thought in Russia was unthinkable without an analysis of the ideological influence of Orthodoxy, the conceptual relationships between secular and ecclesiastical historical science are revealed. A gap has been filled in the historiographical heritage,

DOI: 10.4018/978-1-6684-4915-8.ch001

which considered the scientific activity of church historians either with a high degree of tendentiousness or casually, characterizing their contribution not so much to church history as to Orthodox theology. The result of this was distrust of the scientific competence of these historians and, as a result, ignoring the research potential left by the Russian church history school, caused by ideological differences in views on history.

In the pre-revolutionary period, secular and church historians carried out considerable work on the collection of materials and their publication. These materials had the character of reference data and historical essays. The content of some of them is still relevant today. In their studies, scientists spoke about the difficulties of the parish clergy and tried to draw public attention to it. As a result of an extensive array of documents, the dissertation shows that from 1901 until the beginning of the February Revolution, representatives of the highest hierarchy of the Orthodox Russian Church carried out activities aimed at limiting the participation of the emperor in church administration and at "distance" of the church from the state. This is confirmed, in particular, by the reduction in February 1901 of the "loyal" part of the oath for the ordained bishop, the abolition of the oath for members of the Holy Synod, and the reduction in the commemoration of the emperor at the proskomedia since 1913. The desire of the hierarchy to limit the participation of the emperor in church administration is evidenced by and "reviews" of diocesan bishops (in 1905-1906) on church reform.

They reflected the dissatisfaction of representatives of the highest hierarchy with the relations between church and state that had developed in Russia. This, as well as the desire to restore patriarchal administration in the ROC, was also mentioned in the materials of the Pre-Council Presence (1906), as well as the Pre-Council Meeting (1912-1913). The aforementioned church commissions proposed to strengthen the sovereignty of the episcopate in the administration of the Russian Orthodox Church.

Historian P.V. Znamensky in his dissertation considered the position of the clergy in the XIX century. He analyzed the legislation on the Church and assigned a large role to state measures regarding the clergy. P.V. Znamensky mainly studied materials on the central and southern dioceses.

Of the pre-revolutionary researchers, the historian D.I. Rostislavov, who considered in his works the difficult financial situation of the clergy, he was one of the first to pay attention to the incomes of the clergy and their economic activities. He paid considerable attention to the monastic economy. In 1876, the D.I. Rostislavov's work, which presents statistics on 290 monasteries.

V.V. Mirotvorcev dedicated his work to the problems of the white clergy. It is noteworthy that the author tried to protect the moral condition of the clergy in the eyes of society. He spoke of the need to transfer the bureaucrats to the state salary.

In the pre-revolutionary period, a lot of literature on the history of church law was published.

Among these works, the study of I.G. Aivazov on the activities of the department of the Orthodox faith during the reign of Emperor Alexander III and church-civil rulings. These works contain information on the property rights of clergymen and their rights to use land.

In the last quarter of the XIX century, works appeared on the history of church charity. A unique publication was a collection in seven volumes, edited by I.Ye. Andrievsky and P.P. Semenov from 1880 to 1886. The collection contains information on church charity in various dioceses, and also presents statistics on charity. This is the most complete description of charitable activities from 1855 to 1880. It may be noted V.M. Benzin's article, which is dedicated to the participation of the church and priests in charity processes. Considering philanthropy at church parishes, the author gives a rather extensive factual material. The main field of his research was the charitable activities of brotherhoods, almshouses and parish trusteeships at churches. He also gave examples and examined in detail the sources of financial and other funds involved in church philanthropy.

One of the major historians who paid attention to church charity was V.O. Klyuchevsky. In his opinion, church charity was not only an auxiliary means of social well-being, but also a necessary condition for one's own moral health. At the beginning of the 20th century, scientists were interested in the history of the emergence of Orthodox parishes. A.A. Papkov in his work showed the continuity of Orthodox parishes from the XVI century to the second half of the XIX century, and at the same time, he drew attention to the need for their religious and educational work.

These authors had similar views on the problem of parochial charity. In the face of growing poverty, this task required special attention from the government and the public. With proper organization, the parish could become a structural unit of the public charity system. Regarding the independence of the parishes, the opinions of the authors differed.

In the 1880-1890s teachers of the Voronezh Theological Seminary N.I. Polikarpov (1871–1934) and S.E. Zverev (1860-1920). N. I. Polikarpov worked on biographies of bishops. S.E. Zverev studied the history of the Church and monasteries. To cover the issues under discussion, he used ancient acts that were stored in Voronezh, as well as in other cities. One can name the publications of the Voronezh local historian, publicist, teacher, historian Pavel Vasilievich Nikolsky. In his work, he revealed the methods and content of training in a theological seminary, gave information about the teachers, inspectors and rectors of this seminary. In the "Voronezh diocesan sheets" P.V. Nikolsky showed the life of the seminary at the end of the XIX century.

In 1910 P.V. Nikolsky was elected to the post of chairman of the Voronezh Church Historical and Archaeological Committee, where his research work was concentrated. He was the editor of the annual Voronezh Antiquities (1907–1912), where he published articles on the history of some monasteries and on monasticism on the Don. P.V. Nikolsky compiled a reference book for the clergy of the Voronezh diocese for 1900, which provided information on 1,060 churches of the diocese, their parishes and clergy. He also owns works on the needs of diocesan life (Voronezh, 1901), on the Assumption Divnogorsky monastery (Uspenskiy Divnogorskiy monastyr'), historical essays on Russian theology (Anderson, 2001).

Among the pre-revolutionary Voronezh researchers of the Church, Dmitry Ivanovich Sambikin stands out. In 1882, he published an article in the Voronezh Diocesan Vedomosti about the history of the Assumption Church, which is one of the oldest churches in the city of Voronezh.

Dmitry Ivanovich Sambikin collected materials about the churches of the Voronezh diocese since 1881. As a result, he summarized data on 950 monasteries, parish, cemetery and house temples in the Voronezh province. In the Voronezh Diocesan Vedomosti, village priests published articles with historical descriptions of the parishes on the initiative of D.I. Sambikin.

Archbishop D.I. Sambikin wrote many articles, essays, brochures, books. For his merits and scientific works, Archbishop D.I. Sambikin was awarded the degree of Doctor of Church History in 1904. Among his works, a special place is occupied by «Mesyatseslov». Professor A.A. Tsarevsky spoke of the important practical significance of the «Mesyatseslov», where information was collected about the saints of the Orthodox Church.

The local historian of the history of the Church of the Central Black Earth Region was Tikhon Mitrofanovich Oleinikov. In 1910, he served as clerk in the Voronezh Church Historical and Archaeological Committee, and in 1913 was appointed its chairman. Under his editorship, three issues of Voronezh Antiquity were issued. He published descriptions of one of the churches of the settlement of Rossosh and the Valuy Uspensky monastery.

The works of P.I. Zlatoverkhovnikov and A.A. Tankov, the Kursk historians of the late XIX - early XX centuries are also interesting. N.I. Zlatoverkhovnikov in his work covered the history of the charity of the Kursk monasteries in medical care for the poor. Important information is also available in the publications of A.A. Tankov, which refers to spiritual enlightenment and education in the Kursk province.

A.M. Vanchakov gave in his study a thorough review of the history of the development of the parish school in the XIX - early XX centuries. He considered the parish school from the standpoint of its efficiency and the right to independent existence. A.M. Vanchakov covered the assistance of the government, private individuals and various public organizations to church-school affairs. The materials of the statistical department of the Synod cited by him allow us to present a true picture of the interaction between the Orthodox Church and secular authorities in the field of education.

In 1887, in the Tambov province, a local historian I.I. Dubasov published essays on the history of the Tambov Territory. They examined the history of the Orthodox Church in the Tambov province. The author sanctified the life of clergy, in particular, the clergy of the first half of the XIX century, Jonah, Theophilus and others.

I.I. Dubasov wrote that the Church played a significant role in the daily life of the population. He was worried about the pastoral activities of rural clergymen, who, due to their illiteracy, could not significantly influence the parishioners. In addition, the local historian noted that they practically did not differ from the peasants. One can single out studies on the history of spiritual female education in the Tambov province. These materials, published by V. Lebedev, show the goals of the establishment of spiritual women's education and consider the draft charter of the Tambov school of girls of spiritual rank.

So, in the XIX - early XX centuries in the provinces of the Central Chernozem region, literature on the history of the church stood out. Local printing houses published little books on the history of the church, and in the printing houses of St. Petersburg and Moscow doctrinal works were published in large numbers. The works of historians performed spiritual and educational functions (Zlatoverkhovnikov, 1902).

Thus, in the pre-revolutionary period, the majority of scientific works were dominated by archival material, problems were identified for future research (Klyuchevsky, 1908).

In the Soviet period, little work was published on the history of the Russian Orthodox Church. The study of religion and the Church was ideological. The clergy was represented by the exploiter of the people. In literature devoted to the history of the Church in the Soviet period, bias prevailed, the pathos of conviction prevailed, and facts were often distorted. Despite the prevalence of journalism, bias in evaluating church activity, scientific methods based on historical material are gradually beginning to penetrate.

In the 1920s the first generalizing studies on the history of the church were published, which highlighted some aspects of its activities in Soviet Russia. More unbiased was the work of B.V. Titlinov — "Church during the revolution." In general, the author impartially examined the state of affairs of the Russian Orthodox Church, noting that the diocesan authorities cared little for her moral duties during the monarchical period, being essentially one of the structures of the power system, which resulted in the negative attitude of the clergy to the religious policy of the state. The work of B.P. Candidov — "Church and 1905", in which the author cited significant source material, which made it possible to identify the connection between the tsarist regime and the Orthodox clergy. According to B.P. Candidov, in general, the activity of the church was of a counter-revolutionary nature, most of the priests persistently supported the autocracy. The work "Church and 1905" carried a vivid political subtext.

The fundamental work of the Soviet historian V.I. Pisarev gives an unbiased assessment of the activities of the Orthodox Church in the Russian state. The author made conclusions about the crisis of the Church, about the increasing interference of the Church in state affairs, about the growth of the material well-being of the clergy. V.I. Pisarev examined the reforms of the 1860s, which made it possible to remove estate restrictions in the formation of the clergy and change the professional training of clergy.

Professor A.V. Kartashov in his book gives a not so pessimistic assessment of the synodal period of the Russian Church. The author explains that in the 19th century religious and secular philosophers took part in the educational and theological activities of the Russian Church (Khomyakov, the Aksakov brothers, Vladimir Soloviev, the Trubetskoy brothers). N.M. Nikolsky in his work "History of the Russian Church" on a large historical material tried to show the social role of the Church. His book contains a lot of factual material on the history of the Russian Orthodox Church. Therefore, his research is relevant to this day, as the author carefully studied the events, as a result of which this book can be used as a reference. N.M. Nikolsky spoke about the relationship of the Church and human activities. The author emphasized that the causes of the crisis of the Church were related to its economic situation.

It should also be noted the study of S.L. Frank, in which the scientist tried to apply a sociological approach to the study of the history of church reforms, the history of the Russian Church, and social mobility in the clerical class. S.L. Frank revealed the low material position of the clergy. Noteworthy is the author's conclusion that reforms led to the Church's crisis, which entailed a hostile attitude of the clergy towards the state. However, the author claims that there were many complaints against the clergy, as clergymen did not carry out their official duties so diligently.

In Soviet historiography, the work of N.S. Gordienko, in which he argued that the union of the Church and the state was not voluntary, and the state put pressure on this union. He identified three groups of clergymen, between whom there were strong contradictions: priests, high hierarchs, and church officials. In terms of income, clergymen were closer to the middle peasantry. N.S. Gordienko also subdivided the urban and rural clergy according to their material situation.

However, a more objective approach to the history of the Russian Church begins in the 1960s. In 1969, a monograph by E.F. Grekulov. In his work, E.F. Grekulov emphasized the inextricable connection of the Church with the autocracy and considered the Church as the main conductor of state policy. Historian S.S. Dmitriev was also occupied with the problem of church-state relations. At the same time, he noted that the Church in Tsarist Russia was subordinate to the State.

Soviet historians paid great attention to the study of the problems of the Russian Church. They analyzed the confrontation between the state and the Church, the clergy and church hierarchs. However, the lives of ordinary clergymen, their way of life, experiences, and thoughts were out of sight of scientists.

In the modern period, research topics related to the study of the history of the Russian Orthodox Church have expanded significantly. Scientists have become more interested in the daily life of clergy. Recently, new works have appeared on the history of the Orthodox Church, which is of great importance for the present study.

V.A. Fedorov in his book examined the main points of the history of the Russian Church of the XIX century, highlighted the policy of Russian emperors. M.A. Babkin and S.L. Firsov the main problem of the Church in the late XIX - early XX centuries. considered its nationalization. In their opinion, the authorities used the Church to restore their authority, and in the eyes of the people the Church itself was associated with the ruling regime.

Most modern scholars objectively approach the study of the history of the Orthodox Church. B.N. Mironov published the monograph "The Social History of Russia of the Period of the Empire", in which he examines the formation and development of the clergy in Russia. He believes that the spiritual estate in Russia is quite independent in the state system. B.N. Mironov reveals how the clergy from the estate was transformed into a professional group.

L.A. Andreeva in her monograph analyzes the relationship of religion and power in Russia. She believes that in the second half of the XIX - early XX centuries the state used the Orthodox Church as an instrument of ideological support for its power. This, according to L.A. Andreeva, and was the main problem of the Orthodox Church. At this time, the rights of the Church were declining, and responsibilities were increasing. The church was not able to solve its internal problems, as the dictates of the state intensified, which led to the decomposition of the clergy. The first work on the history of church procedural law is the monograph by E.V. Belyakova, where the author reflected the contradictions between secular and church norms. In his article D.V. Pospelovsky examined the relationship between the Orthodox Church and the state at various stages of their coexistence. He believed that "thanks to the new spirit of the time, the Church gained freedom".

S.I. Alekseeva in her writings analyzed the history of Russian church administration. Until 1917, it reduced the entire church history to the crisis of the Synod, and did not cover other important problems of church life. Further study is needed of the emperor's influence on the affairs of the Church.

S.V. Rimskiy dealt with the history of the church. He systematized little-known historical sources. S.V. Rimskiy was the first scholar to propose the term "church reform" in relation to the changes of the 1860–1870s and put these transformations on a par with other reforms of Alexander II.

In recent decades, works began to appear on the church reforms of the second half of the 19th century. Among them should be called a monograph by A.Yu. Polunov, which analyzed the changes in the position of the church that are associated with the activities of the Chief Prosecutor of the Synod K.P. Pobedonostsev. According to the scientist, these changes were, in essence, a revision of the paramount transformations of the 1860-1870s. The author believes that it was practically impossible to really raise the role of the Church and stabilize its relations with other faiths in an authoritarian-bureaucratic system. A.Yu. Polunov rightly believes that the contradictory and incomplete transformations in the Church led to a decline in the authority of the clergy and a decrease in its social activity (Vargunin, 1897).

In the post-Soviet period, historians are interested in the charitable activities of the Church. Volgograd historian V.G. Bobrovnikov writes about the versatility of church charity. He believes that the charitable activities of the Church extended to the whole of society. G.N. Ulyanova wrote in her work that parish trusteeships were structural units of charity in the Russian Empire.

In the P.N. Zyryanov's monograph and in a collective monograph edited by N.V. Spitsina Russian monasteries and monasticism in Russia in the 19th - early 20th centuries were studied. These works show the life of Orthodox monasteries, their economic activities, as well as methods and forms of land use.

In a collective monograph edited by Kh.V. Poplavskaya and O.V. Kirichenko, as well as in the monograph by T.A. Listova, examines the relationship between the clergy and the peasantry in the post-reform period. The authors talk about the spiritual evolution of the peasantry and assign a large role to this clergy. The influence of the clergy on the development of the peasant economy is also shown. T.G. Leontieva in her monograph considers the life and work of women of the clergy, the intrafamily relationships of a simple priest, his everyday life. The author deeply analyzed the economic activity of the parish clergy.

Famous Voronezh historian A.N. Akinshin investigated certain aspects of the Church's activity in the provinces of the Central Black Earth Region. In the book "Temples of Voronezh" he presents historical information about all the churches of the city of Voronezh and its suburbs. A.N. Akinshin also gives information about new and under construction churches. In 2003, A.N. Akinshin published an article in which he examined how the modern Russian Orthodox Church is developing.

In 2003, the book "Voronezh Archpastors" was published, edited by Metropolitan Methodius of Voronezh and Lipetsk (Nemtsov), dedicated to the memory of St. Mitrofan, the first Voronezh bishop, and St. Anthony Smirnitsky, archbishop of Voronezh and Zadonsky. In this work, the life of St. Mitrofan is described, an analysis of the miracles that took place, which made it possible to carry out canonization. O.D. Popova in her article considers the participation of the Kursk clergy in educational activities.

The history of the Kursk monasteries was devoted to the study of the Glinskaya pustyn' of Archimandrite Ioann Maslov. Schiarchimandrite Ioann Maslov described the history of the Glinskaya pustyn' from its foundation to the present, showed its significance in the history of the Russian Church. In his study, the Glinskaya pustyn' is defined as the center of spiritual enlightenment. The book is based on a large archival material, on documents of the Russian State Historical Archive (RGIA, 1900).

The history of the Glinskaya pustyn' in the XIX - early XX centuries described in one of the sections of the book. The abbots of the monastery, Archimandrite Innocent (in 1862-1888) and Scheiarchimandrite Ioannicius in 1888-1912, were distinguished by mercy and charity. The whole monastic brethren were engaged in charitable activities in enlightenment, education, and the spiritual and moral sphere.

S.N. Emelyanov's research allows revealing the position of the Orthodox Church in the Central Black Earth Region in 1917-1922. S.N. Emelyanov writes that the Orthodox Church during the revolution of 1917 was in a crisis. The dominance of administrative methods in the leadership of the church over clergy and the lack of connection with the lower echelons of the church apparatus - parishes, increased disunity between clergy and the episcopate, which ultimately led to a decrease in the activity of the parish life and helped to lower the cultural and intellectual level of the clergy.

Here you can also note the work of S.S. Zhirov in which the author examined the history of the development of monasticism and monasteries of the Russian Orthodox Church in the second half of the 19th century. This researcher came to the conclusion that monasticism did not solve most of the questions that arose before him. Despite external successes (growth of material well-being, increase in the number of monasteries and the number of their inhabitants), the monasticism of most Russian monasteries of this period was in a spiritual crisis. Many aspects of the life of the monasteries did not meet the requirements that were imposed on them by the post-reform Russian society.

E.V. Zavyalova's research contains valuable information on the history of the Orthodox canonization of Russians at the beginning of the 20th century. She notes that over the centuries the institute of canonization of saints developed gradually, taking in the names of the famous ascetics of the Russian Church, namely Theodosius of the Caves, Alexander Nevsky and many others. This process culminated at the beginning of the 20th century, when saints were honored: Anna Kashinskaya (1909), Joasaph Belgorodsky (1911), Seraphim of Sarov (1903) and Pitirim Tambovsky (1914). This process was aimed at strengthening the spiritual feelings of believers and the influence of the Church in the social sphere and state affairs. T.N. Artsybasheva made a significant contribution to the history of the development of the monastic culture of the Kursk province. In her studies, she analyzes not only the specifics of the formation of monastic culture in the Kursk province, but also the various factors of its formation. According to the author, monastic culture was a significant component of the spiritual and social prevalence of the Orthodox faith throughout the region. T.N. Artsybasheva considers the history of monasteries not only as educational and spiritual centers, but also as special economic structures, which were a complex functional organism that combines several areas of church activity.

The educational and charitable activities of the Kursk Region Church are covered in a 10-volume work, which was edited by V.I. Zhukov, B.D. Bespartochnyy, M.D. Cherkashin, V.L. Yurkovetsky. This publication is important scientifically, since it examines the functioning and emergence of theological schools, Orthodox monasteries and their role in the development of public education. A.Yu. Drugovskaya and L.S. Gatilova reveal various aspects of the moral and charitable activities of the church in the Kursk province in the XIX - early XX centuries. They write about the various areas of charity of local churches and monasteries. Kursk historian Yu.A. Bugrov in his work "History of the Kursk diocese" describes the state of Orthodoxy in the Kursk province in the late XIX - early XX centuries. He paid special attention to the study of the life and life of priests from ancient times to the end of the 20th century. A.Yu. Bunin's research helped uncover the activities of the Orthodox clergy of the Kursk Territory at the beginning of the 20th century. In his work, the author emphasized that the Kursk priests in 1905-1916, thanks to the policy of the Russian state, aimed at strengthening the principles of tolerance. The Kursk priests intensified cultural, educational, social and missionary activities, which were aimed at preserving the Orthodox identity of the state-forming Russian nation. In 2005, historians of Belgorod State University published a monograph on the development of the estate society of the Central Black Earth Region in the post-reform period. V.S. Kulabukhov in one of the chapters of this monograph examined the issue of the evolution of the social status of the Orthodox clergy in the post-reform period. This work is one of the most important studies on the history of the modernization of the clergy in the post-reform period in the provinces of the Central Black Earth Region. The author studied such problems as the placement of the Orthodox clergy in the territory of the Kursk province: its size, charity, estate-corporate activity and the level of education (Titlinov, 1924).

V.V. Reutov's research made it possible to uncover the social ministry of the Orthodox Church in the Kursk diocese in the 20th century. It is shown in the work that the Church tried to provide the society and the population with the necessary assistance in all spheres of life in the difficult conditions of life of the people that were caused by revolutions, the construction of a new society and its restructuring, wars.

Studies on the relationship between the Orthodox Church and the Old Believers are also very important for history of the Church.

O.A. Pavlova's research allowed us to draw parallels related to the history of the emergence of Old Believers in the Oryol province, and to find the specifics of the development of Old Believer communities in the studied province.

A.V. Apanasenok's research in which the history of the relationship between the Old Believer communities and the Orthodox Church is studied should be especially noted. In this work, the author concludes that despite opposing himself to the Church and defending the status of the bearer of the "true faith", the Old Believers turned out to be actually a useful form of religion. The fact of the existence of Old Belief and the successful struggle against it by the Orthodox Church forced it to maintain religious activity in parishes at the appropriate level, to cultivate oneself, to work more actively with the laity. The Znamensky readings are held annually in Kursk, which are devoted to pressing issues of interaction between government agencies, society and the Church. Representatives of the authorities positively assess the work of the Znamensky readings as a successful experience in solving pressing problems of a spiritual and moral nature. Studies in the Tambov province on the socio-demographic situation of women from the clergy are also of interest. These aspects are reflected in the work of V.L. Dyachkov, A.N. Ul'yev. The authors examine the role of women in the marriage and family relations of the clergy. L.F. Chigrinskaya in her article studies the reasons for overcoming the estate in the Orthodox clergy. She analyzes the numerical and social composition of women's monasteries and determines the demography of the clergy of the Tambov diocese. Foreign works include the works of many learned historians. For example, I.K. Smolich in his studies describes the entire synodal period of the Orthodox Church, shows the connection of church history with cultural history in Tsarist Russia. He drew attention to the fact that the state influenced the affairs of the Church, he argued that the parish priest depended on secular and ecclesiastical authorities. The scientist studied the trends that affect the number of clergymen: the departure of students of seminaries in secular educational institutions, the low material position of the clergy, the unpopularity of the profession of a priest. I.K. Smolich carefully analyzed church and civil law. The scientific work of the German researcher Julia Oswalt is dedicated to the revival of church parish life. She writes that the Russian clergy was restrained by secular bureaucracy, which was afraid of clergy activity on public grounds. The scientific works of the American historian John Shelton Curtiss - «Church and State in Russia», «Russian Church and the Soviet State, 1917–1950» — provide an objective assessment of the position of the Church. The author examines the role of the clergy in the 1905 revolution and concludes that the pro-monarchical position of the

Church leadership caused the exclusion of not only parishioners, but also a large number of lower clergy, with both radical and liberal moods among the clergy. The repressive policies of the Synod and the autocracy prevented expressing these sentiments. The historian John Shelton Curtiss was the first foreign scholar who tried to study the problems of the Russian Church and to reveal the currents in it. However, the limited sources did not allow the author to support his conclusions more clearly. Among foreign studies, the work of A. Schmemann deserves attention. The author analyzes the history of the Russian Orthodox Church in the synodal period. A. Schmemann wrote that the Church has become essentially a state institution. According to the researcher, in the synodal period in church life there was a revival of patronage of arts. In the article by G.L. Frieze reveals the history of the interaction of the Church and the state at the beginning of the 20th century (Kartashov, 1959). The author considers the crisis in relations between the Church and the authorities. He concludes that the strict constant control of the Church by the state has led to the fact that at this time the Church began to advocate for a change in its status. Therefore, the Church ceased to be the guarantor of the stability of the autocracy. These works contain various information about the history of the state and the Church. Some of these studies are narrowly focused, while others are limited in time.

CONCLUSION

Thus, despite the availability of scientific literature, the topic of the monograph did not receive sufficient reflection in Russian historiography. Therefore, it is necessary to conduct research, both at the federal and regional levels, devoted to the history of the Russian Church and the state in the 19th - early 20th centuries.
All this allow us to achieve the following goals and objectives, namely:

- study the relationship of the Church with society and authority more deeply,
- identify the socio-economic situation of the Church; analyze the system of spiritual education,
- assess the role of the Church in the life of nobles and peasants, to trace the dynamics of the relationship between spiritual and secular authorities,
- identify the main areas of parish charity,

- consider the specifics of Orthodox spiritual and moral education and missionary work.

REFERENCES

Anderson, L. W., & Krathwohl, D. (2001). *A taxonomy for learning, teaching, and assessing: A revision of Bloom's Taxonomy of Educational Objectives.* Longman.

Aydın, Z., & Yıldız, S. (2014). Using wikis to promote collaborative EFL writing. *Language Learning & Technology, 18*(1), 160–180.

Benzin, V. M. (1906). *Parish charity in Russia after 1864. Labor Assistance 2.* Academic Press.

Bolkhovitinov, E. A. (1800). *Historical, geographical and economic description of the Voronezh province.* Voronezh.

Index of temple festivals in the Voronezh diocese. (1885). *Voronezh, 4.*

Kartashov, A. V. (1959). Essays on the history of the Russian Church. Academic Press.

Klyuchevsky, V. O. (1908). *The course of Russian history. Part 2.* Academic Press.

Milyukov, P. N. (1896). *Essays on the history of Russian culture: Part 2. Church and school (faith, creativity, education).* Academic Press.

Nikolsky, P. V. (1899). Historical note on the state of the Voronezh Theological Seminary for the last 25 years. *Voronezh Diocesan Sheets, 10,* 426–440.

Sambikin, D. I. (1882). Assumption Church in the city of Voronezh. *Voronezh Diocesan Sheets, 19,* 623–632.

Titlinov, B. V. (1924). *Church during the revolution.* Publishing House "Past".

Vargunin, N. A. (1897). The results of the activity of zemstvos in the field of public education. *Russian Wealth, 9,* 56–69.

Zlatoverkhovnikov, N. I. (1902). Monuments of antiquity and new time of Kursk province. Academic Press.

Znamensky, P. V. (1873). Parish clergy in Russia since the time of Peter. Academic Press.

Chapter 2
Study Sources

ABSTRACT

It is shown that sources of research include several groups of documents from unpublished archival materials to memoirs, which only partially compensate for the ability to trace the development of state-church relations. This mainly relates to the field of church legislation, memoirs, and reference and statistical publications. At the same time, one should take into account, in general, a good knowledge of sources on the history of the orthodox church in the 19th-early 20th centuries. The peculiarities of the archival documents under study include the fact that they reflected issues of the economic life of monasteries and churches, prescriptions and orders received in monasteries, and churches from spiritual consistories.

INTRODUCTION

Sources for writing the monograph were archival and published materials. The first group of sources includes materials from the Russian State Historical Archive (RGIA), which include the funds of the Office of the Chief Prosecutor F. 797, the Office of the Synod F. 796. The 796 fund contains the correspondence of the Chief Prosecutor with secular persons and bishops, documents on the state of the church schools, about the "white" clergy, about the situation of theological schools and seminaries, about the emergence and development of church journalism, about the activities of clergy.

Fund 797 investigates cases of reform of censorship of clergy (Op. 87), reconstruction of church administration (Op. 96), and information on

DOI: 10.4018/978-1-6684-4915-8.ch002

relations between clergy and rural parishioners. The material of these funds made it possible to study the historical role of the parish clergy in the social structure of Russian society, to consider the mentality of the lower and higher hierarchs of the Orthodox Church, and also to analyze the organizational and pedagogical aspects of the activities of the clergy.

The fund 804 (Presence for the affairs of the Orthodox clergy) was used in the work. It shows the life and life of the clergy during the reforms of the second half of the XIX century. The documents reflect the general picture of transformations in the spiritual department. The income of theological schools is stated in the materials of the State Historical Archive of Moscow. The monograph contains materials of the State Archive of the Russian Federation (GARF) F. 678 (Alexander II), which provide information on the reform of church life during the reign of Alexander II. These materials disclose the content of the crisis of the Church during the renewal of the state and the contradiction between the spiritual and secular authorities. The fund 677 (Alexander III) was used, where religious policy under the emperor Alexander III is considered. The State Archives of Russia contains information about St. Ioann Kronshtadtskiy (St. John of Kronstadt), who in 1882 built the «House of Diligence». This «House of Diligence» («Dom Trudolyubiya») gave everyone the opportunity to receive help as a reward for work. The goal of the «House of Diligence» was to stimulate labor activity(RGIA, 1900).

The monograph also used materials from the Central State Archive of St. Petersburg (TsGASPb) (F. 19 Petersburg Spiritual Consistory). This fund has information about the opening of the Study Committee at the Holy Synod in 1867, which made it possible to analyze the activities of the Study Committee in the methodological guidance of theological schools and seminaries. Most of the archival materials in connection with the regional aspect of the topic were information from the State Archives of the Kursk Region (GAKO), the State Archives of the Voronezh Region (GAVO), the State Archives of the Tambov Region (GATO), and the State Archives of the Oryol Region (GAOO). The peculiarities of the archival documents under study include the fact that they reflected issues of the economic life of monasteries and churches, prescriptions and orders received in monasteries and churches from spiritual consistories.

The materials of the State Archive of the Voronezh Region reflect a tendency to increase the social role of the Church. The documentation of theological schools, hospitals and almshouses, as well as various charitable organizations, allows us to draw conclusions about the size of the monastery and church charity. In the monastery documents, the role of Voronezh monasteries as religious centers is shown, liturgical life, ceremonies and religious processions are reflected. The documents also presented various accounts and payrolls related to the introduction of the holding. Property records of clergy reflect the nature of movable and immovable property, for example, an inventory of the property of Archbishop Anthony, who died in 1849 (Kulabukhov, 2005).

The service records and receipts of the Voronezh province were the main forms of the current clerical work of archival materials. The most important documents relating to the personnel of the monasteries were the service records of monks. They contain information about social origin, age, education of novices and monks, biographies of priors and abbesses. There is evidence of the opening of new parishes in the villages. The income books of the Voronezh province included church ownership plans, lists of leased real estate, and construction and repair documents.

Of great value for the study are the evidence that is contained in the State Archives of the Kursk Region (fund 20). This fund, one of the few dedicated to the Kursk Spiritual Consistory, contains deanery reports, decrees, collections of paperwork, as well as reporting documents from the Kursk monasteries on the situation in the cloisters, and "receipts and consumables" of the monasteries. The reports of the priors of the Kursk cloisters contain information on the economic activities of the clergy, and there are cases on the charge of the clergy in violation of the church charter. This fund helped to reveal the material and financial situation of the clergy, as well as to determine the degree of indifference of the clergy.

You can find out about the number of Churches in various districts of the Kursk province from the fund 483 "Deanery districts of the Kursk province". This fund examines the Clearing lists of churches of the 1st deanery district of the city of Kursk for 1898-1910, which says that in the Kursk province in 1910 there were 12 monasteries, 57 chapels, 479 wooden churches, 638 stone and three churches were built.

Archival materials from the 187 fund, which provides information on the Kursk Glinskaya Korennaya Rozhdestvo-Bogorodichnaya Pustyn', are of great importance. This foundation made it possible to study the internal way of life of the Pustyn', which was distinguished by spirituality and asceticism.

In the course of work on the monograph, from the fund 217 of the Church of the Kursk Province, data were taken on the condition of the churches of the Kursk province and the material situation of the parish clergy. The fund 792 "Theological seminaries, colleges and parish schools of the Kursk province" was used, which contains information on the educational and educational activities of the diocesan schools, the life of his students, the change in the number and social composition, as well as the quality of education. The fund contains materials such as curricula, magazines, information about payment for studies, examination sheets, reports of representatives of the spiritual department on monitoring the quality of education in theological educational institutions. This fund made it possible to highlight the educational activities of the clergy. No less valuable archival sources are materials from the Oryol Spiritual Consistory, which includes documents of secular and spiritual authorities (the important one was the permission of the Synod to open a parish); financial statements of deaneries, churches, theological schools and seminaries, consistories; correspondence of spiritual and secular authorities; Investigation of complaints by parishioners. In the churches of the Oryol diocese, confession sheets, metric books have been preserved, where information was given about the born, married and deceased inhabitants of the Oryol province. Researchers' interest in these documents is constantly growing, since they are the main documentary sources in the compilation of pedigrees.

Fund 183 "Tambov branch of the Russian Bible Society" was studied, which explains that the Bible Society had 57 branches and 232 "partnerships" in provincial and district cities. An analysis of this fund made it possible to determine the goal of society, which was to distribute religious books in Russian, Slavic, and other languages of the peoples of Russia. The Fund 186 "Tambov Theological Seminary" is interesting. It contains "reports of the Tambov Theological Seminary", "information about the schools of the Tambov Diocese", which show the criteria for the educational activity of church educational institutions. It also contains information about convents: personal data of abbess, information on the social and numerical composition of monasteries, information on sources of income of the cloisters and their economic situation, data on the upbringing and education of girls from the clergy.

The published sources were represented by the legislative acts of the Church, church and secular periodicals, publications of reference and statistical literature, materials of monastic congresses, and memoirs. The legislative code of the Church includes the "Code of Laws of the Russian Empire", which made it possible to show the directions and trends of government policy in the 19th and early 20th centuries on the provision of benefits to the clergy. Until 1885, there was no complete code of church legislation in Russia, and this interfered with the activities of local church authorities. Only in 1869 the multivolume book "Complete Collection of Decisions and Orders on the Department of the Orthodox Confession" begin to be published, where legislative acts on church issues for 1825-1835 were published. The publication of judicial and peasant reform documents began, which contained information that pertained to the ecclesiastical department (Akin'shin, 2003).

Thanks to this group of sources, it was possible to trace changes in the legal status of the Orthodox Church, the specific content of the religious policy of the Russian Empire, reconstruct its stages and evolution, and reveal the mechanism for changing its priorities.

The monograph uses periodical materials, the most important secular and spiritual publications of various kinds. Secular publishers were more decisive in the publication of church information, since they had a certain independence of judgment. In the Voronezh province, magazines such as Voronezh Antiquity were published; "Voronezh diocesan messenger"; "Index of temple festivals in the Voronezh diocese." Since 1866, the Voronezh Diocesan Gazette began to appear. In the "Voronezh diocesan sheets" in 1893 A.M. Pravdin published the Alphabetical List of Church Parishes of the Voronezh Diocese. This list included settlements of the Voronezh province, which indicates the number and names of Orthodox churches in them. Thanks to this, modern researchers can find out the history of the name of a settlement by the temple located in it (Nikolskoye, Novobogoroditskoye, Borisoglebskoye, Petropavlovka, Pokrovskoye, Troitskoye).

The activity of non-Orthodox faiths was also devoted in the 19th century to a large number of publications. Diocesan missionary T. Rozhdestvensky in 1896-1900 in the city of Voronezh, he collected information about sectarianism, conducting correspondence with parish priests. He summarized the data he collected and issued in the diocesan sheets more than ten Open Letters.

In the second half of the 19th century, an upsurge in church scientific thought was observed. In the middle of the 19th century, the History of the Russian Church was introduced into the programs of seminaries and academies, from this time articles on the history of the Church began to be published in periodicals at theological academies: in 1855–1917. in Kazan, in the "Orthodox Interlocutor"; in 1821–1917 in St. Petersburg, in Christian Reading; in 1892–1918 in Sergiev Posad, in the Theological Bulletin; in 1843–1891 in Moscow, in "Additions to the creations of the Holy Fathers in the Russian translation". Statistical information on the family composition of the clergy is presented in the journal Voronezh Conversation.

In the Kursk province, by decree of the Holy Synod No. 2637 of December 1, 1870, the newspaper Kursk Diocesan Vedomosti was published, which began to appear on January 1, 1871. It published articles on church events, various reports, essays on theological topics, reports of parish schools, and historical information. Publications in the Kursk Diocesan Vedomosti helped to study the educational activities of the Church, to highlight the true life in the late XIX - early XX centuries. and the spirituality of the people. The Kursk Diocesan Vedomosti contained information on the participation of the monasteries of the Kursk diocese in charity and public education, highlighted the activities of specific monasteries aimed at the development of public education. In 1865 secular periodicals were published: the Oryol Fact Sheet and the Oryol Provincial Gazette. Along with this, thanks to Bishop Polycarp, the Oryol Diocesan Bulletins began to be published at the theological seminary, which published orders of church hierarchs and articles that dealt with church problems. The "Oryol diocesan sheets" also published data on the participation of merchants, clergy, the nobility in the cultural and public life of the Oryol province.

In the Tambov diocese, St. Theophan the Recluse (Feofan Zatvornik) was the founder of the Diocesan Vedomosti newspaper. In 1859, he was appointed to the Tambov pulpit, and two years later the first issue of the Tambov Diocesan Vedomosti appeared, where he published an essay by Archpriest Stefan Bereznyagovsky "The History of the Tambov Diocese," instructions from the Holy Fathers, catechism teachings, verses by seminarians, and sermons of bishop Theophan, biography of St. Tikhon Zadonsky. "Diocesan sheets" appeared in connection with the clergy's need for local information in order to know the history of their diocese. The study of such publications made it possible to present the type, classification, specifics and problems of the church press, its significance in the socio-political life of the Russian state.

A.I. Razdorsky' book refers to reference and statistical publications. This book contains data on reference publications in the amount of 230 pieces in all 57 dioceses of the Russian Orthodox Church of the 19th - early 20th centuries. The work contains a directory of books, periodicals, historical and statistical literature, systematized by individual dioceses of the Russian Orthodox Church. The directory provides a list of parishes of the Voronezh diocese and Churches for 1888; contains indexes of names, monasteries and diocesan printing houses, geographical names. Information about the stone church in the name of St. Apostle John the Theologian is contained in the Nizhnedevitsky Museum of Local Lore, where descriptions of churches and parishes of the Nizhnedevitsky district of the Voronezh province are available.

The writings of the Kursk Statistical Provincial Committee contain data on the development of church schools in the 19th - early 20th centuries in the Kursk province; their quantitative ratio with zemstvo schools is shown. In the field of primary public education, Zemstvo schools competed with parochial schools.

Tambov province had complete historical and statistical descriptions. Two such descriptions were prepared: in 1888 a book by N. Molchanov was published and in 1899 a book by I. Pokrovsky about a parish in the rural settlement of Raev. 27 dioceses, including the Tambov diocese, prepared reference and memorial books for the clergy (1876, 1893, 1902). The "Reference and commemorative book on the Tambov diocese for 1876, 1902" contained information on the personnel of the diocesan administration, theological seminary, as well as a list of churches and monasteries of the diocese.

In addition, it is possible to note the work of church-historical-archaeological committees. The committees studied the church and religious life of the Central Black Earth provinces, their past and present, examined church antiquities in the dioceses. To carry out their tasks, the committees described the archives of churches, various kinds of church antiquities, studied local religious customs, traditions, observed the preservation of ancient temples, church utensils, icons and took measures against their damage or destruction. The work of these committees attracted interest in the history of the Orthodox Church and helped preserve ancient temples.

In the second half of the XIX century in the Tambov province there were church-local history organizations, and since the 1870s a church-historical committee functioned, and since 1912 - a church-archaeological committee. Separate editions were published in these organizations, but no specific "Labor" was organized.

The Tambov Scientific Archival Commission (TUAK) assumed the functions of a church-local history organization. Researcher of the church V.A. Kuchenkova claims that many sources on the church history of Tambov did not die for modern scholars thanks to the activities of TUAK. The permanent publication of the TUAK published the work of researchers from 1884 to 1918. At first it was called "Meeting Journals," and from 1887 this journal became known as "Izvestia TUAK". In 1887, 100 documents on the history of Tambov monasteries were published in it, these numbers were collections and mainly included lists of archival affairs (Apanasenok, 2010).

Documents of zemstvo-statistical surveys of private ownership farms are of great value for studying the problem of the development of private land ownership of the clergy. These collections systematize estates according to the estates of landowners; there is also information about rent, working cattle and wage workers, the amount of land, inventory. Separate statistical collections contained information on representatives of the clergy who owned land. Each statistical compilation contained statistics for a specific county of the Central Black Earth provinces. Reference and statistical publications covered with maximum completeness all the parishes of the Orthodox Church, and gave a historical description of this territory from a religious point of view. Valuable information is available in the official materials of the monastic congresses, which took place in 1906 and 1917, and in the works of the Pre-Council Presence. These documents show the reasons that led to the crisis of the church, monasteries and monasticism, identify the problems and challenges facing the monasteries in the 19th and early 20th centuries, and identify ways out of the crisis Posternak.

One of the published sources was memoir literature, which is important when studying the relationship between the state and church leadership, the material situation of the clergy, and the mood that prevailed among the clergy.

In 1992, the book of Metropolitan Yevlogiy Georgievsky was published in Russia, which is one of the memoirs sources. Evlogy Georgievsky was a representative in Western Europe of Russian Orthodoxy, a theologian, an outstanding church figure. In his work, Evlogy Georgievsky examines the life of the clergy in Russia in the pre-revolutionary period, and also talks about his participation in the work of the Holy Synod. In general, the sources are quite extensive and informative. Their analysis made it possible to solve the tasks and fully reconstruct the history of the Russian Orthodox Church in the Central Black Earth provinces in the 19th and early 20th centuries (Frieze, 1991). It can be noted that a review of historiography and sources on the investigated problem allows us to distinguish individual periods in the study of the topic, which is not adequately covered in domestic and foreign historiography. Based on the analyzed literature, the history of state-church relations is generalized. It was revealed that the beginning of a systematic scientific study of the history of the Church was associated with church reforms that were carried out in the middle of the XIX century, as well as the entry of theological schools into the system of secular education.

CONCLUSION

It is shown that sources of research include several groups of documents from unpublished archival materials to memoirs, which only partially compensate for the ability to trace the development of state-church relations. This mainly relates to the field of church legislation, memoirs and reference and statistical publications. At the same time, one should take into account, in general, a good knowledge of sources on the history of the Orthodox Church in the 19th - early 20th centuries. This allows us to analyze data from various sources on the activities of the clergy in the structure of public administration and develop an idea of the development of the church as an institution in the Russian state and in the provinces of the Central Black Earth Region.

REFERENCES

Akin'shin, A. N. (2003). *Temples of Voronezh*. Kvarta Publishing House.

Apanasenok, A. V. (2010). *The formation and functioning of the Old Believer communities of the Central Black Earth region of Russia: The last third of the XVII - The beginning of the XX century*. Dr. East. Sciences.

Frieze, G. L. (1991). Church, religion and political culture at sunset of old Russia. *History of the USSR*, (2), 107–115.

Kulabukhov, V. S. (2005). *Evolution of the social status of the Orthodox clergy. Evolution of the class structure of the society of the Central Black Soil in the post-reform period (on the example of the Kursk province)*. Academic Press.

Kursk region: An anthology of social work. (2001). Publishing House of MGSU Soyuz.

Oswalt, J. (1993). Clergy and parish life reform. 1861-1865. *Voprosy istorii, 11-12*, 140–149.

Smolich, I. K. (1996). History of the Russian Church. 1700–1917. Publishing House of the Transfiguration of the Valaam Monastery.

Chapter 3
State Legal Regulation of the Church

ABSTRACT

By the beginning of the 20th century, enormous changes had taken place in the state system of the Russian Empire. In addition to the emperor, the State Duma and the State Council, which included not only Orthodox people, became the supreme legislative bodies. But laws that related to the Orthodox Church, for example, on the finances of the Synod, were considered by the State Duma and the State Council. Until 1917, preparations were underway for the convocation of the Local Council. Documents related to this event are church-historical and church-legal monuments, as they show the spiritual consciousness of the episcopate, clergy, and parishioners.

INTRODUCTION

In the XIX - early XX centuries the position of the Russian Orthodox Church was determined by legislative acts that were adopted under Peter I. The fundamental articles of the Spiritual Regulation were included in the Code of Laws of the Russian Empire (Askochensky, 1900). It provides a religious justification for the power of the emperor and thereby secures a strong union of the state and the Church. The law proclaimed Orthodoxy the "dominant" and "primitive" faith in Russia. The emperor was supposed to be only of the Orthodox faith. He was declared guardian of law and supreme defender of the dogmas of the Orthodox Church. This gave the state the right to administer

DOI: 10.4018/978-1-6684-4915-8.ch003

the affairs of the Church, down to canonical topics, and to prosecute religious dissent.

The law allowed all religions to be professed in Russia if they were tolerant of the existing system. Orthodoxy took precedence over non-Christian confessions. The law allowed the transition from non-Christian religions to Christian ones. Transitions in the opposite direction were prohibited. The law obliged the Church to carry out acts of civil status. It required all Orthodox Christians to receive communion and confession (at least once a year). Clergy should report cases of persistent evasion from this to secular authorities.

By the beginning of the 19th century, the "Book on the Position of Parish Presbyters", adopted as early as 1776, compiled by Bishops Parfenius (Sopkovsky), George (Konissky), which contained important Synod decrees, served as practical guidance for pastors. In this book there were instructions allowing during the baptism of Orthodox children to allow heterodox to accept. Also, this book was used in the application of penance by church courts and confessors. Until the mid-19th century, this book was studied in theological schools, and many generations of Russian priests prepared it for pastoral parish service.

The authoritative church-legal collection was the "Helmsman's Book" (Kormchaya Kniga, 1902), however, the rules in it were reduced, and some of the documents became outdated. In 1839, instead of the "Helmsman's Book", the "Book of Rules" began to be published, where there was a translation of canons into Church Slavonic. The canons were reproduced in full, and the rules were separated from various legal material that had lost force. In the 19th century, 10 volumes of the "Complete Collection of Decisions and Orders for the Department of the Orthodox Confession of the Russian Empire" were published.

The description of the documents was contained in 11 volumes of the collection "Description of documents and files stored in the archives of the Holy Synod", which were published from 1868 to 1917.

Lay people («miryane») who worked in churches were also subject to trial for financial fraud. This confirms the case of the parishioners' complaint about the wrong spending of money by the builder of the church of the village of Tolstyj Kolodez of the Shchigrovsky district of the Kursk province Grigory Barkov for 1884. This case contains a petition from a retired captain of Kosmodemyansky, in which he explains that he and some other parishioners of the Church of the village of Tolstyj Kolodez were informed by the Kursk diocesan authorities about the refusal of the builder of the Church, Grigory Barkov, to report on the amount of money spent on building the Church.

Captain Kosmodemyansky asked to appoint a commission to clarify the circumstances of the money spent on the construction of the church and, in case of loss of money, to punish the culprit. According to the investigation, it was found that the church was built in violation of urban standards. In particular, a cellar was excavated under the church, which was not originally planned during the construction of the church. In addition, the cellar interfered with the foundation of the church. As a result, part of the money for the construction of the church was spent on excavation work on the construction of the cellar. By agreement with the district architect and the Kursk diocesan authorities, the builder Grigory Barkov undertook to put cast-iron supports and strengthen the foundation of the Church, without charging extra money for this. In this case, the Kursk diocesan authorities decided: in view of the fact that the church builder admitted his guilt and undertook to fix everything, this request of the captain of Kosmodemyansky was left without consequences (Dudzinskaya, 1983).

The Charter of the Spiritual Consistories of 1883 and the notes to Articles 152 and 175 made the application of Article 414 of the Statute of the Criminal Procedure mandatory. In accordance with this article, when accusing a clergyman of committing a crime, justices of the peace and judicial investigators directly began to carry out the investigation, informing the higher-ranking consistory authorities. In 1883, a judicial investigator of the Voronezh District Court sent a petition to the Assumption Church in the village of Kastorny Zemlyansky Uyezd to inform about the birth of Mitrofan Podpyshnikov, who, according to his testimony, was 22 years old. He was born in the village of Kastorny and was baptized in the Assumption Church. This information is necessary to clarify the circumstances of the criminal case on the basis of article 414 of the Charter of criminal proceedings.

These notes, obviously, were made by the State Council, which decided that the conduct of the initial investigation in the ecclesiastical department on misconduct by clergymen, who in the ordinary course of affairs are considered in secular public places, is unlawful. Such an order contradicts the principle of non-interference of administrative authorities in court cases proclaimed in the Charters (decision of the Governing Senate No. 594 of 1867, Decree of the Holy Synod of June 23, 1868).

According to Article 148 of the Charter of the Spiritual Consistories, persons of a clergy rank for crimes against the office were subject to diocesan court. This circumstance is confirmed by the case on the charge of the priest of the village of Mashkova Surena, Tambov province Lev Zvonarev of a malfunction in office. In particular, this case contains a resolution of the district police board stating that the priest Lev Zvonarev did not fulfill the duties assigned to him by interrogation of the parishioners. The peasants Nikiforov, Rogov and Chernyshov explained that Lev Zvonarev did not serve the liturgy, did not accompany the dead from the church to the cemetery, and refused to be congregated to parishioners. During the investigation, Lev Zvonarev did not object to the testimonies of Nikiforov, Rogov and Chernyshov. In view of this situation, the diocesan authorities ordered the priest Lev Zvonarev not to not satisfy the requests of the parishioners for the celebration of liturgies, unification, and communion. As a result of the fact that Zvonarev's actions in clarifying the circumstances of the case were random in nature, 12 rubles of legal costs should be recovered from Lev Zvonarev in this case. Archpriest of the Tambov Ecclesiastical Consistory Alexey Kornilov signed this resolution in 1898.

In addition, this article of the Charter contained cases related to mutual disputes between clergymen, which could arise when using the real and movable property of the Churches, on complaints against priests of secular and clergy in violation of obligations and on requests for strict payment of certain debts. On the basis of the Charter, the following were also punished: clergymen who beat someone (with a hand or a gun) in the church during a priesthood (Article 179), clergymen who spoke unseemly words in the church, which resulted in a stop in the priesthood (Article 180). Such is the case on the charge of the clerk of the Dmitrievskaya church in the village of Repetskie Butyrki of the Timsk district of the Kursk province Georgij Pozhidaev of insulting the parishioners. The case file contains a report from peasants Ignat Nefedov and Ivan Zlobin to the clerk of the Dmitrievskaya Church, Georgy Pozhidaev, that Georgy Pozhidaev spoke insulting words to parishioners during the service, led a drunken and violent life. As a result, parishioners of the Dmitrievskaya Church asked to remove Georgy Pozhidaev from the diocesan service. During the investigation, it turned out that the violent behavior of the priest is true. The Kursk ecclesiastical consistory decided to remove the deacon George Pozhidaev from the Dmitrievskaya church, with a subsequent ban on holding services to him in churches. Signed this decree in 1886, the bishop of Kursk and Belgorod Mikhail. According to the Charter, the actions of clergymen, expressed in disrespect for the House of God and sacred things with words or actions (Article 182), improper conduct by priests and accountants of receipts, consumables, metrics and search books (Articles 192 and 193) were also punishable.

On December 23, 1889, a decree of the Holy Synod was received at the Voronezh Spiritual Consistory, which stated that the Holy Synod, when checking the records in the metric books in the consistories, discovered their inconsistency. It was also reported that metric records are inherently very important, such as documents on civil rights, so they are necessary for each individual person in the various conditions of his personal, family and social life. The Voronezh Spiritual Consistory decided: to prescribe to local rural deans for the diocese that they pay special attention to the timely and error-free maintenance of metric records. Those guilty will be subject to certain penalties on the basis of Articles 192 and 193 of the Charter of the Voronezh Spiritual Consistory.

The secular courts could not initiate cases of misconduct of clergy, for these offenses lawsuits were filed immediately with the ecclesiastical court, except for cases involving criminal offenses, in these cases documents were submitted to the criminal court of general jurisdiction. The lords of the nobles were left the trial of the laity and the white clergy only in civil matters; if it was a clergyman, then in the presence of a representative of the clergy. If a clergyman was suspected of unlawful acts for which criminal punishment was provided, then under Article 150 of the Charter, the investigation was first conducted in the clergy in the presence of a zemstvo or city police official, and if the accused could not prove his innocence, then by definition of the Consistory he was transferred to criminal court. When the matter was of particular importance, secular persons approached him immediately in the presence of a representative from the clergy, and sometimes without him (Veselovsky, 1867)

In cases of priests and clerks who were suing for criminal offenses, a representative from the spiritual side, who had the right to vote along with other members of the public place, should certainly have been present. Deputies from the clergy had the right, in accordance with Art. 152 of the Charter, get acquainted with all the necessary documentation and make copies. In addition to the above rules, the Charter of the Spiritual Consistories contained the following instructions regarding diocesan jurisdiction. According to complaints from clergy and secular persons against insults caused by clergy, legal proceedings were carried out by the Consistory if misconduct was not related to criminal offenses (Article 199), if clergy were sentenced to deprivation of dignity by a decision of criminal public places for any criminal offense, and if the diocesan authorities did not have anything to justify them, it led to a decision effect by virtue of which the Holy Synod notified (Article 175). Complaints about violation by clergy of obligations, as well as requests to induce these people to fulfill these obligations and to pay undisputed debts in those places where the Judicial Statutes were not introduced, were brought to the diocesan authorities (Article 203).

The activities of the ecclesiastical courts, in addition to the Charter of the Spiritual Consistories, were determined by other regulatory acts of the Russian Empire. Regulation took place by direct reference in law either to the necessary actions, or by default. Thus, article 374 of the "Status Law" stipulates that clergy in certain cases prescribed by the Charter of the Spiritual Consistories were subject to a spiritual court, and in other cases, they were tried in general judicial places, that is, there was a blanket link to specific regulatory acts. The same method of reference was contained in the Institution of Judicial Establishments of November 20, 1864: "The judicial power of the ecclesiastical courts was determined by special decisions about them".

The issue of jurisdiction was resolved in more detail in the Charter of the Criminal Procedure, article 218 of which stated that cases of misconduct by clergymen were considered by secular or ecclesiastical courts in the manner specified by Art. 1017-1029 of this Charter. In accordance with these articles, persons who belonged to the clergy of any of the Christian confessions, for violation of official duties defined by the rules of the Church and other documents of the ecclesiastical department, and for unlawful acts for which, at the discretion of the ecclesiastical authorities, it was necessary to subject them to liability, were subject to spiritual court. If the actions of these persons caused material damage, then the recovery of losses was carried out in the general civil procedure. On November 20, 1822, minor children were stolen by clergymen of church property in the settlement of Trinity Starobelsky district of Voronezh province. In this case, the Voronezh Spiritual Consistory decided: since young children committed the theft of church property, it was ordered to recover from the children's parents the amount of money necessary to purchase new property.

Clerics were sued for criminal offenses in the general criminal procedure, but subject to certain rules. When judicial investigators and justices of the peace began to conduct an inquiry and investigation into the misconduct and crimes of monks and clergy, they informed the higher clergy about this, and also informed them of the results of the search activities throughout the investigation. In this case, the clergy was obliged to take measures to prevent stops in worship and the administration of other demands. Clerics could only be detained on suspicion of committing serious crimes, which entailed the loss of all special rights and all rights of state and advantages only in cases of emergency.

These persons, while in custody, should have been separate from other prisoners. In cases of clergymen to be examined by jury, all investigative acts were sent by the Prosecutor before their consideration by the Trial Chamber: regarding persons of the Orthodox confession - to their diocesan authorities, regarding persons of other confessions - to their spiritual pastors in accordance with confessional affiliation. Higher church instances had to inform the prosecutor of their opinion on the merits of the case and the prosecution, which was attached to the case and sent to the Trial Chamber, within two weeks, and when considering the merits of the case, this conclusion was not binding on the court and jury.

In the same manner, accusations of non-marriage unions of incest were allowed. The spiritual courts, and only then secular ones, initially allowed cases of marriage in unlawful degrees of kinship or property, cases of forbidden marriages of Christians with persons of other confessions, as well as of the fourth marriage of Orthodox Christians (Lisichkin 1984).

In 1891, the Decree of the Holy Synod on the procedure for marriages between persons of the Orthodox and Catholic confession entered the Voronezh spiritual consistory. The Decree stated that measures should be taken to ensure that Catholic priests are steadily complying with the legal requirements of the Orthodox clergy regarding the issuance of metric records of Roman Catholic people who marry Orthodox Christians. But the Catholic clergy avoided issuing such evidence, which in most cases led to the fact that marriages were not carried out. The Voronezh Spiritual Consistory decided that marriages with persons of Catholic confession should be conducted with the provision of a mutual premarital certificate.

Defendants in cases of derogation from the Orthodox faith and church ordinances were subjected to a criminal court only for those actions that under the criminal laws were subject to any punishment. Moreover, those accused of deviating from the Orthodox faith were initially notified by the shepherds and transferred to the court only if they refused to remain an adherent of Orthodoxy. The facts of deviation from the Orthodox faith were encountered in the Voronezh province. This is the correspondence of the office with the commander in chief in the Caucasus on the issue of the return of the peasant of the Voronezh province Andrian Shirinkin to his homeland, who had abandoned his former views and had again entered the Orthodox religion. The case says that on December 7, 1900, the peasant Andrian Shirinkin was exiled to Transcaucasia for insulting the teachings of the Orthodox Church, as well as being carried away by false doctrine of sectarians. According to the Ministry of Internal Affairs, Andrian Shirinkin changed his attitude to the Orthodox faith, was distinguished by conscientiousness and sincerity. As a result, the Ministry of the Interior does not encounter any obstacles to sending him home to the city of Novokhopyorsk.

Special rules were also established when the clergy served their sentences. So, monks and clergy, convicted by justices of the peace under Article 5 of the Charter of Punishments for arrest or imprisonment, were sent not to places of detention, but to execute a sentence by order of the diocesan authorities.

The priests of the white and black clergy, in accordance with the "Code of Criminal and Correctional Penalties" of 1885, for punishing the deanery in the churches and any other unlawful actions, were punished only by the definition of their spiritual authorities, on the basis of existing decrees. On October 9, 1816, a report of the Voronezh Spiritual Consistory was compiled, which said that priest Alexei Polonsky prevented the residents of the settlement of Raigorodka, Voronezh province from coming to church for confession and communion. It is explained that a sick woman came to church, whom he did not partake and confess. In addition, it is said that the priest did not give due attention to widows and orphans. The Voronezh ecclesiastical consistory referred the facts to the Zemsky district court, which ruled that priest Alexei Polonsky, at the request of the diocesan authorities, unconditionally fulfill all church canons regarding widows and orphans, as well as infirm people, if they cannot come to church for health reasons. If possible, Alexei Polonsky should pay attention to such people in the church. According to the same provision, the clerk, who allowed himself to be beaten with a hand or an instrument in the church during the service, after being expelled from the spiritual department, was punished according to secular laws.

Persons of the white and black clergy for unauthorized absences from parishes and monasteries were subject to transfer to higher authorities for punishment according to church rules. More detailed regulation of this provision was entrusted to bishops. Thus, Bishop Epiphanius, Bishop of Voronezh and Cherkassky, issued a directive in 1896, according to which "for no reason should any of the clergy go away from their parishes without the permission of their dean and without a ticket from him. Punishment is a fine. " Analyzing the above rules of jurisdiction of cases to the ecclesiastical courts from various regulations of that time, we can draw the following conclusions about jurisdiction. Since both clergy and laity were subject to the diocesan court, this jurisdiction can be considered mixed or complex.

By the decision of the Holy Synod and the Senate, the following offenses were recognized as a jurisdiction: dissemination of false rumors and unnecessary causing general alarm (Article 37 of the Charter of Punishments, cassation decision No. 239 of 1867, Decree of the Holy Synod of December 15, No. 42 of 1867), insulting officials in the discharge of their official duties (cassation decision No. 12 of 1868 and Decree of the Holy Synod No. 34 of May 31, 1872).

In these categories of cases, there were two exceptions: cases of insulting a clergyman of a church elder and insults of a clergyman of a clergyman were subject to a spiritual court - these offenses were recognized as crimes against the management and subordination procedures (cassation decisions No. 321 of 1874, No. 1 of 1869 and Decree of the Holy Synod of November 22, 1877 No. 1699).

This conclusion about the jurisdiction of the clergy and laity can be found in two major scientific works. The first one is A.A. Dorskaya's monograph and the second one is the monograph by E.V. Belyakova, which was the first significant work on the history of church procedural law. Of particular interest is the monograph by A.A. Dorskaya, in which ecclesiastical law of the late XVIII - early XX centuries is considered. in the Russian Empire, its role in the system of law, and also the balance of church and state elements in the legal regulation of public relations in Russia.

According to the circular Decree of the Holy Synod of October 24, 1886 No. 19, cases of insults and insults that could result in reconciliation were subject to the conduct of a spiritual court, the latter, despite the amicable agreement of the offender with the victim, should punish the guilty if the insult was connected with an offense nasty to the dignity. This confirms the case on charges of Igor Ubrantsev, priest of the village of Kotorovo in the Tambov province, in excessive requisitions in the execution of the claim. The case contains an extract from the journal of the Tambov Ecclesiastical Consistory stating that priest Igor Ubrantsev was taking excessive payments for the demands of peasants Ivan Ryabinkin and Karp Spirin. Peasants are asked to remove the priest from their parish. By a decree of the diocesan authorities, priest Igor Ubrantsev in 1896 was exempted from the requirement in the Michael-Archangel Church, due to the aggravated relations between parishioners, and transferred from this church to the newly opened parish.

Church courts examined cases of slander of one priest by another according to the explanation of the Governing Senate under number 67/181. Based on the foregoing, it can be concluded that all crimes and misconduct of persons of a clerical rank, not related to violations of the duties of their ranks and not provided for by the Charter of the Spiritual Consistories and other provisions applicable to the church department, were subject to general court orders, and general laws applied to them . The governing Senate and the Holy Synod also found guilty of misconduct for accusing the clergy of insulting officials. The question naturally arises - was the expression "clergy" used in Article 1017 of the Charter of the Criminal Procedure applicable to "clergymen" and "clergymen" or acted selectively?

According to the explanation of the Governing Senate (cassation decisions No. 181, 238, 256 of 1867 and No. 800 of 1869), clergymen accused of insulting honor and punished by the diocesan authorities should be understood only as clergy and religious, but not clergy who for acts that do not contain a violation of official duties, obeyed the general procedure for legal proceedings.

When executing sentences against clergy convicted by general courts for common crimes, in accordance with Art. 1029 of the Statute of the Criminal Procedure, Art. 5 of the Charter of Sentences and Art. 86 Penalties, clergy and religious, sentenced to remarks, reprimands or arrest and short-term imprisonment, when this does not result in loss of dignity or expulsion from the clergy, are not placed in places of detention, but are sent to the clergy for the execution of the sentence. In its Decree No. 2 of January 11, 1873, the Synod permitted these persons to serve a similar sentence in a monastery instead of a prison. In the Voronezh province, there have been cases of encouraging clergymen who served in prison churches. On December 17, 1899, the prison department of the Boguchar Prison Church notified the Voronezh governor that the clerk of the Boguchar Prison Church, Georgy Kotelnikov, who has been in this position since May 25, 1894, made valuable donations to decorate this church. These are icons, a silver cross, a chandelier. For donations, George Kotelnikov undoubtedly deserves encouragement (Bogoslovskij, 1860).

Persons with a clerical rank could receive remuneration for work in the judicial department. This fact is confirmed by the humble petition of the spiritual and judicial investigator Semyon Tverdov to the Tambov spiritual consistory that Semyon Tverdov is a spiritual and judicial investigator of the 2nd Temnikovsky district of the Tambov province, and for this he does not receive a certain annual remuneration. True, Semyon Tverdov receives legal costs from each case, but payment is too long and untimely. Therefore, Semyon Tverdov requested the Tambov Spiritual Consistory to appoint him a decent annual remuneration. The Tambov spiritual government decided on the basis of Article 643 of the "Charter on the Servants of the Spiritual Government" to appoint an investigator Semyon Tverdov 60 kopecks per diem, and for a pair of his horses 7 kopecks. The Tambov Spiritual Board made this decision in 1903.

Based on articles 148 and 197 of the Charter of the Spiritual Consistories, clergy on mutual disputes arising from the use of movable and immovable church property, and on the retention of church income from each other, were subject to the conduct of a spiritual court. However, they were also involved in litigation and lawsuits between them and secular persons on unfulfilled contracts and obligations and in penalties for violation of rights by damages and losses, and self-possession, under paragraph "a" of Article 149 of the above Charter, were subject to a secular court in designated public places.

In 1819, the wife of the priest of the church of the settlement of Novotroickaya in Starobelsky district, Tatyana Yurchekiva, turned to the Voronezh spiritual consistory with a request to consider the petition for giving her part of the inheritance of her father, priest Leonty Bedin. Tatyana Yurkechiva asked to resolve the dispute regarding the property left by her father. The petition said that Tatyana Yurkechivoy has a sister who claims to inherit from her according to the law. This is a half-house with a garden and part of the property, which includes valuables left by their father, priest Leonty Bedin. The Voronezh Spiritual Consistory sent the case to the district court, which decided to split the property and the house in half. Similarly, under Article 1018 of the Statute of the Criminal Procedure, clergymen were liable to civil court after the consideration of the case by the church department to recover remuneration from them for harm and losses caused by the crime.

The courts of general jurisdiction dealt with the cases of not only individual, but also collective clergy - monasteries and churches, subject to special rules and exceptions provided for them. In Voronezh province, a report was written by the letter-supervisor of the Starobelsk ecclesiastical administration Semyon Kozhin about permission to write reports in the form existing in secular office work. In this case, the Voronezh Spiritual Consistory decided: to declare a letter to the inspector Semyon Kozhin that he would write papers in the current form, and would not complicate himself and his superiors in this matter. Archimandrite Voronezh and Zadonsky Samuel signed the decree on December 20, 1820. Exceptions could apply both to the field of substantive law (for example, transactions for the acquisition of property and the conclusion of contracts were regulated by Section 397 of the State Law) and to the area of procedural law. Separate exemptions were found in specialized laws governing specific types of public relations - for example, there were a number of articles on the legal capacity of church subjects in the Commercial Charter (Afanasyev, 2008).

In accordance with Article 203 of the Charter of the Spiritual Consistories, complaints about violation by clergy of obligations, as well as requests to induce them to pay undisputed debts, were accepted by the diocesan authorities if they were not disputed by the defendants, i.e. clergy. Thus, if a clergyman to whom a lawsuit was brought before a magistrate or district court to recover an uncontested debt or the fulfillment of another such obligation would, in turn, bring an action against non-jurisdiction, then both the justice of the peace and the district the courts were obliged to refer the matter to church authorities or to grant the plaintiff the right to appeal to the latter. If the clergy did not object to the consideration of their case by secular institutions, then the proceedings took place in a general manner. Particularly, the time for filing a protest against jurisdiction should be stipulated - only before the start of the court session; if the protest was brought after the start of the consideration of the case, or the deadline for appealing against the final decision was missed, the person lost his right to appeal or cassation in accordance with the explanations of the Civil Cassation Department No. 256 of 1867.

Part 2 of Art. 148 and Art. 206–220 of the Charter of the Spiritual Consistories, Art. 723 and 724 of the Law on Crimes and Art. 1012–1015 of the Charter of the Criminal Procedure determined the jurisdiction of secular persons to the ecclesiastical court. Such crimes were considered a departure from the faith and from the decrees of the Church, the investigation of these offenses was initiated by order of the spiritual authorities. The decision, which in this case was taken by the court in a case instituted without a formal requirement of the diocesan authority, was subject to cancellation.

When the investigation ended, information about acts that contained real facts of abrogation was transmitted to the consistory in order to decide on the initiation of criminal prosecution, and before this decision was made, secular authorities took measures to suppress crimes, for example, the suspect was detained. In the Voronezh province there were cases of accusations of priests in anti-government protests. In 1895, priest Fyodor Andrievsky was sent a notice from the Valuysky district police officer, which said that priest Fyodor Andrievsky, in the presence of clerk Beloborodov, stated that several letters addressed to different posters were received at the post office in the settlement of Nikitovka, Voronezh province, on the first day of Easter persons where there was an appeal of the people to revolution. In Voronezh, 200 people were arrested in this regard. The priest's son, Yevgeny Andrievsky, said that such riots reign in the Kharkov and Poltava provinces. In view of the foregoing, a search was conducted by the Voronezh provincial gendarme administration in the priest's apartment. During the search, nothing was found. As a result, it is concluded that the persons mentioned were not seen in political unreliability. This case was left without consequences (Tvardovskaya, 1978).

In 1902, Nikolai Vasiliev, the psalmist of John of the Theological Church of the Valuysky County, was charged with insulting remarks against the emperor. In particular, Nikolai Vasiliev saw the tsar's inaction in that the emperor did not decide all important state affairs on his own, but shifted everything to ministers. As a result, mass unrest of peasants and students took place in many cities of Russia, which demanded an improvement in their plight. Having examined this complaint, the Voronezh Provincial Gendarme Administration finds no reason to proceed with the said case because each person, including the priest, can express his opinion on political issues if this does not threaten the preservation of the autocracy. In this case, the priest expressed his opinion.

In 1904, a report was compiled by the Novokhopersky district police officer at the request of the priest of the village of Abramovka, father Nikolai Bazhenov, about the teacher of the parish school Petr Pissov agitating the peasants against the war with Japan. The report said that the teacher of the local parish school is among the military ranks talking that they should not go to war with Japan, the emperor can be changed, how elders are replaced, and that the Japanese should be helped, under whose authority they will be to live better, because the Japanese will not rob the peasants of the earth. It is said that the teacher of the parish school is 19 years old, and he is of the Orthodox faith. The Voronezh Provincial Gendarme Administration determined to judge Pyotr Pissov for a state crime.

An interesting figure stands out in the normative documents of that time - the churchwarden. By social status, he did not belong to the clergy, but, nevertheless, carried out functions closely related to the activities of the Church. Regarding the jurisdiction of church elders, the highly approved "Instructions to Church Elders" of July 12, 1890, article 58 states that a church elder who evades the fulfillment of the rules provided for in the instruction and the requirements of the diocesan authorities, if there is information about this, as well as in case of unsuccessful exhortation of him, he is dismissed from office by the definition of the consistory, approved by the diocesan bishop. In 1891, a decree was followed by the Voronezh Spiritual Consistory regarding church property. It said that due to the numerous thefts from the churches of church utensils, it is necessary to establish special night guards at the churches. The Ministry of the Interior takes care of this, which reports that these guards should consist of church leaders who are entrusted with the protection of church property.

Diocesan proceedings in cases of misconduct of persons of a clergy rank could be twofold - either directly to the bishops, or through the consistory.

Bishop proceedings were expressed by the consideration and resolution of disputes and crimes directly by the archbishop. According to the Charter of the Spiritual Consistories, he was judged: misconduct committed by ignorance and inadvertence, which required correction by the action of the bishop and hierarchy, not exposed to the publicity of an ordinary court, all misconduct against the congregation and office, not related to harm and temptation, noticed by the clergyman, previous behavior whose complaint was made, complaints brought precisely in order to correct those who stumbled by the archpastoral court and edification without formal proceedings. In these cases, the diocesan bishop could directly instruct the dean or other trusted clergyman to conduct an unspoken inquiry, and if the validity of the slander or remark was confirmed, the bishop would call the accused to talk with him and, looking at the wrongdoing and about signs of repentance, could release him or apply pastoral penance for up to two weeks. Complaints were not allowed against these orders of the bishop, nor were they included in the formulary lists. In all other cases, an investigation was appointed, that is, the case was examined in a consistory order. Such, for example, is the case on the complaint of the foreman («starshina») Ivan Firsov against the clergy of the Cossack settlement of the city of Shatsk, Tambov province, for unjustly bringing him to trial. The case contains the most humble petition of the foreman («starshina») Ivan Firsov to Bishop Tambovsky and Shatsky Theodosius that the priests of the Cossack settlement accused Firsov of not allowing them to their lands, where they must plow and sow winter bread. As a result, priests lost 220 rubles. The Tambov Spiritual Consistory conducted an investigation in which these facts were not confirmed. The Consistory has decided not to bring Ivan Firsov to court. The case is dated 1870. The above rules related to the determination of jurisdiction and jurisdiction of disputed cases to church courts. So, both clergy and laity were under the jurisdiction of the church courts. If the court in relation to clergymen was of a corporate nature, then the norms of spiritual law were applied to other members of the society in the manner and on the grounds that were determined by state legislation. Representatives of the clergy who were present during the investigative actions showed corporatism in determining the punishment of the higher church authorities. The Senate, making precedential decisions, leveled the contradictions between secular and church norms. Since the time of Peter I, there has been a closer merger of the state and the Church. In the 19th century, the Orthodox Church became an integral part of the state machine. But complete unification did not happen. The church remained an independent institutional body of government.

CONCLUSION

By the beginning of the 20th century, enormous changes had taken place in the state system of the Russian Empire. In addition to the emperor, the State Duma and the State Council, which included not only Orthodox people, became the supreme legislative bodies. But laws that related to the Orthodox Church, for example, on the finances of the Synod, were considered by the State Duma and the State Council. Until 1917, preparations were underway for the convocation of the Local Council. Documents related to this event are church-historical and church-legal monuments, as they show the spiritual consciousness of the episcopate, clergy and parishioners. The newest period in the history of the Orthodox Church began in 1917-1918. convocation of the Council of the Russian Orthodox Church and the restoration of the Patriarchate. The Local Council was the highest canonical body at which the most important issues of church life were discussed. However, the program of the Council was not completed until the end due to the circumstances of that time, the Cathedral worked a little more than one year. Thus, being partly a state mechanism of governance, the Church felt the administrative pressure of secular authorities, which, undoubtedly, limited its initiatives in state-legal service and led to the bureaucratization of the Christian worldview.

REFERENCES

Askochensky, V. I. (1900). In and. In *Russian Biographical Dictionary*. Academic Press.

Dudzinskaya, E. A. (1983). Slavophiles in the social struggle. Academic Press.

GATO (State Archive of the Tambov Region) F. 181. Op. 1. D. 1683. L. 430.

Lisichkin, V. M. (1984). Ideology and politics of modern Russian Orthodoxy. Academic Press.

RGIA (Russian State Historical Archive) F. 797. Op. 31. D.18a. Art. 3.

The memorial book of the Voronezh province for 1878-1879. (n.d.). Voronezh: Publishing House of the lips. Stat. Committee.

Tvardovskaya, V. A. (1978) The ideology of the post-reform autocracy. Academic Press.

Veselovsky, G. M. (1867). *The city of Ostrogozhsk, Voronezh province and its county*. Voronezh: Type. Governorate. Board.

Chapter 4
Church as a Social and Spiritual Institution of Society

ABSTRACT

Spiritual awakening began in Russia in the 19th-early 20th centuries, the main meaning of which was to try to purify the spiritual image of Russia, return to the origins of Russian Orthodoxy, and comprehend the historical mission of the Russian people. Education in society was increasingly moving away from church foundations, and despite the awakening in Orthodoxy, the prejudice in society towards the clergy was already rooted historically, and overcoming the negative features of the perception of the clergy could not be overcome by a sharp jump, even with increased social activity of the clergy.

INTRODUCTION

In the XIX - early XX centuries. The Orthodox Church occupied a crucial place in the life of the Russian people. Priest A. Borisov spoke of its influence in this way: "The existence of the Russian Orthodox Church was for the people a sign of the presence of God in the world". The social role and functions of religion in the 19th century changed dramatically. The church was presented as a legitimate institution, playing a huge role in human life, elevating spirituality over social, aesthetic and economic values.

In connection with significant changes in the country, new trends arose in church-state relations. The role of the Church began to prevail not only in the socio-cultural, but also in the political life of the Russian state. The

DOI: 10.4018/978-1-6684-4915-8.ch004

Christian ideology of the Orthodox Church influenced the consciousness of Russian citizens.

The Russian Orthodox Church was able to cultivate in a person such qualities as love for people, patience, compassion, mercy, honesty, the ability to put oneself in the place of others, modesty, respect for the interests of one's neighbor, which forms the moral and spiritual basis of the individual. An objective assessment of any event cannot be given without a complete picture of the interaction of the Church and the state. In this regard, the Church can be characterized as a social institution. On the one hand, the Church was a community of communities, and on the other hand, it was a church hierarchy. In the era of the new era, the Church organically merged into civil society. Being a part of civil society, the Church has always been independent of the state and even competed with the state not only in the social sphere, but also in the spiritual.

Religion is the spiritual component of the Church. The ontology (picture of the world) and axiology (value system) that religion offered were different from the ideology of the state. Since the Church has always relied on traditions, it was perceived as "eternal" and unchanging, starting from its origins, and therefore it was an alternative to the "changing" world. The church professed an image of fidelity to tradition. Cultural beliefs, symbols and values were the sphere of religion, and they solved the issues of human existence.

In the 19th century, the Church exerted a great influence on society through church journalism (tserkovnaya publitsistika, 1880). In the early 1860s church journalism arose, which had its own laws. The religious needs of the estates and groups were reflected in church journalism. Along with the state, it was an important social institution. Two types of journalism appeared: religious and spiritual. Religious journalism relied on religious ideology and served for internal use in the Church. Spiritual journalism was created not only by ecclesiastical, but also secular figures. Ecclesiastical journalism differed from ecclesiastical journalism in that it illuminated secular issues related to relations in society, but at the same time it relied on church dogma. By studying such publications, one can imagine the type, classification, specifics and problems of the church press, its significance in the socio-political and church life of the Russian state. Periodicals in all regions played the role of an information center, which allowed for the exchange of information between the authorities and the population and a dialogue on the most important events in local life. The press united the local intelligentsia and made it possible to exchange information between different sectors of the population.

The main objectives of these societies were: creating historical descriptions of dioceses, studying the history of the Church, local archives, religious customs and rituals, taking monuments under protection.

Before the revolution, in Russia there were several types of church and local history organizations:

1.   Archaeological and historical committees and commissions,
2.   Commissions for the study of archives,
3.   Historical and statistical committees for describing dioceses,
4.   Church treasuries.

These organizations included a museum and a library. At first, museums (ancient repositories) were created, in which written and material monuments of church antiquity were stored. From this began the activity of church archaeological committees and commissions. When studying the history and life of the local community, the result could be when a large number of interested parties took part in this activity. Propaganda activity was one of the aspects of the Church's local history activity. The dioceses occupied vast territories, so parish priests, teachers and students of parish schools and religious schools were involved in their study as members and correspondents. The committees, in addition to clergy, could include secular people. In the provinces of the Central Black Earth Region, printing houses of provincial boards were created in which provincial sheets were published. The editorial offices of the provincial Gazette were associated with statistical committees. Interest in regional issues brought together committees and statements. Statistical committees in the provinces in their publishing activities were very active in the production of commemorative books.

In 1856, a series of the "Memorial Book of the Voronezh Province" was published, which had a common program in all the provinces of the Russian Empire. First, reference information about the temples was printed, then tables and materials for statistics, and then articles on ethnography and history.

Diocesan statements were of great importance for historical and statistical descriptions of dioceses. Diocesan Sheets began to be published in 1860. They had information about local church life, history, and ascetics. Since 1866, the Voronezh Diocesan Vedomosti began to appear, they covered the history of the emergence of parishes and villages. "Voronezh diocesan sheets" included two parts: official and unofficial. The unofficial part was called "Additions" to "Vedomosti". The Voronezh Diocesan Gazette was published at the seminary. At first there were 4 editors: the rector of the seminary, archimandrite Theodosius, hegumen Arseny, and priests Theodor Nikonov and Mikhail Nekrasov. Their work aroused interest in history among readers. In 1867 and 1868 in the "Voronezh diocesan sheets" was published an article by priest F. Nikonov "Description of the Voronezh diocese." In his article, the priest used the books of Bolkhovitinov, "Voronezh Acts" and the affairs of the consistory. This work was of great value. The author gave a geographical description of the Voronezh diocese, showed the importance of the city of Voronezh among other cities, described the initial space of the Voronezh diocese and subsequent changes in its borders. These publications were closer in spirit to the reader, since they described the church life of their land, local shrines and ascetics; published tips on the Orthodox upbringing of children, family relations, and moral materials.

In 1836, provincial statistical committees opened in Kursk, and in 1838 the Provincial Gazette began to be issued. At first, in the Provincial Gazette there were few publications on a church theme. The provincial statistical committee collected various information, including church statistics, but for a long time did not publish its works. Only in 1863, after the abolition of serfdom, was their first issue released. Of great importance for the development of the Church and society was the Manifesto of Emperor Alexander II on the abolition of serfdom. He influenced the unity of the flock and pastors in the rural community. The "Works" of the Kursk Provincial Statistics Committee contained information on the population for 1861: in total there were 1863079 inhabitants in the Kursk province, of which the clergy constituted 12%, that is 21451 people. In the Central Black Earth provinces, there were about 200 parishioners for each pastor, and in Kursk, there were 28,205 inhabitants for 391 clergymen, which was two times less in comparison with the Tambov, Voronezh and Oryol provinces.

Subsequently, the Kursk Provincial Statistics Committee in its works began to print information about church history and statistics. In 1865, a Russian press decree was adopted. This decree paved the way for the appearance of the Kursk diocesan sheets (Kurskie eparhial'nye vedomosti, 1900), their release began in 1871 according to the decree of the Holy Synod No. 2637 of December 1, 1870.

It was printed by the printing house of M. Gordon in Belgorod. Matvey Nevsky and Professor Grigory Voznesensky were their first editors. The newspaper immediately earned the love of flock and shepherds. The newspaper published sermons, materials on the history of the Church, and theological materials. The provincial church newspaper played a large role in the election campaign of the clergy. Some articles reported on the election campaign of the clergy in other provinces. The article on the elections to the IV State Duma said that an appeal to members of the State Duma from the Tver diocese appeared in the "Tver diocesan sheets". Elections are important for the entire imperial clergy, therefore, to give this issue wide publicity, information about the elections must be placed in the «Kolokol».

The issue of elections is of great importance, the time is approaching for elections to the IV State Duma, whether the clergy is ready to give the future State Duma to Russia. In Kiev, a meeting of the clergy on the election of the IV State Duma was held with the participation of Archpriest Tregubov and chaired by Bishop Chigirinsky. There was a meeting on the same topic in Kursk. If elections are held on holidays, the diocesan authorities must serve the liturgy, and not miss elections. The clergy of the Tver diocese also need to prepare in advance for the elections to the IV State Duma".

In 1859, Bishop Theophanes the Recluse («Feofan Zatvornik») was appointed to the Tambov Department, and two years later the «Tambov Diocesan sheets» (Tambovskie Eparhial'nye Vedomosti, 1902) was founded. Until the 1870s The Diocesan Gazette was published weekly in two parts - the official and the addition. The official part published reports of various societies, orders of the Tambov Spiritual Consistory, information about vacant priestly, deacon and psalm-priest places, decrees of the Holy Synod, announcements, discharge lists of students of religious schools of the diocese. Articles of theological, church-historical, spiritual and moral content and various sermons were printed in additions.

In the first year of publication, the "Diocesan Vedomosti" published catechetical teachings, the instructions of the Holy Fathers, the sermons of Bishop Theophanes, the biography of St. Tikhon Zadonsky, verses by seminarians and the essay "History of the Tambov Diocese" by Archpriest Stefan Bereznyagovsky.

In 1877, the Tambov Church Archaeological Committee was opened, by the decision of which the number of articles on church history was increased in the "Tambov diocesan sheets". Biographies of the saints Hilarion Troekurovsky, Pitirim Blessed, John Sezenovsky, essays on the history of Lebedyansky, Kozlovsky, Voznesensky, Trinity, Tambov monasteries were first published in the Tambov diocesan sheets. Much attention was paid to official documents, therefore, reports of missionary and charitable fraternities, reports on cash collections for various diocesan needs, and reports of guardianship of the poor were published. At the beginning of the 20th century, two more supplements to the "Tambov Diocesan Vedomosti" began to be published: "Church Antiquity", and "Brotherly Word".

The editors of the Diocesan Gazette tried to make the publication interesting; for this, they published historical, archaeological, ethnographic material, historical and statistical descriptions of the dioceses. The local clergy, according to the creators of the Diocesan Vedomosti, should have been not only readers, but also authors of articles. On the pages of «Eparhial'nye vedomosti» in the Central Black Earth provinces appeals for cooperation were published. This should have improved the Diocesan Gazette.

The editorial staff determined the topics of information that they needed from the local clergy: "descriptions of the faiths preserved in the people, church and folk customs, descriptions of the ritual and religious-moral life of the parishioners are needed". The clergy and the "Diocesan Gazette" cooperated in several areas. This was a description of the holidays, rituals, customs, that existed among the local population. It combined history and modern life of the parish. However, the main part of the ordinary parish clergy of the dioceses of the Central Black Earth Region in the 19th century was not accustomed to social activities, closed in its corporation, which the authors of the Diocesan Vedomosti lamented from time to time. In a number of publications, priest authors clarified the point of view of clergymen of the diocese - the revival of parishes is hindered by the dependence of pastors on parishioners, however, the indifference of an educated society that has lost its faith was called one of the most important problems. In view of this situation, in 1890 a decree of the Holy Synod was issued on teaching the Orthodox people in churches the truth of Christian faith and piety.

The Decree stated that many residents of the Voronezh province, calling themselves Orthodox, are in spiritual ignorance, do not know what they believe in, do not know prayers, do not know the spiritual significance of rituals. In this regard, the Holy Synod decided the heads of the dioceses and local churches to conduct conversations on all days, aimed at explaining to the people of the Christian faith. In addition, it is necessary to give a complete and accurate interpretation of the Divine Scripture, reasoning about the rules of life. The Holy Synod also decided to establish at each parish religious interviews, which concerned the doctrine of the three persons of the Divine, the sacraments of the Church, and the holding of the liturgy. Archpriest of the Voronezh Spiritual Consistory Michael Nekrasov signed this Decree .

The clergy was also instructed to abide quite clearly by the church charter. This is confirmed by the resolution of the bishop of Tambov on the meeting of rectors and abbesses of the monasteries of the Tambov diocese held on February 5 and 6, 1892. At the meeting, decisions were made on worship, private life, admission and dismissal from monasteries. The resolution says that worship, prayers and requiems, laid down in the charter, should not be rushed, on holidays to select and appoint readers who can read with meaning, reading should be psalmodic, separate, and melodious during the holidays. In addition, to have monitors and novices to read the holy gospel, the life of saints and other books of spiritual and moral content, for which open a library, if not (Klyuchevsky, 2000).

In the XIX century, popular church magazines gained popularity, they were designed for a wide age category of citizens and were intended for family reading. For example, the magazine Kind Word was addressed to every believing Russian family, and the spiritual and folk magazine Kormchiy was approved as a useful reading for soldiers. Religious editions "Sunday", "Sunday" and others were recommended for Sunday reading in the family, but their circulation was small, delivery and distribution met difficulties, the population was poor - this affected the mass of their audience.

Great importance was attached to the historical and statistical description of the dioceses, which covered as much as possible all parishes and churches, and gave a historical description of this territory from a religious point of view. Descriptions of the parishes, compiled by local priests, served as the basis for publications.

Those also applied to the history of the monasteries of the Voronezh diocese. There are voluminous works and essays about these monasteries. Archimandrite Demetrius and Hieromonk Gerontius were prominent historians of the monasteries of the Voronezh diocese. Archimandrite Dimitri published historical essays about the monasteries of the Voronezh diocese. His essays were published in the book Index of Temple Festivals in the Voronezh Diocese. He published articles on the Korotoyak, Voznesensky, Shatrishchevsky, Divnogorsk, Valuy, Belokolotsky monasteries. Hieromonk Gerontius composed essays on the history of the Zadonsky Bogoroditsky, Eletsky Holy Trinity, Zadonsky Tikhonovsky and Tolshevsky monasteries. These works contain a lot of material on the history of monasticism in the Voronezh diocese. Reading these articles, some general conclusions can be drawn, since the monastery archival documents were used in the articles. Archimandrite Dimitry also used the archive of the Voronezh Spiritual Consistory in his works (Bunakov, 1907).

Parsing consistory affairs on the history of monasteries, we found that some papers have pencil marks, apparently belonging to a researcher of antiquity. In the description of the dioceses, not only religious issues were raised, but the Church was also interested in the economic situation of the population, its life and social life.

The Church Gazette promoted missionary ideas in Russia. The historian F. Znamensky, F. Orantsky, and the missionary S. Seoji (S. Seodzi) published articles on this subject. The weekly promotes sobriety. In addition to the "Church Gazette", there were other periodicals: secular "Government Gazette", "Russian Word", "Russian Gazette", church theological and philosophical magazines "Theological Bulletin", "Proceedings of the Kiev Theological Academy", "Christian Reading". The "Church Gazette" with these publications conducted polemics on various church and socio-political issues. In pre-revolutionary Russia, church publications were systematized into groups: 1) publications that fulfill the tasks of religious and moral education; 2) publications for the people; 3) purely theological, catechism publications; 4) highly specialized church publications; 5) missionary publications; 6) official chronicles. For several decades, starting from the 80s of the XIX century, the journal "Guide for Rural Shepherds" was published. In this journal, explanations of prayers, advice to priests on relations with rural residents, materials of the Synod, recommendations for rituals and demands were published, problems of rural life were consecrated. Developing, church publications worked with their audience and created it (Pospelovsky, 1995).

Among the Voronezh Orthodox publicists of the 19th century is Viktor Ipatievich Askochensky, who was born in Voronezh in the family of a clergyman on October 1, 1813. His father was a mentor to all clergymen of the Voronezh province in musical singing. First V.I. Askochensky received a home education, and then entered the Voronezh seminary. Studying at the seminary, he kept a diary in which he described the mores in the seminary. Since 1839, he was published in the magazines Mayak, Moskvityan, Sunday Reading, which at that time were considered Orthodox conservative publications. In 1846, his book "A Short Outline of the History of Russian Literature" was published, in which he described the work of Russian secular and church writers.

At that time, Askochensky became a deeply religious man and a convinced conservative, which was reflected in his novel Asmodeus of Our Time, published in 1851. In his novel, he exposed the immorality and atheism of Russian society. From 1858 to 1877 Askochensky in St. Petersburg published the weekly newspaper Domashnaya Conversation. This newspaper brought him all-Russian fame. On its pages there was a polemic with manifestations of Westernism, nihilism, atheism, liberalism and revolutionism in Russian periodicals. For 20 years, the direction and nature of the materials in the Conversation did not change, mainly, it was "Useful Tips", "Wise Sayings", instructions to parents about raising children in the spirit of the Orthodox faith, stories about the dangers of drinking, theft, adultery.

Researchers connect the development of the church press with the growth of freedom-loving moods in Russia in the 19th century. The Orthodox periodicals of this time were diverse in type and quantity. In 1855, the Orthodox Interlocutor magazine was published, articles published in this journal called for opposing material and other "liberal teachings" and "moral depravity". The journal Faith and Reason answered the demands of the spiritual life and religious thought of modern society and opposed rationalism and unbelief. From 1860 to 1891, the Orthodox Review was published, which was a bright and significant magazine. This journal was founded by learned priests - G.P. Smirnov-Platonov, N. Sergievsky, P.A. Preobrazhensky. The objectives of the magazine were "to promote increased attention to religious needs and issues in Russian society, to be a body of rapprochement between society and the clergy, between life and spiritual science".

Slavophiles A. Koshelev, A.S. Khomyakov, I.S. Aksakov, the Kireevsky brothers published «Russian Antiquity» and «Russian Conversation» (Russkaya starina, 1901, and Russkaya beseda, 1865), in which church journalism occupied a large place". The publishers themselves, as well as authors close to them in spirit, carefully examined the problems of church and religious life. Recognizing the originality of the autocracy, they were opposed to any state interference in public life, the most important component for them was the religious field.

The foundations of religiosity are not manifested in these years in general philosophical constructions, but in specific, practical issues of church life in Russia, in considerable attention to its long-standing diseases, to the search for independent ways to solve them. Perhaps the main problem that the Slavophiles tried to solve during these years was ways to revive religious and social activities in Russia. The famous Slavophil I.S. Aksakov advocated the revival of the importance of the Orthodox parish in everyday life, defended the direct right of the religious community in the management of the church economy and in the control of church funds. He wrote a lot about the self-government and independence of the parish community in accordance with the general catholic system of our church, so that the community, temple and clergy form one organic whole. The pages of spiritual journals began to actively discuss issues of the struggle against materialism - they started talking about foreign experience, and regretted the underestimation of the danger of materialism by the Russian clergy. Differentiation within the clergy testified to the intense search for their own face against the background of public unpredictability. The boundaries between the church and society gradually blurred, the barriers to their rapprochement were removed. The role of Russian spiritual journalism consisted in the affirmation of Orthodoxy in the mass consciousness; the formation of an official religious ideology; in bringing to the population state, secular, socio-political ideas.

In the XIX - early XX centuries society and the clergy were active. Some changes in the social system, hopes for church reforms aroused the minds. Priest Konstantin Bogoyavlenskij, who lives in the Tambov province of Kirsanovsky district in the village of Morshan-Lyadovka, was an exponent of such sentiments. In his article, he wrote that "if out of a dozen written articles at least one spiritual thought finds a response in the heart of the reader, it will be a great thing." His political views were: "Orthodoxy, Nationality, Unity of Russia." The main theme of Konstantin Bogoyavlenskij was "Unity", he called on the clergy to this and suggested: "We will organize" fraternal leaflets "to combat disorder and anarchy, distributing these leaflets".

The country underwent processes of urbanization and modernization, as a result of which the society was divided into polarizing warring parties that protect their own corporate interests. Among the priests, modernization was stressful, the new conditions of entrepreneurship and management were contrary to Orthodox ethics, which was protected by the clergy. His Grace Gregory, vicar of the Tambov diocese, in 1909 spoke of the church in the village of Arzhenka: "The church in the village of Arzhenka is good; the choir, which the manufacturer Aseev supported at his own expense, was talented, but the people in the church behaved noisily. People who worked in the factory did not go to church. Work at the factory begins at 6 a.m. on Monday, and ends at 6 a.m. on Sunday. "The priest asked to let people go on Saturday at 5 pm, but the manufacturer did not agree, as this was unprofitable and unnecessary for him by law."

The church awakening emerging in the 19th century made the creative intelligentsia turn to the search for a spiritual image adequate to the attitude of the era. The rapidly changing spiritual atmosphere (including under the influence of foreign contacts) for the first time demonstrated the greatness of the power of public opinion, which influences the positions of the "leaders". The abolition of serfdom and civil liberties of the individual are the main topics of the then circulating manuscripts. The church theme at first arose only spontaneously, in connection with other problems, but gradually the trends of the time captured the church environment. It was society that became the generator of subsequent reform processes in the church. At first, however, church issues were touched upon extremely generalized, without specifying. The main attention of the then ideologists of transformations was drawn to the civilian sphere, to the crisis of the old system as a whole. Therefore, church issues were mechanically woven into the general context of domestic policy assessments. On the other hand, secular figures themselves were afraid to widely affect the religious environment, lacking serious theological knowledge and fearing competition with the authority of the higher clergy. The meaning and correlation of the concepts of "church" and "society" then caused a different interpretation. The church was no longer reduced only to the clergy, estranged from the laity, and society was not limited only to the educated noble minority, and new forces entered the arena of public life.

A sign of spiritual renewal in the XIX - early XX centuries. was a return to national origins. The phenomenon of the miracle of holiness in Russia was one of the signs of spiritual renewal. In the Voronezh province, a case was known that occurred with Father Nazarii, Abbot of Valaam. Choosing a place for desertification, father Nazarii went to the Black Sea Cossacks. He stopped on the way to live with a priest. The priest told the elder that he never in the church serves the Sunday liturgy, since the church is empty and there is no one to serve. The temple is never empty, it contains the guardian of the throne of the Lord - an angel, Father Nazarius answered and advised him to serve the all-night vigil, which they held together in office. 30 people gathered in the Church. Leaving the Church, the elder explained to people that it was necessary to go to the Church, and by Sunday afternoon more people gathered. The number of parishioners gradually increased, and the priest began to serve the Divine Liturgy daily. There were cases when the parishioners themselves chose a priest. Parishioners of the Church of the settlement of Yevsyug of the Starobelsky district (Uyezd) of the Voronezh province on April 3, 1812, asked to be appointed to the post of priest Matvey Velikhov. The petition said that in the settlement of Yevsyug of Starobelsky district (Uyezd), one of the priests was suspended from diocesan affairs due to his illness, and Matvey Velikhov was appointed to his place at the request of the parishioners (Korf, 1906).

Parishioners of the Intercession (Pokrovskaya) Church of the settlement of Kobychina, Starobelsky district, asked to identify the son of the priest Simeon Grekov as a sexton. It is said that the son of the priest Simeon Grekov, Fyodor Semenov, is a kind person, not lazy in housekeeping, conscientious in behavior. It was decided to give Fedor Semenov approval. The Bishop of Voronezh Athanasius approved this request.

Thanks to a strict ascetic life and fervent prayer, significant events took place in the lives of individuals. In 1740, a daughter, Maria, was born in the family of the Ukrainian Cossack Konstantin Bosoy in the county town Biryuch, Voronezh province. Growing up, she expressed a desire to become a nun. However, parents opposed this. Konstantin Bosoy, after the conversion of the Ukrainian Cossacks to state-owned settlements, moved with his family to the settlement of Belogorye, Ostrogozhsky district. They lived poorly, and Mary after the death of her father was in great need. Concerns and difficulties drowned out her dreams of monasticism. At the age of twenty-five, she married Samuel Sherstyukov, a military resident of the settlement. The marriage was unsuccessful. In this marriage, the children of Gregory and Simeon were born, but Mary, finding herself in extreme poverty, gives the children to serve. When she was 45, Mary remained a widow.

She had no firm faith in God, no support and ideas about her future. Under the weight of circumstances, she plunged into vice. Maria learned from the pilgrims about the Kiev Pechersk Lavra and, in order to confess, she decided to take the path to a place holy for every Russian person. On foot, without a livelihood, she reached Kiev and spent a year in the Lavra. Every day, Mary visited the caves, stood services, confessed, and communed with the Holy Sacraments of Christ, praying to the holy saints Anthony and Theodosius and other Kiev-Pechersk miracle workers. Prayers, relics of saints, labor of cave diggers change it.

By the will of God, Mary came to confession to the hieromonk, who knew Belogorye well. He saw her remorse and desire to be saved, so he blessed Mary for charitable works, fasting, prayer, sobriety and constant contrition of her sins.

But Mary wanted more and asked for blessings to repeat the exploits of the cave diggers. She returned to Belogorye and at the age of 56 she began to dig a cave in the chalk cliff on the right bank of the Don, not far from the Bricks Farm. The highest capital circles learned about the ascetic Mary. The local population supported and respected Mary. But appeals to the closure of the caves began to come to the highest state and spiritual authorities. At this time, the emperor issued a decree on a thorough investigation of the case of Mary.

A special commission examined the case, she confirmed Maria's good intentions, and the persecution was stopped. The state treasury, by decision of the emperor, allocated 2500 rubles for the construction of the cave temple. Mary decided to dedicate the temple to the heavenly patron of the emperor, the Right Prince Alexander Nevsky in gratitude for the mercies shown. Archpriest Athenogen Pechersky on August 30, 1819 consecrated the church, which increased the number of like-minded and assistants to Mary, and stopped the ill-wishers. For 20 years, the feat of the founder of the Belogorsk caves continued, the length of the caves during the life of Mary reached 212 meters. Forces began to leave her, and in recent years, Mary only showed how to properly perform the work. On June 22, 1822, Mary died, but her cause continued to live. The caves that dug under Mary were called old caves, and the caves that were dug after her death were called new. The efforts of many volunteers quickly grew new caves. The case was continued by Ioann Alekseevich Tishchenko. He was a contemporary and like-minded Mary, a deeply believing old man. He supported Mary in her labors, and he dug cave passages in old caves. Their remains are buried in special crypts on top of a cave mountain. The tombs of Mary and John, which they dug in the depths of the caves, now serve as monuments of the contrition of their sins.

The idea of founding in the caves of the monastery in the 19th century began to be confirmed by the fate of hardworking, humble, simple and benevolent hermits. The life of the cave diggers was filled with a deep sense of hermitism. The cave society from 1822 to 1866 increased from 4 to 25 people. Dmitry Lyapin, Andrei and Petr Mandrusenko, the Vasilchenko brothers saw the meaning of cave hermits in awakening the soul. The deeper the caves became, the brighter were the spiritual aspirations, stronger faith in God, more expensive every day and hour sent by God. The faces of the elders living in the caves radiated joy and peace. By a special brotherly disposition to each other, they were called brothers. Each performed the work most successful in his hands. The source of strength was prayer, so hard work was a joy for the brothers. Communication and staying with the elders inspired and strengthened people, and they increasingly began to come to Belogorye.

Particular attention of believers in the provinces of the Central Black Earth Region was paid to visiting the Churches. On June 30, 1822, residents of the settlement of Osipova, Starobelsky Uyezd, petitioned the Voronezh Spiritual Consistory for the appointment of a second priest in their parish due to the lack of priests in the village in two churches. The priest has a long time to get to the Church, which is called Pokrovskaya. The second Church is located on the outskirts of the settlement and was built in honor of the Ascension of the Lord. According to the certificate of the Voronezh spiritual consistory, it turned out that the second priestly place was granted and assigned to the Voronezh district spiritual teacher Grigory Rudinsky. The diocesan authorities in the provinces of the Central Black Earth Region tried to timely repair the old Churches and maintain cleanliness and order in them (Selivanov, 1987).

In 1890, the diocesan authorities in the Voronezh province decided that, due to the dilapidation of many churches and church and public buildings, drafting and the necessary control over work are allowed without coordination with the provincial government on the basis of Article 213 of the charter of the Voronezh Spiritual Consistory. The essence of the resolution consisted in updating the iconostases in many churches of the Voronezh province, covering the buildings, repairing floors, and roofing.

Article 322 of the charter of the Voronezh Spiritual Consistory stated that schools, almshouses, churches and other institutions had important social significance. Therefore, supervising them was very useful. Art workers also participated in the church awakening of the provinces of the Central Black Earth Region. Ivan Nikolaevich Kramskoy was engaged in religious painting, in 1870 he was commissioned by S.P. Sinelnikova, for the Trinity Church of the Ostrogozhsky district of the Voronezh province completed nine images. In the provinces of the Central Black Earth Region, a "thaw" («ottepel'») actually began, although not so pronounced. But with all the differences in colors and shades, a common worldview was formed, based on a unifying desire to return the Church a corresponding high role in society, to awaken the moral forces of the clergy, to revive the religious consciousness of the laity. In the Voronezh province, there were cases of rewarding clergymen for the conscientious performance of their duties.

In 1835, a report was received from the horse factory workers in the Voronezh Spiritual Consistory, who unanimously testified to the honest and selfless service of the priest Fyodor Klimentov of the Assumption Church. The report says that Fedor Klimentov diligently fulfilled spiritual requirements, despite the fact that the plant was far from the Church, he always came to worship on time. And therefore, the workers of the horse factory applied for the award of the priest Fedor Klimentov with the insignia established for the clergy. The Voronezh Spiritual Consistory decided to satisfy this petition and reward the priest for selfless service with a distinction. Archpriest Vasily Postnik signed the report. The inclusion of Orthodoxy in public life became one of the central achievements of the era and was regarded as a guarantee of increasing the moral strength of the Church. The understanding of the Church began to include the harmonious unity of the clergy and laity with a significant emphasis on the role of the latter in the broad framework of the Orthodox society, while highlighting the most active part of it - the Orthodox public. The limits and forms of the social mission of the clergy were expanding - not only as a connector of the heterogeneous parts of the "world" into a single whole, but also as a carrier of Christian love, a source of trust in society.

At the end of the 19th century, the parish clergy was placed in strict subordination to the local episcopate. The diocesan consistories were subordinate to the diocesan bishops and the Synod; they were to inform the Synod of the mood of the parish clergy. These reports contained information that the authority of the clergy was declining, and the issue of the morality of the clergy was discussed many times in the Synod. The bishops were ordered to recognize the worthy, the weak to support and instruct, and the unworthy to punish. In this regard, one can note the decree of the head of the Voronezh provincial gendarme administration stating that the paramedic of the Zemlyansky district of the Voronezh province Vasily Andreev spread anti-religious convictions among the peasants, inspiring them not to recognize God and the sacraments of the Orthodox faith. The head of the Voronezh provincial gendarme administration admitted that Andreev is a person who is extremely harmful in all respects to the local population. It was ordered to remove from the province paramedic Vasily Andreev in the interests of protecting public order and preserving the Orthodox faith. This decision was approved on June 29, 1905. As a social and ideological institution of society, the Church has its own specific feature, it is more closed and conservative in comparison with other institutions. State laws, secular institutions, economic formations change, and only for many centuries church canons and dogmas remain unchanged.

The state, relying on religion and the Church, first, perceives the spiritual and moral aspect, and only then - the social norms of regulation of public life. Spiritual awakening began in Russia in the 19th - early 20th centuries, the main meaning of which was to try to purify the spiritual image of Russia, return to the origins of Russian Orthodoxy, and comprehend the historical mission of the Russian people. Education in society was increasingly moving away from church foundations, and despite the awakening in Orthodoxy, the prejudice in society towards the clergy was already rooted historically, and overcoming the negative features of the perception of the clergy could not be overcome by a sharp jump, even with increased social activity of the clergy (Listova, 2001).

The contradictions between the Church, the state and society escalated at the beginning of the 20th century; they caused a crisis in church-state relations. As a result, research has emerged in Russian historiography. At the very beginning of the 20th century, the first works that had a philosophical and journalistic character were published. Church and government circles showed great interest in the article "Requests for Life and Our Church Administration", which appeared in the Moscow Gazette in December 1902. The author of the article is populist L.A. Tikhomirov concluded that subject to some reforms, the monarchy and the Church can be preserved.

In his article, he analyzed the activities of the Orthodox Church after the reforms of Peter I. L.A. Tikhomirov concluded that the synodal administration does not meet the established church traditions. L.A. Tikhomirov proposed returning to the ancient canons of Orthodoxy so that the Church could more effectively serve people in political and public affairs and could speak in its full voice on its behalf. Researcher of the Church B.N. Mironov agreed with this point of view. He gave a clear picture of the development of the social status of the spiritual estate of Russia in his work. B.N. Mironov devoted his considerable attention to the problems of social mobility and the development of the class position of the clergy.

Analyzing the historical events of the 19th - early 20th centuries, the researchers took into account not spiritual and moral characteristics, but mainly socio-economic ones. Among the many works stands out work, the author of which is A.N. Bokhanov. A.N. Bokhanov's monograph was published in the post-Soviet period. In it, the author considers, from the point of view of the Orthodox faith, various forms of Russian self-consciousness from the very initial historical stages to the end of the 19th and beginning of the 20th centuries. He sees the "historical destiny of Russia" in the preservation of Orthodoxy.

CONCLUSION

Thus, the Russian Orthodox Church as a social and spiritual institution of society showed interest in the history of the local community. The Russian Orthodox Church understood its uniqueness, collected and published facts of local history, ethnography, archeology, economic and public life, drew public attention to the vital aspects of the Central Black Earth region.

REFERENCES

Bunakov, N. (1907). *Rural school and public life*. Academic Press.

GAOO (State Archive of the Oryol Region) F. 580. Op. 1. D. 2063 L. 7-8ob.

GAVO (State Archive of the Voronezh Region) F. I-84. Op. 2. D 47.L. 225.

Klyuchevsky, V. O. (2000). Orthodoxy in Russia. M. 310 p. Personal archive. Certificate N°. 7118. Personal archive. Certificate N°. 10104.

Korf, M. A. (1906). *The nobility and its estate management for the century XVIII-XIX centuries*. Academic Press.

Listova, T. A. (2001). National Orthodox rite of creation of a family. *Orthodox life of Russian peasants of the 19th - 20th centuries: Results of ethnographic research*, 31–35.

Litvinov, V. V. (1911). Temples and limits dedicated to St. Tikhon Zadonsky. *Voronezh Antiquity, 10*, 19–25.

Pospelovsky, D. V. (1995). Russian Orthodox Church in the XX century. Academic Press.

RGIA (Russian State Historical Archive) F. 796. Op. 442. D. 1420.L. 26.

Selivanov, V. V. (1987). Year of the Russian farmer. *Letters from the village. Essays on the peasantry in Russia in the second half of the XIX century*, 104-108.

Tvardovskaya, V. A. (1978). The ideology of the post-reform autocracy. Academic Press.

Chapter 5

The Role of the Church in the Life of Nobles and Peasants

ABSTRACT

The parish played a special role in the life of the peasant; he was an integral part of village life and life. The closure of the church in the village was perceived negatively, since it was believed that with the closure of the temple the village itself would disappear. All this stimulated the ardent desire of the peasants to have a temple in their village, which was most often built at the expense of peasant families and rural communities. Most of the temples and churches built in Russia in the 19th century were wooden: serfs could not afford to build a stone temple. (They were usually erected by landowners.)

INTRODUCTION

To study the past, scientists need to study all groups and classes of Russian society. The nobility and the peasantry, which was an integral part of Russian society, aroused the interest of scientists interested in the history of the country.

In the 19th century, in the relationship between nobles and peasants with the clergy, unlike other layers of society, a certain isolation is traced. One could become a nobleman, having earned one of the Russian state orders, or by length of service in the civil service, and it was difficult for a layman to become a priest. In addition to his desire, in order to transfer to the spiritual estate, a person needed to have the consent of many authorities, pass the test of knowledge of the conduct of divine services, church singing, prayers, and

DOI: 10.4018/978-1-6684-4915-8.ch005

sacraments. To do this, the candidate for a place in the clergy had to get a special education. But in theological educational institutions under the law of 1808, in addition to the sons of the clergy, only children of noblemen could study. In all spheres of life, the position of the nobility was privileged.

With the help of the government, the nobility preserved and strengthened their estate, did not allow the dissolution of the estate in other wealthy sections of the population. Hereditary nobility in the Oryol province in the second half of the XIX - beginning of XX centuries. accounted for half of the total population in the province. Of local origin in the Oryol province there were 51.5% of hereditary nobles living in their counties - 33.1%, natives of other counties of the province - 18.4%. In the second half of the 19th century, 48.5% of the nobles moved to the Oryol province, of which 45% were natives of other Russian provinces and 3.5% came from other states. 62.9% of the nobles lived in cities, the noble urban population was 1.7 times the number of rural nobles.

In the Oryol, Bryansk, Yelets, Trubchevsky industrial districts there was a large percentage of the urban noble population, and the rural nobility dominated the Kromsky, Sevsky, Bolkhovsky, Mtsensky, Dmitrovsky, Livensky, Maloarkhangelsk agricultural districts. Men among hereditary noblemen of the province made up 46.7%, and women - 53.3%. Literacy among the noble population was 95%, literate women were 52%, and men 48%.

The social position of the nobility was gradually changing. The basis of the material well-being of the Russian nobility was landlord tenure, which was reduced during this period. In 1877, landlords and merchants among the nobles were 56%, in 1895 - 40% and in 1905 - 30% [90], which indicates a reduction. And the percentage of small estates with less than 100 acres increased. These persons could no longer be considered landowners, their situation was difficult. They existed under the same conditions as the peasants, but were deprived of the advantages that the rural population had in the form of seed assistance and allowance during the years of crop failure. Many were poorer than the peasants, but the zemstvos and the administration did not provide assistance to them, sending them to the noble estate bodies. Noble societies could not help them. In the 19th century, there were cases when the nobles were tonsured as monks, but not a single nobleman joined the parish clergy (Fedorov, 2005).

The rural clergy, like the peasants, raised livestock, plowed the land, and mowed hay. In the first half of the 19th century, the peasantry was the most numerous class. Peasants were divided into four categories: landowners - there were 23 million, state - 19 million, specific, belonging to the imperial family - 2 million and church peasants - 1 million people. All peasants, except the landlords, paid state taxes and tributes.

The peasants understood the holiness of the Church and its significance for man, therefore their attitude to clergy was respectful, but taking into account the personal qualities of the priest. The rural clergy in the province maintained their archaic traditions. Despite the fact that the inheritance of places by the clergy was canceled, this custom continued until the beginning of the 20th century.

The prosperous tops of the village were shopkeepers, moneylenders, and representatives of agricultural capitalism. The number of middle peasants also continued to increase. Opposing social groups in the village have not yet formed. The peasant devoted all his time to his household, but the clergy did not have such an opportunity, since they had to conduct services in the Church and constantly perform religious ordinances, so the clergy could not feed themselves from the earth. The bulk of the rural clergy was poor, which greatly depressed the representatives of this estate.

The government tried to help the rural clergy, and since 1842 began to pay them a salary from the treasury, but it was small and could not firmly provide for the well-being of the clergy, and only half of the Churches received this help. The government saw the problem of material support for rural areas and understood that with the abolition of serfdom, it would become acute.

In 1897, in Russia 77.1% of the population were peasants. Three peasants in tsarist Russia fed one citizen. Such a huge number of people who were employed in agriculture was kept in the village only because unproductive manual labor was used.

All these negative phenomena caused conflicts in the relations of peasants with the clergy, degraded the authority of the priests and the influence of the clergy on the peasants. By rights and education, the clergy considered themselves superior to ordinary people, they wanted a better fate and sought to communicate with landowners and officials. But the clergy experienced a feeling of bitterness and disappointment, because nobles, officials, burghers, and peasants did not consider the clergy to be "their own."

With the abolition of serfdom, the isolation of the spiritual estate could no longer be maintained. Under the conditions, when the whole of Russia's acquisition of personal freedom, the restriction of clerical rights of the clergy looked like nonsense.

The clergy as a whole fulfilled the above-stated, purely ideological task of combining the traditional legal worldview (with all the features of its perception in the "lower classes") with faith in the incomprehensible ideal of the intercessor king, and thereby directly ensured a relatively quiet course of the abolition of serfdom .

An important aspect of the study is seen in determining the importance of fasting, icons, church holidays, Bible knowledge in the life of the nobility and peasantry. Moreover, this value had a religiously meaningful meaning, in particular, the limitation was made that limiting the telepresence is necessary for a great deal of success.

All elements inherent in the needs of the nobleman were reproduced in his possessions. In this regard, the religious paraphernalia («atributika») constantly rested his place in the estate.

The Church occupied the central place among the manor houses. The church is not only an organization, but also a separate building, standing in the way of activities and the intermingling of two cultures — noble culture (dvoryanskaya kul'tura) and peasant culture (krest'yanskaya kul'tura). The church was the pride of the village (by the way, the village with the church was already called a village), therefore, the nobles considered it necessary to help the Church and its servants. People of that era unchallengedly accentuated the Church with a family burial vault. In the church and on church graveyard, all family members were interrogated.

The posts were observed quite strictly in the noble environment (among the people which is called «dvoriane»). Fasting for the nobility meant not only restricting oneself in food, but to a large extent "fasting" meant not to add anything inadequate to the neighbors and those who were ok. In the days of rest, reading of the literature was forbidden, it was forbidden to be publicly dis- cussed, which was necessarily done.

Speaking of the nobility, it should be noted that the nobles attached great importance to baptism, confession and communion (Kuchenkova, 1993).

In the Kursk province on February 6, 1890, in the Nicholas Church, priest Vasily Popov performed the sacrament of the baptism of Lev Ershov, whose parents were the nobleman Ilya Sergeevich Ershov and his legal wife Varvara; both Orthodox. The receivers were merchant Mikhail Volkov and Maria Falkova. A baptismal certificate was issued from the Kursk Ecclesiastical Consistory to Collegiate Assessor Ilya Sergeyevich Ershov, who lives in the city of Grayvoron, Kursk diocese. In the Kursk province of the Belgorod district of the village of Gorodishche on December 10, 1888, at the Nativity of the Theotokos Church, priest John Maltsev performed the sacrament of baptism of Anna Semirnina, whose parents were non-commissioned non-commissioned officer Ivan Semirnin and his legal wife Maria; both Orthodox. The prisoners were the bailiff of 4 camps Vasily Sokolov and the city of Belgorod cemetery church, the priestly wife of Thekla.

On August 16, 1898, nobleman Mikhail Alexandrovich Landinsky was given a certificate by the clergy of the Intercession Church of the city of Voronezh that Mikhail Landinsky confessed and communed during the Assumption Lent. The priest of the Intercession Church Dmitry Mitrofanov signed this certificate. Among the population there were a sufficient number of "freethinkers" who believed that fasting was acceptable only for the common people, and therefore the moral exploits of the nobility should be judged as they deserved.

After the Liberty Manifestos, the nobility began to return to the village, which marked a return to the old patriarchal norms of life. True, the land was already experienced by urban, metropolitan people, with education and, often, with new cultural needs, but nevertheless they were people who, in their own way, were very susceptible to living, who had some kind of economic activity. The bishops begin to establish spiritual and administrative ties with them.

Returning to parental roots, landowners begin to rebuild churches or build new parish churches. There was a saturated reprisal with the lords of the eparchy. Requests were submitted for the construction of stone temples to replace wooden ones.

In 1890, the nobleman I.I. Vorontsov-Dashkov from the village of Novotomnikovo of the Tambov province built the Church at his own expense. A feature of the temple was masonry resembling wood carvings; and the internal painting of the temple was similar to the painting of the old Moscow Annunciation Cathedral. The church had fine work ceramic iconostasis with tiles. In the XIX century, 13 convents were founded in the Tambov province, seven of which were built by nobles, and one Sezenovsky was not without their participation.

Six monasteries were opened in the manor estates, the conditions of the estates were perfectly suitable for the cloisters, as there was already a residential building - the manor house, in most cases, the Church, manor land, courtyards and outbuildings that already existed on the estate. Basically, all these monasteries, in addition to the Ottoman, were created after the reform of 1861, which led to the ruin of those noble nests, where the economy was based on serf labor. The estates where the landowners could not or were not able to farm in a new way fell into decay, and the question arose of selling land to neighbors or peasants. The best way out of the situation was the monasteries based on these lands; as a rule, all land was transferred to them. The lords of the dioceses often had to consecrate the parish churches with the landowners. The lords also made long detours of their dioceses. On these trips, as usual, the bishop and his accompanying staff, at the invitation of the landowner, stayed at his house.

At the beginning of the 19th century, Zadonsky Monastery was the most famous among the noblemen. Until 1783, Bishop Voronezh Saint Tikhon lived in this monastery. Nobles who knew the saint came to the monastery for spiritual advice and blessings. Count Stepan Fedorovich Tolstoy often came to the monastery and sent letters, and in his will he expressed a desire to stay in the monastery after his death. Saint Tikhon was exclusively located for some of the pilgrims. So, the holy ascetic often visited the landowner of the Voronezh district of the village of Podgorny Nikifor Mikhailovich Marin. Nikifor Marin was an assistant to the Voronezh governor, was merciful and pious. For example, he bailed the peasants sentenced to death for participating in the Pugachev riot, and with their help in the village instead of the wooden one, a stone church was erected in memory of St. Tikhon, Bishop of Amafunta. In gratitude for the mercy of the condemned, the saint presented the pious landowner with his belt portrait. Already after the death of the saint, in Mary, in the place where he exclusively loved to sit the holy patriarch, a church was erected. A spring and a well were nearby, and this place was visited by pilgrims. A religious procession was going from church to chapel on church holidays, pilgrims applied to the icons and took holy water in the well. Often, lay people from their homes transferred great Christian icons to monasteries and temples. There were several reasons: to help the monastery financially; for the blessing and remembrance of family members who have already been buried or should rest in the future on the territory of this monastery; and enable parishioners to worship the holy image on the icon. Marriage icons were also valued, there were always several of them: the icon of the Savior, one or several Mother of God, several saints of God, revered in the family or in the family.

In the Kursk province, many leaders of the county nobility "humbly" asked local priests and "law teachers" to take part in the 1897 census. "In view of the special importance for the population of the first universal census, the successful execution of which depends on the good composition of the enumerators, is that it is desirable to involve clergymen in the census. And they will not refuse; at the invitation of the census department managers, to assume the responsibilities of enumerators for the remuneration offered to them".

The census forms of the 1897 General Census were supposed to be processed in St. Petersburg and published in separate final issues in the provinces, but the process dragged on for a long time. For example, data on the Kursk province were published only in 1904, i.e. 8 years after the census. This led to the fact that on the ground they tried to count the population on their own, as a rule, on the initiative of local authorities. In a number of provinces, zemstvo backyard censuses were carried out (in the Kursk province in 1883-1885), but they did not give figures for the total number of inhabitants, and their purpose was somewhat different. Therefore, for all demographic collections published in the last decades of the 19th century, the main source of information was church statistics.

Some noble families considered the heavenly cover-body a kind of one or another saint. To strengthen faith, through the prayers of living or deceased ancestors, signs of heaven were given through miraculous icons. Endowed with graceful power, shrines encouraged a person to seek high prayer and aroused the gift of repentance in him. In the orthodox noble house, new pilgrimage shrines appeared after a personal visit to holy places or a gift from a familiar pilgrim. For the price, they were inexpensive, but priceless, depending on the revered saint and his monastery.

In one box, there were the Voronezh relics of St. Mitrofan of Voronezh. During the life and after the death of St. Mitrofan, who died in 1703, the nobles served requiem for him, came to the grave, prayed and turned to him for help. After 1717, the incorruptibility of the relics of Mitrofan was discovered, and their mass veneration began, but they began to record miracles only at the beginning of the 19th century. Judging by these records, people of all classes turned for help. In the records of the miracles of St. Mitrofan, a case of the wonderful healing of the landowner I.N. Ladygin, cured of paralysis in 1829. It is also necessary to say how faithful nobles treated the shrines in their homes. People kept great Christian shrines, and this made them reverently try to fulfill the commandments of God, pay attention to their spiritual life, prayer, and know church service.

For example, at the beginning of the 19th century, a Moscow official S.P. Zhikharev knew the church charter, the text of the Bible, as it was raised by religious parents - landowners of the Voronezh province. The nobles preserved personal archives, memoirs, diaries, notes, documents that were published in the 19th and early 20th centuries, which left evidence that many nobles had Christian shrines: particles of holy relics placed in the arks, icons, crosses that have come to their owners in various ways. The attitude to the shrines among the believing nobles speaks of the depth of their awareness of human,

64

civil and Christian duty. The best representatives of the Russian aristocracy considered their social and state ministry as a religious ministry given by God. And therefore, pious nobles relied not only on themselves, on their minds, on knowledge, on power, but, first of all, on God's blessing for their work, their home. Shrines gathered in the houses, in which they saw the pledge of the protection of the saints of God, heavenly help in the difficult work of power. Shrines: icons, particles of relics, came to the houses of noblemen in various ways, but this happened through a high bishop or royal blessing. The icons and relics of the nobles were awarded for their service and for church blessings. Also, the shrine made its way inside the family through a parental blessing or blessing of relatives. The icon was inherited by the eldest son or by someone who had the right to do so. The place of honor in the homes of noblemen was occupied by shrines after miraculous circumstances, therefore, the acquisition of shrines can be considered as God's blessing. A letter was attached to the royal gift, in which the argument of gift was indicated (Tarasova, 2005).

In a noble, merchant, and petty bourgeois environment, along with exceptional examples of rule enforcement, fasting, Christian holidays, there were still deviations, although rare, from church discipline. But the numerous Russian estate - peasants - strictly observed fasting, Christian holidays, this was the usual line of their behavior, not going beyond the traditional forms of communication. In the 19th century, Russian peasant Orthodoxy was perceived not as a body of dogma, but as a truth addressed to every person, which shaped life principles and relationships. In the Voronezh province there were many peasants of the Orthodox faith. In the metric book of the village of Mozurka, the Archangel Church of the Novokhopersky District is mentioned, containing information about birth, marriage, and death for 1862-1863, 1866-1870. This metric book contains the names and surnames of the born peasants of the Orthodox faith in the village of Mozurka, who visited the Archangel Church. The names and surnames of the receivers at the Arkhangelsk Church are also included in the metric book. In particular, Alexander Ivanovich Eresiev and Erofei Petrov are mentioned, both Orthodox, the peasant Sergey Petrov and his legal wife Elena Ivanovna, who have the Orthodox faith. The priest Andrian Makarovsky served at the church. In the Transfiguration Church of the village of Spassky Mtsensk Uyezd, a metric book is preserved, in which there is a record of the marriage of parents of I.S. Turgenev January 14, 1816. In the church of the village of Pankovo, Sevsky district (Uyezd), there is a metric record of the birth and baptism of the artist Grigory Myasoedov in 1834.

Thanks to the materials of the Russian Geographical Society, it is possible to show a big role of confession («ispoved'») in the life of the peasants. It is worth noting that the peasant, who for a long time did not confess and did not partake of the communion, was deprived of the right to be a witness in the community. Such data can be found in the biographies of domestic devotees of the faith, especially since many of them were born into a peasant family.

In the XIX century, there were cases of the sale of peasants to priests. The peasant woman Theokla Demina was sold with her family to the priest Stefan Orzhelsky on May 12, 1821. The peasant woman Theokla Demina of the Starobelsky district reported in a petition that she and her husband and children had come under audit with the former Mr. Fedor Ryndin and had been sold to the priest Stefan Orzhelsky, who had mistreated her. Therefore, she asked His Grace for a return to the former owner. The Voronezh ecclesiastical consistory decided: to report this case to the Voronezh provincial government, and to the priest Stefan Orzhelsky to gain meekness.

In the middle of the XIX century, during the epochal transformations, the issue of educating the peasants acquired particular importance. In fact, all of the peasants showed an interest in education in a spiritual school. The interest of the peasants to theological schools was reinforced by the fact that the schools were located close to their places of residence, the teachers were people who were well acquainted with the life of the peasants, and also because the teaching in these schools was of a church character.

The Synod's prosecutor («oberprokuror») K.P. Pobedonostsev in his own report repeatedly pointed out that the interest in church schools was spawned as if, according to his statement, the peasants wanted their children to be taught religious subjects. One of the students of the parish school in the Voronezh province said: "My parents from the peasants, who did not receive any education, they, realizing all his need, wanted to give me a modest education". The village teacher N. Bunakov wrote at the beginning of the 20th century that, according to the peasants, the church school provides knowledge of the Law of God and allows children to participate in worship. In 1892, one of the Tambov clergymen also shared his thoughts on this topic. In the report on the state of the diocese, he wrote, in particular: "The people look at the education of their children, their literacy and God's law as a highly useful work". The peasants welcomed the participation of their children in the church choir and sought to teach the children to read the Book of Psalms, the Psalter, and Acts. Zemstvo studies data 80–90 years XIX century and modern research convincingly speak of the prevalence of spiritual literature in the reading circle of the peasants. Being mostly illiterate, peasants loved to be read aloud to them. Church literature was preferred; the villagers exclusively loved to listen to the lives of the saints. They said: "Read to us about educated and good people. "We will learn to farm without books, but how to live a Christian life - we want to know about it from the book". In the printed word, the peasants did not seek advice for introducing the economy, but tried to gain spiritual skills. Common in the village was the help of the parishioners to the Church and the clergy. According to the custom, in the village of Yasenach of the Nizhnedevitsky district of the Voronezh province, each parishioner, passing the Church during harvesting, dumped several sheaves here. Thus, 1000 rubles were raised, for which the Church was repaired. All peasant life was connected with the church calendar. The peasants were guided by church holidays, with which they associated the most significant events of their lives. The peasants usually spoke as follows: such an event did not occur on October 1, but on Pokrov («na Pokrov»); not October 22, but - on the Kazan Mother of God («na Kazanskuyu Bogoroditsu»).

Reliable milestones in the field work were constant holidays: Christmas, Assumption («Rozhdestvo, Uspeniye») and others; and variables: Easter, Trinity, Ascension («Paskha, Troitsa, Vozneseniye»). Centuries-old observations convinced the peasants that haying must begin after the Trinity. Scientists are unanimous in the opinion that the peasants honored the holy days, did not work on holidays and weekends, since they considered this a great sin. The religious and moral basis of the relationship of two generations in the family was extremely clearly expressed in the views of the peasants about the meaning of parental blessing. "They attached great importance to parental blessing," the correspondent of the Ethnographic Bureau from the Voronezh province categorically asserted in 1900. Children received a parental blessing before leaving on a long journey, before the wedding, before the death of their father or mother. The blessing was simply given in front of some responsible or dangerous business. The son, who was in a bad relationship with his mother, going into huts, had to ask her for blessings, as an observer from the Novokhopersky district of Voronezh province told.

According to the notions of rural residents, marriage was not only a vital necessity, but the fulfillment of a divine commandment, and the peasants believed in the holiness of the crown. The marriage was preceded by rural ceremonies, which in their content, in most cases, were Orthodox. When during the matchmaking an agreement was reached on a future marriage, all those present lit candles, prayed, and then made promises to each other and kissed each other. Promises were held tight, because the violation was considered a sin. The peasants said that breaking the word is a sin, although people have not heard it, a witness God can punish parents for pride. The most significant event in the life of the peasants was the sacrament of wedding, which took place in a rural church. "The peasant respected the rite of marriage, he was anxiously preparing for it and met with fear, since God blesses man for a new life". The metric book of the village of Malaya Privalovka, Voronezh province, contains information on the marriage in Kazan Church in 1867 of the peasant Peter Andriyanov, who was married the first time, with the peasant Evdokia Sergeyeva. Priest Peter Yakovlev and sexton Vasily Posolsky conducted the wedding. The peasants believed that "faith without works is dead," and judged a man not by his outward piety, but by how he fulfills the commandments of Christ. The peasant population observed the religious canons in which Orthodox customs found expression. According to the memoirs of the Voronezh peasant I. Stolyarov about his childhood, church posts were observed very strictly in the village. In total, there were more than two hundred fasting days in a year, and fasting determined the diet and the diet of the products of a rural family. In fasting, it was impossible to drink milk not only for adults, but also for children, and these days they ate only potatoes, millet porridge, kvass and sour cabbage. Peasants believed that outside the Church it is impossible to save and gain the kingdom of heaven. After the birth of the children, it was necessary to baptize on the second or third day. This event could be postponed, but not more than a month, due to the remoteness of the rural temple, spring thaw or suffering time. Since child mortality was high, parents tried to christen the child as early as possible, because they believed that babies who died baptized become angels. The godparents were present in the village temple when the sacrament of Baptism was performed. Now they were accountable to God for the righteous life of their godson. Then people, coming from the church, celebrated christening, laying the festive table. The place of honor was occupied by the godfather and godfather, as the peasants attached great importance to spiritual kinship. In the middle of the XIX century in the Tambov province in the Morshansk district it was considered an unforgivable sin to quarrel with the godfather or godfather. Therefore, to avoid sin, the peasants tried to take the godparents from another house and not have a spiritual relationship with the household. The peasants' attitude toward death was completely Christian. They believed that the soul is immortal and there is an afterlife, and therefore they did not have a sense of fear of death as a physical phenomenon. From childhood, the proximity of death was common for peasants: in their presence, their grandfathers and grandmothers, brothers and sisters, they also became witnesses to the last minutes of their neighbors' lives. The peasants were only afraid that the death hour would not find them "unprepared". The peasants considered death an inevitable event, and therefore, before death, they confessed, communed, and reunited. The funeral in the village was a church, the deceased was buried in a church and buried in a rural cemetery, graveyard.

The Russian peasant, working on the earth, realized his responsibility to God, fulfilling his commandments in relation to the earth, and to economic activity. The authors of the collection "Russians" argue that "Christianity helped to develop a conscientious attitude to work and strict discipline, since the peasants believed that labor was blessed by God." Public prayers and religious processions were widely practiced in the villages, and the Orthodox faith of the Russian peasant was expressed in this. Such prayers took place at the initiative of the community or individual laity. Moreover, those prayers were widely spread throughout Russia. In the memoirs of the village priest of the Tambov province, it is said that such prayers could be performed in the fields and on a variety of occasions. The reason for the prayers could be the beginning and end of field work, drought, the first cattle pasture. Sometimes prayers and religious processions were performed for prevention. For example, in Kursk province, on the feast of the Epiphany, the grain was poured in the form of a cross in the courtyard, and while the animals were eating grain, they walked around the cross three times with icons and sprinkled it with holy water to keep the animals alive and healthy. To avoid the death of cattle, prayers were served on February 11 on the day of St. Blasius. On April 23, St. George's Day, prayers were held on the occasion of the first cattle pasture. In the Oryol province, prayers from drought annually served in the field on the Sunday before the Ascension, on July 8, at Kazan, prayers from hail were served. The peasants widely used holy water in the household and in everyday life, which brought grace: it was sprinkled with fruits, vegetables, fields, cattle, crops, seeds. Epiphany water was especially appreciated (Pospelovsky, 1996).

In the last quarter of the 19th century, the government attempted to distinguish between the spheres of life of the rural world and the parish community. By the circular of the Minister of the Interior of March 21, 1887, rural and rural parish gatherings were forbidden to interfere in the affairs of church administration, in the affairs of the parish, drawing up sentences on these issues. By prohibiting rural and volost gatherings from making decisions regarding domestic parish life, this act deprived the peasant world of the right to actively participate in church parish administration, and transferred the emphasis in management from institutes of peasant public self-government to the religious community of parishioners. This attempt was not entirely successful due to the deep penetration of Orthodoxy into the consciousness of the Russian peasantry, the unity in this consciousness of the secular and church. Some types of misconduct that were prosecuted by the law, such as murder, deceit, fraud, embezzlement, combined the properties of sin and crime in the eyes of the peasants. Understanding by the state legislation of a crime as an act combining the signs of a criminal offense and a crime against faith formed the basis the law on the provision to the community after 1861 of the right to "remove from the society perverse peasants" and placing them at the disposal of the government. One can also say that blasphemy was so alien to the Russian religious type that the first cases on these charges appeared only after the 1905 revolution.

In such cases, the peasants made a worldly sentence about the removal of a person from society for bad behavior. The same sentences were drawn up against peasants who were convicted of theft by the circumstances of the case, but did not admit what they had done in court, which aggravated their guilt. When the state introduced the "General Regulation on Peasants" in 1861, it was guided by the idea of gradually introducing customary law into the framework of state law. The force of existing legal norms was recognized as custom: property and family property disputes and legal relations for the most part continued to be resolved on the basis of customary law practice. The government understood that these norms were organic for the religious and moral views of the peasantry, and, on the contrary, civil law did not always agree with the religious and life ideals of the peasantry, with their ideas about truth, goodness, and justice. The rise of the priest's authority not only as a spiritual shepherd, but also as an adviser to peasants in household, household, and other matters, had an impact on the decision of the Synod to introduce teaching of medicine, natural history, and agriculture in theological seminaries. In the late 1860s, these church departments were abolished due to the lack of allowances, classrooms, however, the dioceses began to supply rural priests with folk medicine books, agricultural books or practical instructions for educating the peasants. The priests helped the peasants with advice, "and sometimes with possible measures, in illnesses and in domestic life, for which they enjoyed their special location, landlords and peasants willingly helped such priests in their households." The peasants rendered reverence to the priest constantly. Meeting the priest, they without fail took off their hats, bowed low and asked for blessings; they called the priest "father", the deacon - "father deacon", the psalm-maker - by the name of the patronymic. To insult a clergyman, according to the peasants, is a great sin. Respect for the priesthood was combined with the exactingness shown by parishioners to its bearer. According to their conviction, the pastor should, with due observance of the church charter, perform divine services and requisition, be attentive to questions and appeals of parishioners. He had to know the needs and concerns of his parishioners. The priest himself was a farmer, and agricultural occupations even more closely connected clergy and parish. All the main stages of the life cycle of the Russian peasant were inextricably linked with the parish: the christening of the newborn, the marriage of the couple, the funeral service of the dead and their constant commemoration. Thus, the parish played a special role in the life of the peasant; he was an integral part of village life and life. The closure of the church in the village was perceived negatively, since it was believed that with the closure of the temple the village itself would disappear. All this stimulated the ardent desire of the peasants to have a temple in their village, which was most often built at the expense of peasant families and rural communities. Most of the temples and churches built in Russia in the 19th century were wooden: serfs could not afford to build a stone temple (they were usually erected more often by landowners). The parish in Russia of the 19th century is not only a church with a clergy, it is also an administrative unit. It could be formed in the presence of funds for the maintenance of clergy. Moreover, in the XIX century they called the clergy, consisting of this temple. As a rule, a clergy of 3-4 people was present at the church: a priest, deacon, clerk, and psalm-reader. It is necessary to mention the church elder as a person who was elected from the community and helped the priest in his affairs. A parishioner was considered a male or female person who has his own house in the parish and is in this peasant community. The problem of relations between church authorities and parish clergy with the parish community in the late XIX - early XX centuries studied by historians. Church historians A.A. Papkov and N.Ya. Vinogradov, the reason for the gap between the parish and the clergy was considered the isolation of the spiritual estate. The parish strengthened and stimulated the love of the temple, sacrifice and mercy. A regular visit to the temple corresponded to the idea of the peasants about a righteous and pious life. The parish was a certain religious and moral institution that participated in the formation of the spiritual and moral image of the peasantry; moral concepts of a citizen were formed within the framework of parish life. The attitude of the peasants to certain events, their assessment, was often based on the judgments of the priest himself: the peasantry trusted him as a smart and educated person.

CONCLUSION

Thus, the material examined by us shows that the interaction of nobles and peasants with the Church in the provinces of the Central Black Earth Region in the 19th and early 20th centuries. It was aimed at serving the Fatherland, the Church and the people and was blessed by Christian shrines. In the second half of the 19th century, the peasants still changed their attitude towards the priest and the Church for the worse, however, never to the questions of faith.

REFERENCES

Extract from the journal of the Special Department of the Scientific Committee of the Ministry of Education on December 4, 1879 on the teaching of the Law of God in public schools. 143 p.

Fedorov, V. A. (2005). Theological education in the Russian Orthodox Church in the 19th century. *Pedagogy*, (5), 67–83.

Kuchenkova, V. A. (1993). Shrines of the Tambov diocese. Department of Moscow.

Oryol diocesan sheets. (1873). N°. 4. 200–207.

Pospelovsky, D. V. (1996). *The Orthodox Church in the History of Russia*. Biblical and Theological Institute of St. Andrew.

Tarasova, V. A. (2005). The Higher Theological School in Russia in the late XIX - early XX centuries. In *History of Imperial Orthodox Theological Academies*. New Chronograph.

Chapter 6
Church and Secular Authority

ABSTRACT

In the 19th-early 20th centuries, civil and church authorities, interacting with each other in the provinces of the Central Black Earth Region, had to take into account the opinions and the possibility of interference in decision-making by spiritual and secular authorities, while observing mutual interests. Deanery of the parish churches, personally appointed by the bishop from the most experienced and active clergy, and who had great oversight rights to various parties of the churches and clergy of their district, were the main business partners of the church organization with the county administration. In the county town, the deaneries were "status figures" in provincial life; they were among those "nomenclature" posts that had a great influence on decision-making in the county.

INTRODUCTION

In the XIX - early XX centuries the secular world began to gradually move away from the Church, and therefore Christian denominations experienced difficulties, since the Church needed to find its place in a changing society, comprehend the new time and solve various religious issues. And the Church was to be "renewed" and solve the old tasks in a new way. Various social and political forces could not leave the Church without attention, since the Orthodox Church was too important, especially since the solution of a huge issue for the future of the country - the abolition of serfdom - was put into practice. In the process of peasant reform, the Church's calls for respect

DOI: 10.4018/978-1-6684-4915-8.ch006

for each other's people, for mercy, for honest work, preaching about the "contrariness" of slavery were voiced with increased strength — such was the Church's centuries-old activity in educating Russian people. The judgments were contradictory, but everyone believed that the Orthodox Church was necessary for Russian society, and the future of Russia would be unthinkable without it.

In the 19th century, the Orthodox Church was an instrument of state policy, an institution that merged with state structures. The Church was ruled by the Holy Synod and the spiritual consistories. Although the Synod was the executive branch and did not have legislative initiative, it issued decrees that the ecclesiastical departments were required to fulfill.

The composition of the Synod changed, but in the XIX - early XX centuries. it included 10 bishops representing the black clergy, as well as the confessor of the emperor and the main priest of the army and navy, who were representatives of the white clergy. Some members of the Synod were permanent, who were required to attend all meetings of the Synod: for example, the confessor of the emperor, the main priest of the army and navy, Metropolitan of St. Petersburg; the provisional members took part in the meetings of the Synod in turn, once or twice a year. The bishops led the spiritual consistories, they were appointed by the Synod and confirmed by the emperor. The bishop, together with the spiritual consistory and with the support of the deans - senior priests in the diocese - exercised administration and judgment. The members of the clerical consistory were representatives of the white and black clergy, who were elected by the bishop, and the bishops appointed deaneries and approved the consistory. In the consistories, the white clergy were better represented than in the Synod: in 1801, parish priests comprised 38% of the consistory, and in the 1860s. - 79%.

The chief prosecutor, who was appointed by the emperor from secular persons, supervised the work of the Synod. But the control of the chief public prosecutor was superficial, and therefore the spiritual consistories controlled themselves. The development of the institute of public prosecutor's office can be divided into two phases: the first - from the day it was established until 1803, the second phase began in 1817 and lasted until 1903–1917, i.e. until the end of the synodal period, this was a transitional time for the public prosecutor's office. Until 1803, the influence of the chief prosecutor did not have a decisive role in the activities of the Synod, which was in direct connection with the sovereign himself. The monasteries were ruled by the monks themselves. By the beginning of the reign of Alexander I, the Synod consisted of 5 representatives of the black clergy. This composition was established by Catherine II and did not change under Paul I.

But still, the chief prosecutor began to restore order in the synodal administration. On October 21, 1803, A.N. Golitsyn took the position of Chief Prosecutor of the Synod. Despite a superficial understanding of the life of the church in Russia, knyaz' (prince) A.N. Golitsyn was able to arouse respect and trust of the members of the Synod. The bishops did not dare to speak out against a friend of the emperor's youth. To strengthen A.N. Golitsyn's power in the Synod, a new instruction of the chief prosecutor was approved. According to the new instruction, the chief prosecutor was obliged not only to hold, open and close the meetings of the Synod, not only to announce to the clergy present the decrees of the emperor that were already contained in the previous instructions, but also to personally supervise the fulfillment of the will of the emperor.

To the former duty of the chief prosecutor of disobeying him to no court other than the imperial court, Alexander I added the right of a decisive vote in the adoption of synodal decisions. These important additions in the new instruction of the Chief Prosecutor enabled the emperor to strengthen his decisive influence on the work of the Synod. The public prosecutor became a full representative of secular authority in relation to the Church. The chief procurator had a deputy and a chancellery like the departments under the ministries, as he was a state dignitary, equated with the rights of ministers. The Office of the Chief Prosecutor was founded in 1839. There was also a chancellery of the Holy Synod, but it was also subordinate to the Chief Prosecutor.

Until 1819, updating the composition of the Synod for various reasons happened quite often. This form of participation of clergy in the work of one of the highest institutions of state power made it possible for all bishops to partake in the service in Petersburg.

Since 1819, Alexander I stopped the practice of meeting each bishop personally. There were 7 people in the Synod by this time. All of them entered the state, approved by the emperor on July 9, 1819. It consisted of archbishops, archpriests, metropolitans and bishops. This act ended the process of updating the members of the Synod (Ershov, 2019).

At the beginning of the reign of Alexander I, changes were made to the synodal clerical work. Bureaucratic activity has become an element of state administration of church affairs. The essence of the main task of the Synod was to prepare in practice the implementation of the decrees of the emperor, for example, on the formation of the composition of the Synod. To solve this problem, a linear clerical system was formed, which was engaged in the distribution of synodal decisions formed on the basis of personal decrees and approved by the Synod. First, the necessary decisions were printed in the synodal printing house. Then these copies were sent to the Consistory and the Board of the Deanery, where bishops, archbishops and metropolitans should have become acquainted with the contents of these decrees. Churches and monasteries also received a certain number of copies of synodal ordinances for clergy. A special branch of law - church law - regulated relations within the Church, as well as its relations with the state and society. Its constituent parts, which concerned the Church, were dogmatic and canonical law (Weinberg, 1886).

In the XIX - early XX centuries civil and church authorities, interacting with each other in the provinces of the Central Black Earth Region, had to take into account the opinions and the possibility of interference in decision-making by spiritual and secular authorities, while observing mutual interests. Deanery of the parish churches, personally appointed by the bishop from the most experienced and active clergy, and who had great oversight rights to various parties of the Churches and clergy of their district, were the main business partners of the church organization with the county administration. In the county town, the deaneries were "status figures" in provincial life, they were among those "nomenclature" posts that had a great influence on decision-making in the county.

Therefore, the cathedral and city deans were mediators between church and government structures and had great power over the clergy. The reports of the deaning rural districts contained data on the composition and activities of the clergy, on its financial situation and moral condition, on religious education in parish and parish schools on the territory of the deanery. The consistory studied the reports and drew attention, first of all, to the shortcomings, and quickly took measures to eliminate them. The deanes carried out spiritual supervision of both the clergy and the laity. The role of supervision at the county level in the first half of the 19th century belonged to the clergy. They were intermediaries between the administrative authorities, parish clergy and higher church authorities.

Control of religious morality was formal. The idea of control was based on the theory of Nicholas I, that good morality is the best theory of law, and it should always be in the heart and have religion as its foundation. Important Christian holidays had folk Orthodox customs, which differed both in neighboring counties and in volost's. In the provinces of the Central Black Earth Region, the icons of the Mother of God were venerated the most: the Sorrowful Bogoroditsa, Bogoroditsa the Burning Cupina, the God-Loving Bogoroditsa, Kazanskaya Bogoroditsa, Smolenskaya Bogoroditsa, «Znameniye». Numerous religious processions were made with the icons. In the Kursk province, the icon of the Kursk Mother of God "The Sign" was the most revered. The abbot of the Korennoy Monastery Makarii turned to Alexander I with a petition, which allowed the miraculous icon of the Kursk Mother of God «Znameniye» to be in the Korennaya pustyn' not two weeks, but from the ninth week before the feast of the Nativity of the Blessed Virgin Mary (September 12). For seven centuries, that icon was the patroness of the Kursk land.

In May 1852, in the Kursk province, the State Council decided to make non-working days of the procession («krestnyy khod»). The traditions of the procession were strengthened for centuries and represented a well-developed order and ceremonial part. In 1833, Kursk received the status of a diocesan administrative center, and at this time, the significance of this rite increased. The procession is elevated to the rank of a provincial holiday, it unites the smokers, brings together secular officials, clergy and ordinary people. Particularly solemnity and significance of this rite was given by participation in religious processions of governors and clergy. The Archbishop of Kursk and Belgorod Seraphim recalled that, on the eve of the removal of the miraculous icon, in the Znamensky Cathedral, in addition to the bishop's all-night vigil, another all-night service was served in a special place in the middle of the Krai Square. It began in the evening, at eight o'clock, and ended after midnight. Burning candles lit up in the darkness tens of thousands of faces, and a choir, consisting of hundreds of voices, carried sacred songs around. The ringing of all the Kursk Churches poured into the ringing of the monastery bells. And for everyone who gathered from the near and far provinces of Russia for the procession, grace descended.

The church was one of the state ministries - the "department of the Orthodox confession" - throughout the imperial period of Russian history. The emperor received various proposals for the reform of the Church regarding the change in various aspects of her life. The highest political leadership understood that Church reforms were necessary, and the emperor and his entourage were interested in strengthening Orthodoxy. In this regard, the work experience of the General Directorate of Spiritual Affairs of Foreign Confessions and the Ministry of Spiritual Affairs and Public Education is of great interest. The experience of creating such a double ministry was to include church authorities in the state structure, thereby realizing many ideas through education. The initiator of the creation of these state institutions was the supreme power of the state in the person of Emperor Alexander I and his closest assistants, among whom A.N. Golitsyn, who was an active supporter of the inclusion of church authorities in state structures.

The Main Department of Spiritual Affairs of Foreign Confessions was formed in 1810, when the breath of the impending war was felt in Russian society. Under these conditions, a gradual formation of a national idea was going on, aimed at strengthening Russian statehood as the basis of the union of autocracy and Orthodoxy. This idea was first formulated by N.M. Karamzin in a memo to Alexander I "On Ancient and New Russia" of 1811. Emphasizing that the clergy never opposed the spiritual authority, supported it in state affairs and the conscience of random evasion of virtue, he concluded that it is better if the consent of the monarch and the clergy in matters of state good "has the form of freedom and inner conviction, but not submissive humility". Strengthening the legislative framework, it was necessary to strictly determine the place of the Russian Orthodox Church and other religious denominations in the state structure of the empire, where Orthodoxy was the state religion.

In accordance with the Decree of August 17, 1810, the competence of the new institution included:

1. Mandatory submission to the Highest Consideration of proposals on the determination of bishops and other clergy of the Catholic and Uniate confessions, the appointment of commanding monastic orders and theological seminaries, the filling of vacant seats (including secular persons) to the posts of directors of Catholic consistories, super-general quartermaster
2. Consideration of various complaints of harassment by diocesan authorities - bishops and clergy,
3. Supervision of theological seminaries, monasteries and other faith-based institutions,
4. Monitoring the state of spiritual estates and their financial situation,
5. Construction and closure of churches.

The further fate of the Main Directorate of Spiritual Affairs of Foreign Confessions is closely connected with the activities of the Ministry of Spiritual Affairs and Public Education, because, on the basis of the decree of Alexander I of October 24, 1817, it was merged with the Ministry of Public Education and became part of the Department of Spiritual affairs (Vvedensky, 1905).

May 22, 1822 Epiphanius consecrated the Church of the Holy Trinity, which became in 1836 the cathedral in the city of Voronezh. In the building of the theological seminary was the house church of St. John the Evangelist, which was consecrated by Bishop Epiphanius in 1822.

Voronezh vice-governor M.L. Magnitsky in a letter to Count A.A. From 1817, Arakcheev was given a forest characterization by Bishop Epiphanius: "The Reverend Shepherd is very virtuous and pious, he also knows the real situation here. Bishop Epiphanius from the pulpit's department is opposed to abuses and enemies of the internal order, but those to whom this refers are not being corrected, and the clergy for apostolic sermons are in trouble from various persecutions of the police, which violates the laws. "

In 1805, with the assistance of the Voronezh Governor I.A. Potapov on Bolshaya Moskovskaya Street, behind the rampart, a new church was built in the name of the Holy Trinity. Until 1822, internal work continued, a three-tier bell tower was completed in 1818. And in all its beauty the Trinity Cathedral appeared before the Voronezh residents: the height of the dome reached 37 meters, and the bell tower - 40.5 meters. In 1858, the "renewal" of the church began: they began using pneumatic stoves for heating, marbled the walls in the interior, outside the Church, pediments with four columns were erected over the side entrances. In style, this structure was defined as empire or late classicism.

On January 28, 1830, Dmitry Nikitich Begichev, who was recommended by the Minister of the Interior A.A., became the governor of Voronezh. Zakrevsky. At this time, miraculous healings from the incorrupt relics of St. Mitrofan began, as the historian Litvinov told in his studies. Such miracles attracted many believers to Voronezh, especially a lot of people in the summer of 1830, and the cholera epidemic began, 300-400 people died from the disease every day. D.N. Begichev contributed a lot of his own money to fight the disease and organized fundraising among bourgeois and noblemen. With this money, a hospital for 200 people was built to treat cholera patients, and in 1831 the epidemic was over. For the great zeal of D.N. On February 27, 1831, Begichev was granted a thousand rubles from the State Treasury for 12 years, and on March 9, 1832 he was awarded the title of State Councilor. In 1832, at the ceremony attended by Emperor Nicholas I, the relics of St. Mitrofan were discovered. 128 years after his death, Saint Mitrofan was canonized.

During this visit, Nicholas I did not like the location of the Voronezh Theological Seminary, and he ordered the building to be built in another place. Architect A.F. Shchedrin completed the drawings of the new building, but the seminary remained in the old place, since no money was allocated for the construction of the new building (Ershov, 2020).

In 1810–1813 and 1818–1823 the city head of Voronezh was Samuel Nikitich Meshcheryakov, who donated substantially to the Church. He had a millionaire fortune, since he conducted extensive trade in Voronezh. Two churches were built with the money of S.N. Meshcheryakov.

Those churches were the Ascension Church and the Church of the Prophet Samuel. In addition, S.N. Meshcheryakov donated funds for the construction of the Voronezh Theological Seminary. Voronezh mayor S.N. Meshcheryakov became famous not only in Voronezh for his charity. At his expense in Kiev was built a stone church of St. Nicholas the Wonderworker. In 1809, his wife Alexandra died and was buried in Kiev. In memory of his wife S.N. Meshcheryakov allocated money for the construction of a stone church, before that all the churches were mostly wooden. In 1823, Samuel Nikitich Meshcheryakov died, he was buried at the altar of the Ascension Church. He left a huge fortune of 1.5 million rubles to the heirs, but he did not forget the Church either. S.N. Meshcheryakov allocated the following funds for decorating the holy churches of the city of Voronezh:

- 9 thousand rubles — to the Blagoveshchensky cathedral;
- 20 thousand rubles — to the Cemetery of the Ascension (Kladbishchenskaya Voznesenskaya) Church, which he built;
- 5 thousand rubles — to the parish of the Resurrection (Voskresenskaya) Church;
- 5 thousand rubles — to the Nikolaev parish church;
- 5 thousand rubles — to Theological parish church;
- 10 thousand rubles — for burial, commemoration and distribution to the poor.

It is important that many of the legal provisions relating to the Russian Orthodox Church and other faiths of Russia were worked out and refined in more detail. Despite the fact that the synodal department was actually completely under the control of the Double Ministry, Orthodoxy, unlike other religions, acquired the status of a state religion. The policy of Alexander I contributed to the accession of new, in particular, Western territories to the Russian state with the help of the clergy. Moreover, Minister A.N. Golitsyn on the orders of the emperor in disputes between the Catholic, Lutheran and Orthodox clergy took the side of Orthodoxy. Due to the large duplication of the functions of the Synod and for a number of other reasons, including those related to the Department of Public Education, the Ministry of Spiritual Affairs and Public Education was abolished by Decree of May 15, 1824, and its functions were transferred to the Main Department of Spiritual Affairs of Foreign Confessions, respectively.

By a decree of August 24, 1827, the staff of the Department of the Main Spiritual Directorate of Foreign Confessions was approved as part of the three departments:

- First - on matters of Roman Catholic, Armenian and Greek-Uniate confessions (3 tables);
- Second - on matters of Protestant confession (2 tables);
- Third - on matters of non-Christian confession (2 tables).

There were 24 people in the state. Subsequently, the structure did not change.

In the reign of Alexander II, there was a need to transform the church system, which begins to be publicly discussed. Against the background of the renewal of the state, the contradictions between the spiritual and secular authorities are aggravated, and therefore the problems of reforming church life are acute. After 1861, the governance structure of the Church did not undergo significant changes. Since the time of Peter I, the supreme organ of church administration was the Holy Synod, it consisted of the highest hierarchs of the church, but all matters were decided by the chief public prosecutor, who headed the Synod, who was appointed by the emperor from secular persons, the chief public prosecutor was personally subordinate to the emperor. Law considered the Russian emperor as the official head of the Russian Orthodox Church.

In the 19th century, the number of dioceses of the Russian Orthodox Church increased from 55 to 67. The number of Orthodox Churches increased. At the beginning of the XIX century, their number reached 25.2 thousand, and in 1860 they already became 36.2 thousand, in 1880 - 45.7 thousand, in 1917 - 54.2 thousand. At the beginning of the XX century, there were 23.6 thousand home Churches and chapels. But the number of parish clergy grew more slowly: at the beginning of the XIX century the clergy numbered 102 thousand people, and in 1860 - 113.6 thousand; by 1880 its number dropped to 98.9 thousand, and by 1917 the number of clergymen grew to 112 thousand people.

The number of monks and Orthodox monasteries in the Russian state increases by the middle of the XIX century. In 1808, there were 447 Orthodox monasteries, of which 353 were male and 94 were female, in which there were 5 thousand monks and 6 thousand novices, and in 1860 there were already

614 monasteries, of which 447 were male and 136 were female, in which 8 thousand monks and 13 thousand novices served.

In the 19th century, in the early 60s, in the Voronezh province there were 313 wooden churches and cathedrals, 480 stone, 8 wooden chapels and 9 monasteries, and the number of clergy was 19,328 people. By 1890, there were 973 churches in the Kursk province; 2126 people accounted for one church. In Oryol province in 1840 there were 847 churches, 1 church was attended by up to 1,717 parishioners; and in 1890 there were 992 churches and 1 church was attended by up to 2 110 parishioners. The population grew, as a result of which the burden on the priest increased. In 1796, the borders of the Tambov province were approved, and the Tambov diocese did not administratively leave these borders by 1803. At that time there were 900 churches in the diocese. By 1917, there were 1,500 churches, and the clergy amounted to 3,000 people. The Tambov diocese consisted of 59 districts.

In 1864, decrees were issued on the parish clergy and church parish. Upon arrival from parishioners, elected bodies were formed, headed by parish priests. On February 13, 1910, the Voronezh Dean Archpriest Aristarchus Aristov was sent the decree of the Holy Synod on the distribution of parishes in the city of Voronezh. The decree spoke of the need for each clergy to inform all their parishioners of their belonging to the parish of this church. The reasons for all parish churches, in view of the upcoming reckoning of parishioners from one church to another, must send each other their parish documents to make necessary inquiries about new parishioners. The diocesan authorities, in order to streamline the parish life, to maximize communication and unity with the parishioners, decided: to forbid the clergy to fulfill the requirements in the houses of the residents of Voronezh, who have nothing to do with their churches. Small parishes combined with large ones, as a result of which their number was reduced. Measures were also taken to improve the material situation of the clergy: the state allowance of the parish priest increased by 67%, priests who retired as they were old, as well as their widows, began to receive small pensions. Church clerks who were left out of work did not receive any benefits.

In the second half of the 19th century, Russia turned to meet a contradictory and ambiguous new time. The implementation of the transformation program has changed the face of the country and the way people live. This also applied to church transformations. At that time, the Orthodox Church was ruled by the Synod. People of various directions were waiting for reforms; they wanted freedom and publicity for the Church. In 1867, the division of the dioceses into three categories was abolished: the metropolis, the archdiocese and the bishopric were equated with the rank of metropolis. The bishops of the dioceses received wider rights: they could, without the permission of the Synod, build churches, independently allow entry into monasticism, and solve the problems of spiritual education in their diocese. Now, the parish clergy had the right to elect deans who stood at the head of small church districts, and which included 10 to 15 parishes. Deanes led elected deanery councils. To solve local church needs, the parish clergy began to have the right to gather for deanery, school and diocesan congresses.

From April 23, 1861 to May 9, 1868, P.A. Valuev became Minister of the Interior. He can be considered the author of church reform, it was he who convinced Alexander II to decide on reform of the Orthodox Church. P.A. Valuev opposed state intervention in church affairs and political pressure on religious beliefs; he believed that the Orthodox Church could be strengthened through the development of its internal forces with due government policies. To understand the course of reforms when P.A. Valuev, you need to know his fundamental approach to reforms in general: "Any transformation should take place without internal upheavals and the private rights and interests that were legally established before that and have been in force for a long time should not be neglected."

Church reform was undertaken to preserve the foundations of autocracy, increasing the authority of the Orthodox parish clergy among the people was its main task.

Thanks to church reforms carried out under Alexander II, the activities of the Russian Orthodox Church revived, as the bureaucratic fetters that hindered her softened. But church reforms were shallow, since they did not touch upon issues of church management and its relations with secular authorities. The reforms were inconsistent and therefore fragile, which led to the abandonment of them in the subsequent reign.

Ober-Prosecutor of the Synod Professor of Civil Law K.P. Pobedonostsev (1827–1907), appointed by Alexander II, determined the confessional policy under Alexander III.

For 25 years, K.P. Pobedonostsev was the ideologist of the autocracy. K.P. Pobedonostsev believed that in Russia the Church and the state should be inextricably linked, its violation lead to the death of the Church and the state. "An unfaithful state is a utopia that cannot be implemented, since unbelief is a direct denial of the state." Government, according to K.P. Pobedonostsev, protects the Church from its enemies, helps to ensure its financial situation. At the same time, the Church must act in accordance with the rules existing in the state and take into account the "feedback of knowledgeable persons".

In practice, Pobedonostsev wanted to implement unconditional leadership of the Church. In private conversations, members of the Synod convicted Pobedonostsev of despotism and spoke out against his ideas. Gradually Pobedonostsev picked up like-minded people in the Synod. The church elite supported the policy of K.P. Pobedonostsev in such areas as increasing the number of parish schools, strengthening the Orthodox Church and neutralizing the Old Believers and sectarianism. K.P. Pobedonostsev believed that it was important to make such changes that would not affect the Synodal system, for example, the reform of theological seminaries, and Orthodox hierarchs, priests and lay people expressed the need to stop state pressure on the Church, convene a Council and restore the institution of patriarchate. But the official authorities decided not to notice such statements (Ershov, 2019).

K.P. Pobedonostsev, supported by secular authorities, tried to raise the religiosity of the Russian people, he wanted to widely spread Orthodoxy among non-Russian peoples. During his tenure as Chief Prosecutor of the Synod, the number of church publications, circulation of religious literature increased, and the activity of Orthodox missions increased. He helped organize the Church Brotherhoods, which were called to strengthen Orthodoxy in the western provinces of Russia. The church was to develop, in addition to religious duties, according to Pobedonostsev, to strengthen its authority among the people, and other forms of activity. K.P. Pobedonostsev attached great importance to the organization of church libraries, charity, sermons, conversations of priests with parishioners, and celebrations associated with church anniversaries.

The role of Chief Prosecutor of the Synod increased significantly when K.P. Pobedonostsev was in power. Only K.P. Pobedonostsev, not taking into account the views of the Synod College, decided all the affairs of the Synod. The centralization of church administration intensified. The chief prosecutor tightly controlled the diocesan clergy. The diocesan bishops were supervised by "proxies". These "proxies" were supposed to be with the bishops, they sent the chief prosecutor reports on the moods and behavior of the clergy. The bishops were often transferred from the diocese to the diocese; in 13 years, 180 such movements took place.

The confessional policy of the government under the public prosecutor K.P. Pobedonostsev was contradictory, on the one hand, his department tried to revive the activities of the Orthodox Church. On the other hand, to tighten government control over these activities, petty regulation hindered the independence of the Church, which led to a crisis.

The influence of the Orthodox clergy on the morality of believers has fallen. Local authorities (sometimes negative) had a very big influence on the church. The deacon of the church of the settlement of Osipova, Starobelsky district, Vasily Glagolev, was insulted by volost foreman Fedor Pavlov. Deacon Vasily Glagolev made a complaint to Epiphanius, Bishop of Voronezh. The Voronezh Spiritual Consistory received this complaint. After that, His Eminence sent the complaint to the Voronezh provincial government for consideration. Voronezh provincial government decided: to reprimand volost foreman Fedor Pavlov. In the Voronezh Spiritual Consistory, the rector Archimandrite Methodius, Ioann Tactov signed the complaint.

In the Voronezh province, there were often cases when representatives of the clergy became deputies. On March 28, 1821, after hearing a report from the Dean Archpriest Kirill Mikhailovsky from the settlement («sloboda») of Borovenka Nikolayevskaya Church and Priest Alexander from the settlement of Muratova, it was determined that Archpriest Kirill Mikhailovsky and Priest Alexander were approved as deputies of the settlement («sloboda») of Borovenka and the Muratova' settlement («sloboda»). This statement to inform His Grace Methodius. You may notice that some clergymen were very poor and therefore turned to the Voronezh spiritual consistory with requests for placement in a spiritual position.

On March 16, 1821, the priest of the Assumption Church, Timofey Yablochkov, asked the bishop of Voronezh, Epiphanius, to arrange him for some position due to his plight in the settlement of Lubyanka at the Baptist Church due to the fact that a third staff of clergy was opened at this Church. Timofey Yablochkov was transferred to this state by decree of the Voronezh Spiritual Consistory. But it was said that without the extreme reason for moving to another church, the government should not bother.

In the 19th century, clergymen of various churches collaborated with local authorities. On June 8, 1873, Archpriest Pyatnitskaya Church of the city of Voronezh, Yevlampy Svyatozarov, asked the Voronezh City Council to approve the project for the construction of a wooden wing belonging to him on Dvoryanskaya Street. With this project, Svyatozarov attached three sheets of stamp paper. The Voronezh City Government decided on June 9, 1873 to approve the aforementioned project and inform the Voronezh City Administration about this.

In the Voronezh province, there were cases of petitions by local authorities about the construction of new churches. On March 14, 1821, residents of the settlement of Kuryachevka and the Bondarev farm asked Epiphanius, Bishop of Voronezh, to build a new stone church and explained this with the following circumstances: most people cannot call a priest because of the distance of their farm and settlement from a nearby church to repent and newborn babies christen. The church is asked to be built in the name of the Nativity of the Blessed Virgin Mary. Epiphanius, Bishop of Voronezh, allowed this church to be built.

In the Voronezh province, at the male gymnasium, a church operated in the name of the Holy Right Prince Alexander Nevsky, which was very famous. The merchant of the second guild Peter Alekseevich Zhalin at his own expense built this church in 1885. In the city garden there was a one-story building of the gymnasium, the Alexander Nevsky Church went into the corridor of the gymnasium with three huge doors, inside the Church was a high hall with columns, with windows to the garden.

Since the gymnasium church was considered aristocratic, it was attended by the high society of the city. Former gymnasium pupil M.M. Melentyev recalled: "It was very quiet here, there was no crowd, the service was simple and touching, so it was pleasant to be in it. Only gymnasium pupils served in this church".

Some people asked the local authorities for permission to build the chapel in gratitude to God's help. On May 25, 1893, wine merchants sent a request to the Voronezh city mayor, Ivan Viktorovich Titov, for the construction of a chapel on Starokonnaya Square. The petition says that the Torgovites served a moleben of the Sorrowing Mother of God with a holy passage from the Theological and Smolensk Church. Trade was very scarce. After the prayer, everything was fine. And for this success, merchants sincerely thank God. And for the future, at their own expense, market traders wish to build a chapel in this place in the name of the Sorrowing Mother of God and ask the Voronezh city head to determine a place for construction. Voronezh city government decided to give permission to build a chapel on this site. The decision is dated 1894. The college registrar Ivan Vasilievich Azarov took over the guardianship of this chapel.

An interesting fact is the fact that secular authorities tried to preserve the customs that were observed at various religious holidays. There was an old custom to decorate churches, houses and temples with young birches on the day of the Holy Trinity. According to the Ministry of State Property, this custom could not have bad influence due to the fact that it is a very valuable tree species. It was ordered to instruct the Orthodox clergy to explain to the parishioners about the harm to forestry during the extermination of young birch trees. To convince the parishioners so that on the day of the Trinity it is the same as on other holidays, to use flowers and shrubs, and not to touch the trees. On June 1, 1875 the Voronezh Spiritual Consistory announced this to Archpriest Mikhail Skryabin.

The character of the Orthodox Church was national. She served the Russian state and defended the interests of her people. Therefore, the state turned to the Church for support and blessing, at the same time, providing it with political and material support. The manifesto of Nicholas I clearly traces the unity of the Church and the people. The church fights for the Orthodox faith and protects its brothers, who are united by faith. In the Tambov province from the very beginning of the Crimean War of 1853-1856. the clergy provided assistance to the Russian army. Priests served prayers for the health of warriors and the granting of victory over enemies. On February 14, 1855, a decree of the Tambov provincial government was issued calling on the state militia, which contained a request to the spiritual consistory, so that the text of the manifesto would be read in churches after the divine liturgy to notify parishioners.

Archbishop Nikolai Dobrokhotov (1841-1857) advised the clergy in their sermons to say that Russia's actions were legitimate, and that war was a test that was sent by God. Priests told parishioners that Crimea is a primordially Russian territory, which was invaded by foreign states.

The Lebebyanskoye opolcheniye (militia) was described in the Tambov Provincial Gazette: "The clergy and parishioners of all the city's churches with icons and crosses, while singing sacred songs, to the ringing of the cathedral bell, gathered on the cathedral square in the morning of July 21. The priest Cherneevsky from the Christ-Christmas Church in his speech asked God to grant the Russian army victory over the enemy. The military banner of the squad was consecrated, and M.S. Igumnov conveyed the image of the Mother of God of Kazan to the military commander. "

The church, in addition to spiritual help, also provided militia and material support. Priests and parishioners themselves gave things and money for the needs of the militia. The Znamensky Sukhotinsky monastery donated 30 rubles for the wounded, and for the Tambov squad No. 177 - an icon of the Mother of God of Kazan, 32 measures of vegetables, 3 containers of wine, 3 pounds of bakery products, 50 pieces of poultry and 40 prosphora. Nuns of the Kirsanovsky Tikhvin-Bogoroditsky Monastery gave icons in silver salaries to all the squads that passed through the county. In the Tambov province, until the militia returned in churches and cathedrals, they prayed for the health of the living, for the repose of those who died and died in the war. After the end of hostilities, the militias returned to the province. At home they were met as people who had fulfilled their duty to their homeland, although the Tambov militia did not take part in the hostilities. The troops entered Tambov from June 5 to June 14, 1856, they were met by the clergy in full vestment. Services were held in the Tambov churches in honor of the soldiers, after which the warriors marched along the square in front of the governor's house, and only then dispersed to their counties.

The Orthodox Church, along with secular authorities, took an active part in the course of the Crimean War of 1853-1856.

The synodal church management system created by Peter I existed until the last days of the reign of Nicholas II, despite the fact that the church movement, which was aimed at restoring patriarchate and reviving collegiality, was very strong at the beginning of the 20th century. The clergy and church community, most of the episcopate and individual state dignitaries, supported this movement. The number of parish churches in Russia during the reign of Emperor Nicholas II increased by more than 10 thousand, 250 new monasteries began to operate. In Orel province in October 1899, in memory of the coronation of Emperor Nicholas II, a new church of the Iveron Icon of the Mother of God was built, the main throne of which was consecrated on October 13, 1902. The arrival of Emperor Nicholas II with the heir and the visits of Grand Duchess Elizabeth Feodorovna to the Oryol province contributed to the spiritual development of the Oryol diocese. Tsar Nicholas II arrived in Orel in 1904, while at the Oryol department he led the services of Kirion (Sadzagelov), who became the Oryol bishop on April 23 of this year and reigned until February 3, 1906. For many years, Elizaveta Fedorovna Romanova was the chief of the 51st Chernigov Dragoon Regiment, which was stationed in Orel. The Grand Duchess, together with Grand Duke Sergei Alexandrovich, arrived in Orel Province in 1904 in order to be present when sending the sponsored regiment to the Russo-Japanese war. The Grand Duchess made a review of the regiment, and then she visited the regimental Pokrovsky church, during the consecration by his father Mitrofan Srebryansky.

Emperor Nicholas II donated personal funds for the construction of new churches, he himself participated in their laying and consecration. In 1898, with the direct assistance of Nicholas II and Empress Maria Fyodorovna, a petition was sent to the Voronezh Spiritual Consistory for the establishment in the churches of a circle collection of donations in favor of blind children. The petition said that in Russia there are 250,000 blind children. Each year, the board of trustees of Empress Maria Fyodorovna prepares 25-30 detachments consisting of eye doctors. The guardianship asked to donate who as much as possible for a good cause.

The department of "trusteeship of Maria Fedorovna about the blind" in the city of Voronezh raised 50,000 rubles. With these funds on the territory of the estate of citizen A.N. Klochkova, the famous Voronezh merchant, in 1901–1902. It was decided to build a school for blind children and a church. The first stone of the school building was laid on May 6, 1901. The ceremony was attended by representatives of local institutions, members of the board of trustees, shareholder manager E.K. Istomin, Governor N.A. Sleptsov, Vice-Governor N.A. Khvostov, provincial chairman of the nobility N.I. Szydlowski. The Cathedral Archpriest A. Spassky consecrated the school, attaching great importance to this event, and proclaimed the Sovereign and the entire Reigning House many years. Archpriest A. Spassky put the first stone in the building's foundation, the second - E.A. Shchidlovskaya, then - the governor, followed by the provincial chairman (chairperson) of the nobility and members of the council.

Chairman of the Board of Trusteeship Department Governor P.A. Sleptsov sent Empress Maria Fyodorovna - mother of Emperor Nicholas II, "Patroness of the Guardianship", a congratulatory telegram. The empress replied that she was glad that the construction of a school for the blind and the Church had begun, and she thanked everyone who did a good deed and expressed heartfelt feelings. Nicholas II took the construction of a new Voronezh building seriously. On August 20, 1901, after hearing a message from the Forest Department, the emperor ordered the construction of a house from the Khrenovsky forestry to release 2188 logs for free. To transport the forest by rail, a preferential tariff was introduced for the construction of a school and a church. The consecration of the church took place on September 28, 1902. Since many people came to the consecration of the church, in order to avoid crowding, people could get into the building only by tickets.

The Archbishop of Voronezh, Anastasiy (Dobradin), together with the city clergy performed the service. Chairman of the Board of Trustees Count I.I. Vorontsov-Dashkov, director of public schools of the Petersburg province A.A. Smirnov, Princess Eugene and Olga Oldenburg and other high-ranking officials sent telegrams of welcome. Governor P.A. arrived at the service Sleptsov, Vice Governor A.A. Khvostov, Baron A.A. Iskul von Guildenbrandt. The guardianship report and the article of the Voronezh Telegraph, which were dedicated to the consecration of the building, contained a description of the School of the Blind. These texts said that the new building had 3 floors, it stood on a facade along Bolshaya Moskovskaya Street, from the front door along a stone wide staircase one could go to the Church located on the third floor. In the hall of the church and in the altar, the floors are oak parquet, and in the corridors leading to the church and in the front floor, the floors are made of beautiful metlah tiles.

From the courtyard in the building there were three entrances with stairs, which was necessary in fire protection. The building inside and out was thoroughly completed: in the corridors the arches are made of concrete; there was central heating and electric lighting. On the third floor, in the center, there was a two-light house church. It was built in honor of Mary Yegipetskaya, as she was the Guardian Angel of the mother of Nikolai Alekseevich. Moscow artist Bortsov completed the iconostasis. Rev. Ioann Kronshtadskiy presented the Church with the icon of the Kazan Mother of God. There was a small altar in the temple; it was separated from the hall by a small screen where the believers were. The spiritual mentor of the Church from the time of foundation until the revolution was priest Vasily Rufin, the psalmist was Dmitry Skryabin, the elder was the merchant Nikolai Shuklin. Emperor Nicholas II with all his heart revered the saints, often visited holy places. During the reign of Nicholas II, many saints were canonized. His predecessors canonized the saints Mitrofaniy of Voronezh, Tikhon Zadonsky, Demetrius of Rostov, Innocent of Irkutsk and the Monk Theodosius of Totemsky. And in the years of the reign of Nicholas II, Saint Theodosius Uglitsky was numbered in 1896, Saint Seraphim of Sarov in 1903, and Princess Anna Kashinskaya in 1909.

In 1905, when the revolution especially flared up, the clergy made attempts to restore the cathedral principle in the management of the church. At the head of this movement was Metropolitan of St. Petersburg Anthony Vadkovsky, who was first present in the Holy Synod. On the eve of the revolution, the preparation of legislation on religious freedom began, which culminated in the adoption of the April manifesto "On Strengthening the Principles of Tolerance," as a result of which the government drew attention to the needs of the church. This "manifesto" was being prepared by the Special Meeting, chaired by Count S.Yu. Witte, who headed the Cabinet of Ministers.

During the development of the document, it turned out that with its adoption, the Orthodox Church, which was under the tutelage of the government, would be in a worse position than the heterodox and non-religious communities, which were accustomed to greater independence, as this manifesto got rid of most of the previous police supervision. The synod met three times, after which, on March 22, 1905, the emperor was given a report proposing to change the state of the Church in Russia, the Patriarch should head the Synod and convene the Local Council to discuss church reforms in Moscow. On March 31, 1905, the sovereign recognized the need to convene the Council, but, on the advice of Pobedonostsev, the emperor considered it uncomfortable to convene the Council in an alarming time.

Predsobornoye Prisutstviye (the Pre-Council Presence) spoke of the need to adjust the Basic Laws of the Russian Empire. In paragraph 42 of the Basic Laws it is said that the emperor is the supreme defender, guardian and guardian of the dogmas of the Orthodox faith. The Pre-Council Presence advised editing this paragraph in such a way that the Orthodox Sovereign is the supreme guardian of the state Orthodox Church and its correct order.

Predsobornoye Prisutstviye (the Pre-Council Presence) proposed a more radical change in paragraph 43 of the Basic Laws. Earlier it was written that the autocratic power in church administration acts through the Holy Synod of Government established by it. The new, amended version proposed such a version that the state power carries out its relations with the Orthodox Church in accordance with the All-Russian Church Council, which it recognized, with the Holy Synod and the Patriarch - the Primate of the Russian Orthodox Church. This option implied the rejection of state ecclesiasticality, which was based on the authority of absolute authority, independent over all institutions that were on its territory, including the Church.

In Voronezh province, the congress opened on August 8, 1917 in the building of the Voronezh Theological Seminary under the chairmanship of Archbishop Tikhon.

Representatives of the clergy and laity of the Voronezh diocese, convened for the election of deputies for the upcoming Church Council on August 15, 1917 in Moscow, attended the congress.

In total, it was necessary to elect 5 deputies from the Voronezh diocese: 3 from the laity and 2 from the clergy. 350 people attended the congress. Significantly represented urban and rural clergy, but also a lot of the Voronezh intelligentsia. The townspeople and the Voronezh intelligentsia, together with a significant group of clergy, nominated Tyumenev, a teacher of the cadet corps with a theological education. The candidacy of Fedorenko, a rural teacher, was also approved from the peasants.

In general, Emperor Nicholas II in his church policy showed concern for the well-being of the Church, but burdened by the system of church-state relations established under Peter I and preserved for two centuries, he could not find the necessary answers to the questions of the time in revolutionary times. The emperor understood the need to convene the Council, the election of the Patriarch, in the affairs of church administration, the restoration of canonical principles. But he was afraid that the Council might take the wrong direction, the reason for such fears was given by the mood of some representatives of the clergy, and therefore the emperor did not dare to authorize the convening of the Council.

At the beginning of the XIX century the Church was completely independent, and by the end of the XIX - the beginning of the XX centuries. became one of the departments of the state apparatus. She lost her possessions and began to depend entirely on the funds allocated by the state for its maintenance. Religious reformers in the 19th century considered the Orthodox Church in Russia a victim of autocracy, while proving that in order to revive the Orthodox Church, a break with conservatism must be made. They spoke of the virtues of Christianity and the unworthiness of Christians. This theory was developed by V.V. Rozanov, V. Ern, N.A. Berdyaev, who believe that the main goal is to bring Russian Orthodoxy out of the crisis.

ON. Berdyaev said that true Orthodox spirituality is aimed not only at personal well-being, but also at social transformations, since social life depends on the spiritual state of the population and its moral priorities. V.V. Rozanov believed that only the Church can play a special role in social charity, due to the fact that in an Orthodox church, poverty, squalor, decrepitude, weakness are considered virtue and even merit to God. In print in the 1880s - early 1890s the idea of the emperor's supremacy over the Church is firmly expressed. P.V. Znamensky, who published many historical works on the activities of the Russian Orthodox Church, expressed this idea. One of his most famous studies on the parish clergy since the reforms of Peter I refers to the difficult social, legal, material situation of the parish clergy. P.V. Znamensky published many articles on the history of the Church in the Orthodox Interlocutor and in other secular and spiritual journals. "Church Renovationists," such as I.S. Berdnikov, P.V. Verkhovsky, M.A. Dyakonov stood in opposite positions. Supporters of church renewal spoke out against the inculcation of secular bureaucracy in the church apparatus and advocated the restoration of patriarchate with the inviolability of state autocracy. They proposed the theory of a harmonious relationship between the state and the Church, and at the same time, their existence as independent bodies.

The Renovationist Orthodox clergy spoke only of the formal separation of the Church from the state. This would help her become an independent political force and step up her activities. At the end of the XIX century. this trend in the life of the Church and in literature has intensified in connection with the activation of the movement for the restoration of patriarchate (Vvedensky, 1905).

In the difficult conditions of the renewal of Russia, the clergy tried to assume the role of an independent moral arbiter, insisting on overcoming the discord of estates, calming social upheavals. The state of the Church and the state in Russia at the end of the 19th century was as follows: the Orthodox Church was deprived of independence due to the guardianship and control of the state; dissent in religion was brutally suppressed. However, the union of the Church and the state was a blessing for both sides, as it allowed each side to fully use its reserves for a decent life. The final goals of the state and the Church are different, the state takes care of the earthly well-being of people, and the church cares for the salvation of their souls, they are united by a common desire for truth and good, to limit evil, and to form a worthy civil society. The leading role in this collaboration was to be played by the Church, since it knows the main divine sign that distinguishes man from all living beings - this is his spirit and his spirituality. The Church also, with its Holy Scriptures, convinces the flock that the state is God-given authority and obliges people to respect and pray for it. In the provinces of the Central Black Earth Region, speaking of the prospects for rapprochement between the state and the Church in this historical period, we can say that secular authorities were interested in church problems. At the same time, these interests themselves were dictated mainly by the current deficit of integrative values and integrative ideology. This happened as a result of the fact that the Church positioned itself as the owner of significant capital, the idea was of the secular authorities, who considered the Church to be an "oligarch" with wide opportunities.

CONCLUSION

Thus, summing up, it can be noted that the relationship between the Church and the state was built in the XIX - early XX centuries on the principle of subordinating the Church to state power. In fact, the Orthodox Church was one of the departments of a ramified state apparatus. The emperor was the bearer and source of higher authority in the Orthodox Church. The church was under the tutelage of state power, not possessing the true ability to act as an independent spiritual and moral force. However, it was a public law institution that performed functions such as collecting statistical data, recording civil status, monitoring spiritual censorship, and administering justice. In addition, the Church was responsible for public education.

In the XIX - early XX centuries the confessional policy of the state was implemented differentially, with reference to specific peoples and faiths in a given period of time. In the post-reform period, the state faced the task of unifying legislation in relation to the Church, including by leveling cultural, religious and linguistic differences.

The Orthodox Church and the state during this period intensified their activities in the cause of Christianization. The policy pursued by the state in relation to the Orthodox Church was aimed at increasing the spiritual and moral prestige of the Church, as well as at solving those social problems that the state power could not cope on its own.

In general, the position of the Church in the provinces of the Central Black Earth Region was consistent with the general position of the Church in the Russian Empire as the dominant denomination.

REFERENCES

Archive of the Russian Ethnographic Museum (AREM) F. 7. Op. 1. D. 1140. Ethnographic description of the Oryol province L. 16ob, 20-21ob.

Ershov, B. A., Nebolsin, V. A., & Solovieva, S. R. (2020). Higher education in technical universities of Russia. *7th International Conference on Education and Social Sciences. Abstracts & Proceedings,* 55-58.

Ershov, B. A., Perepelitsyn, A., Glazkov, E., Volkov, I., & Volkov, S. (2019). Church and state in Russia: management issues. *5th International Conference on Advances in Education and Social Sciences. Abstracts & Proceedings,* 26-29.

Ershov, B. A., Zhdanova, T. A., Kashirsky, S. N., & Monko, T. (2020). Education in the university as an important factor in the socialization of students in Russia. *6th International Conference on Advances in Education. Abstracts & Proceedings,* 517-520.

Polikarpov, F. (1907). Historical and Statistical Description of Churches and Parishes of the Nizhnedevitsky County of Voronezh Province. *Voronezh Antiquity,* (6), 12–15.

Vvedensky, S. (1905). *Materials on the history of the Voronezh diocese.* Academic Press.

Weinberg, L. B. (1886). Voronezh jubilee collection in memory of the 300th anniversary of the city of Voronezh. Voronezh: Voronezh. Governorate. Stat. Committee.

Chapter 7
White and Black Clergy

ABSTRACT

Towards the end of the 19th century, Russian society began to change dramatically. Those who are only serving in the church are attracted to the clergy estate. Persons of other classes could join the ranks of the clergy if there were not enough persons of a clergy rank for the corresponding position, provided there was a leave certificate from peasant or city society. The clergy, awarded orders, acquire noble rights: the White clergy receive the hereditary nobility, and the Black clergy had the opportunity to transfer property by inheritance along with the order. Clerics compiled various kinds of statistical documents for secular and spiritual authorities and kept metric books and confessional sheets. An important characteristic of the clergy was the educational level.

INTRODUCTION

The most important part of the church history of Russia in the XIX - early XX centuries is the story of the development of white and black clergy. Representatives of historical science pay great attention to this issue.

The urgent tasks of Russian science are an exhaustive analysis of the specifics of the formation of the clergy, the evolution of the black and white clergy, the study of the historical role of the parish clergy in the social structure of the Russian state, the nature of the relationship between the Church and the laity, and, finally, the special culture and mentality of clergy.

DOI: 10.4018/978-1-6684-4915-8.ch007

This chapter shows that in the XIX - early XX centuries the duties of the clergy have increased significantly. Clerics compiled various kinds of statistical documents for secular and spiritual authorities, kept metric books and confessional sheets. An important characteristic of the clergy was the educational level.

The "black" clergy in the 19th century had a privileged position, because by virtue of celibacy (the vow of celibacy), the path to honors of the highest ranks was open to him. On April 16, 1869, a law was passed according to which the ordination of celibate priests could be possible only after 40 years. The black clergy belonged to the monks who fully devoted their lives to the service of God and who live in monasteries. The black clergy was divided into five categories. The Metropolitan and Archbishop belonged to the highest dignities, "Your Eminence" addressed to them, then the Bishop followed, "Your Grace" addressed to him; they belonged to a common title - "lord". The lower dignities of the black clergy included the archimandrite and the abbot, who headed the monastery, they were addressed to "your high resemblance." The abbess of the convent, that is, abbess, could be a woman. Women did not serve in the white clergy. Priests living "in the world", having a family, children, belonged to the white clergy, which was also divided into five dignities. These are protopresbyter, archpriest, priest, protodeacon and deacon.

In addition to the concept of "clergy", the term "clergy" can be found in literature. The clergy belonged to the clergymen and psalm-goers. Their task was to help the priest during the service. They were not ordained to the dignity. In order to become a clergyman and receive a hierarchical title in the Church, it was necessary to undergo a special act: ordination (or "ordination") from the bishop. Ordination to the dignity gave a number of personal privileges: personal immunity, guarded by especially severe punishments, both canonical (church) and criminal, privileged jurisdiction. This term implied the jurisdiction of the clergy exclusively in church authority in any civil or criminal case, freedom from personal and certain property obligations. Thus, the clergy was a privileged estate, the high social status of which was reflected in the legislation of the Russian Empire. However, the sacred dignity gave its owner not only privileges, he entrusted its owner with serious responsibility and rather significant responsibilities in liturgical life.

The service of the Russian Orthodox Church itself was divided into three circles: Daily, Weekly and Annual. The daily circle of services includes nine services that the clergyman should conduct every day: these are the Ninth hour, Vespers, Compline, the Midnight, Matins, the First hour, the Third hour, the Sixth hour and the Divine Liturgy. In practice, Compline and the Midnight are performed only in monasteries.

In addition to the above-mentioned daily services, special services of the so-called "Weekly Circle of Services" were performed. It was based on the church commemorating special church dates. On Sunday, a service was held in honor of the Sunday of Christ, on Monday - in honor of the Holy Angels, Tuesday - in honor of St. John the Baptist, Wednesday and Friday - in honor of John the Baptist, on Thursday - a service in honor of St. Nicholas. On Saturday, a prayer was made for the repose of all the departed. To all of the above, worship in honor of the great holidays should be added.

The hierarchy of the Orthodox Church was called the "three-princedom", because it consisted of three ranks: the diaconate, the priesthood and the bishopric.

Representatives of the "white" and "black" clergy had their own structures of honorary titles, which were awarded for "length of service" or for special services to the church. An example is the letter of Fedor Loginov from 1874. The letter was compiled by Tikhon, Bishop of Voronezh and Yelets. It was given to priest Fyodor Loginov due to the fact that he truly devoted himself to the church sacrament all the time, for which he was promoted to the rank of.

The internal hierarchy of the black clergy consisted of three degrees: monasticism, monasticism and schema. The majority of monks belonged to the second degree - to monasticism, or the minor schema, they could be ordained to the rank of bishop. The particle "schea" (for example, "schemigumen" or "schemopolitan") was added to the name of the dignity of monks who accepted the great schema. A sexton, a servant in the church, who did not have a dignity, belonged to the lowest level of the church hierarchy; he was responsible for preparing the censer, lighting candles, reading prayers out loud, and ringing the bells. The differences between the "white" and "black" priests were observed in the everyday and everyday life, manifested by feelings of personal resentment and unfair preference.

Unmarried, widowed, and divorced ministers of the church, having received monastic tonsure, could pass from the white clergy to the black clergy. In this case, it was necessary to add up all the church rewards. The largest part of the white clergy was the diocesan clergy. The acquisition of places here rested, as in the previous period, at first on an elective basis - legitimized by spiritual regulation, it acquired only one restriction there, namely, the right of the bishop to test the applicant before delivery and determine his suitability for the place. However, little by little, as the bureaucratization of the Church increases and its component is increasingly included in the state mechanism, the electoral principle is liquidated, weakened by the insignificant interest in the parish population itself, and is replaced by a purely bishopric appointment.

Historian P.N. Milyukov shared this point of view. In 1896, P.N. Milyukov released three volumes of "Essays on the History of Russian Culture". The second part of this book is entitled: "Church and school (faith, creativity, education)". According to his convictions, he was a left-wing liberal and therefore could not sympathize with the Russian Orthodox Church, but his book contains a lot of information about the activities of the Church, theological school and the clergy. According to P.N. Milyukov, at the end of the XIX century in Russia, there were 137178 persons of clergy (Lapotnikov, 1998).

The clergy considered themselves shepherds, leading all parishioners to salvation, into the kingdom of God. The clergy believed in their high mission, which was the "cornerstone" of the mentality of clerics. All parishioners, regardless of their material status and class, were equal before the clergy, and therefore only the priest could commit absolution and other sacraments.

Many clergymen in the 19th century turned for advice on church robes to the Voronezh spiritual consistory. The deacon of the Vasilyevsky church, Dmitry Alekhine, asked for permission to wear black skufu at outdoor services. The Voronezh Spiritual Consistory decided: to declare to Deacon Alekhine that black skufu should only be dressed outside the church during services, funerals, and, moreover, in cold inclement times.

It is possible to speak of the clergy as an estate group only with reference to the white clergy, but not about the black clergy, which had no offspring, or cut off ties with all relatives. As a means of maintaining, the white clergy were state salary, land allotments, voluntary donations of money or agricultural products.

The disagreements between the white and black clergy were especially aggravated with the advent of academic monasticism, these were graduates of theological academies who took monastic vows at the academy or immediately after its completion, which opened up great opportunities for a spiritual career. In 1858, a book by the priest Ivan Bellustin was published in Paris, in which he said that the further life of the academic monks had nothing to do with monasticism, since taking tonsure, they were guided by career considerations. In 1855, the work of A. Smirnov was published, which spoke about the position of the clergy in Russia, and in 1866 the book of Professor D.I. Rostislavov was published abroad.

In their works, based on personal observations, they criticize the activities of the clergy in the Russian Empire. Russian state laws of the 19th century established special rules for becoming a monk, different from the canons of the ecumenical church. First of all, these special rules concerned the age sufficient for taking a tonsure, and the civil duties of the tonsured. For men it was installed at 30 years old, and for women - at 40 (Art. 344 vol. IX of the Code of Laws of the Russian Empire). One of the factors influencing the internal microclimate of the church clergy was age differentiation, which determined the relationship between the priest and the deacon. Also, the habits, inclinations and character of the members of the clergy had a positive or negative microclimate inside the clergy. Age affected the relations of clergymen if the priest was young, and the deacon was old, or the priest was old, and the psalmist was young.

Church rules determined the age at which the degree of church consecration was accepted: for initiation into the deacon's rank, 25 years of age were determined, and in the priesthood, 30 years of age. However, in 1836, in the Kirsanovsky District and in 1911 in the 3rd Tambov District, the age of ordination for the clergy was not a determining factor. Nevertheless, in 1836 they tried to comply with the canonical norm, which was 25 years. This year, the number close to 30 years at the initiation was 11 people, and in 1911 - 8 people.

In the first half of the 19th century, during the formation of clergy, there were some reasons why the principle of family origin was preserved. Fathers-priests could give their children the necessary education, as they had a high income, and the accountants, having a lower income, could not afford it. There was also a tradition of securing a place for one of the sons, a son or son-in-law always took a place after his father, a priest. After the reforms of the spiritual educational system in the 70s XIX century, the principle of family origin was no longer so common. In 1877, in the Kozlovsky district of the Tambov province, among 10 priests, children of the accountants were 6 people; and out of 14 cases, 1 was from the priest's family, but this was due to education.

In urban parishes, the situation was approximately the same. In 1852 in the city of Morshansk, Tambov province, cousins in three cases were close relatives. Compared to rural parishes, there was an earlier age for pre-granting positions: out of 17 people, 7 minors were placed in these places. In the city churches of the two pairs of laureates there were always combinations - the eldest-youngest, this was due to the natural change of generations. So, clergy was a special family, the head of which was a priest, and hierarchical positions were determined depending on age.

In the 19th century, restrictions were placed on the choice of residence, for example, for frustrated monks («monakhi-rasstrigi»), entry into the capital was forbidden for 7 years after they left the monk's title - (clause 4 of article 349 t. IX SZ RI). The consequences for the people who left the clergy were grave - retortion introduced into the Church and the monastery was not allowed when the priests were tonsured as monks (Article 356, Volume IX of the Republic of Ingushetia). Priests were an important stratum of the clergy, occupying a special position among the categories of priests. The priest supervised the parishioners, monitored the confessions and communions of the parishioners, the mood of the peasants, the timing of their departure and return, he led the parish meeting and the parish council.

Social origin was of great importance in the characterization of the clergy. In the Russian Empire, the isolation of the clergy was not encouraged; according to the laws, access to the spiritual corporation was open. In practice, there were many obstacles with some features. In the 19th century, right up to the 70s, due to professional corporatism, it was difficult to get into the ranks of the white clergy. In the late 19th and early 20th centuries, this obstacle was removed, which led to an outflow of people who wanted to connect their lives with the ministry of the Church. The clergy themselves were the guardians of corporate isolation.

In 1814, in 1836, in 1852 among the white clergy, according to the analysis of archival documents, there were no representatives of other classes. The priests became the children of priests or deacons, and the children of the clerks became the lowest members of the clergy. In 1870, in the second Lebedyansky district of the Tambov province, out of 18 priests, only 3 priests were from clerical families, and out of 27 clergymen there were not a single deacon or priestly family. In the 19th century, right up to the 1890s, it was necessary to indicate in the column "origin" in the clerical sheets who the father was, this rule after the 1890s. became optional. And in the XX century it became enough to indicate from which class the clergyman came from.

There were official and unofficial appeals to priests. Unofficially, priests and deacons were contacted: "Father George," "Father Nikolai," or simply "Father." Often you can hear in a speech the word "confessor" from the lips of people who do not know the life of the Orthodox Church, and they don't have Orthodox friends, for example, "my confessor said ...", etc. Extra-church people may think that there are another special step in the priesthood, but it is not. The confessor is a priest, the only peculiarity of the confessor is the nature of the relationship between him and the layman of the Orthodox Church. For example, for confession a person can come to any temple and go up to any priest. The parishioner, who needed to get advice, needed additional conversation, help in solving various difficulties in life, tried to find such a clergyman with whom his church life would be connected in the future. If a priest helped to solve the problems of this person from a spiritual point of view, then he was called a "confessor", and the parishioner was called a spiritual son or spiritual daughter. The name "spiritual father" is due to the fact that he helped to spiritually be born to a person and understand how to live a real spiritual life. The presence of a confessor was not a prerequisite for finding a person in the Church, but it is very difficult to adopt the experience of spiritual life without a confessor. For a spiritual son or daughter, the influence of a spiritual father was based on his authority. Gradually, in the 19th century, the clergy was vested with administrative and police powers: it was monitoring the political trustworthiness of parishioners, recording civil acts. The burdensome duties of the clergy, which had nothing to do with the role of preachers, turned him into a kind of layer of public servants.

Since the 40s XIX century, the white and black clergy expanded and strengthened the direction of cultural and educational activities. The Russian Orthodox Church in the person of the parish clergy was engaged in charity work, historical and regional studies, helping the population in the fight against fires and diseases, opened parish schools and taught in them. The transformations that began, the black and white clergy, were perceived differently, and under the new conditions they tried to morally educate the laity in accessible ways. Reforms that changed the position of various classes and the overall appearance of the country required the clergy to be more actively involved in public life (Benzin, 1906).

Saint Mitrofan, one of the most significant clergymen in the Voronezh diocese, belonged to the black clergy. In 1832, thanks to Archbishop Anthony of Smirnitsky, the canonization of the first glorified Bishop of the Voronezh Region, St. Mitrofan, took place. Saint Mitrofan, Voronezhsky's clergyman, was born in the Vladimir province in November 1623.

Divine saint Mitrofan became a widower in his forties, at the same time he renounced the world so that he could fully serve God. In 1663, in the Zolotnikovsky desert, in honor of the Assumption of the Mother of God, Priest Michael was tonsured a monk with the name of Mitrofan. The local population three years after the ascetic entered the Zolotnikovsky monastery, despite the priest's efforts to hide from human glory, knew the charitable life of Mitrofan.

The Yakhromskiy Cosmin monastery at that time did not have a rector, and the brethren of the monastery, together with the peasants, asked to put the abbot of their monastery, the monk Mitrofan, known for his strict life. In

June 1665, Metropolitan of Sarsky and Podonsky Pavel "blessed the monk Mitrofan in the Superior rank".

In April 1682, Patriarch Joachim, with sixteen archpastillaries, ordained Mitrofan to bishop. The saint at that time was 58 years old. In August 1682, Saint Mitrofan arrived in Voronezh, and he had to put a lot of work into the improvement of the Voronezh diocese. He took care of enlightening the shepherds, built and decorated temples, opened schools at the temples, and fought against the schism that had arisen. The life of Saint Mitrofan of Voronezh covers two eras: the era of Peter I, the period of the kingdom of Moscow led by His Holiness the Patriarch, and the synodal era, when the administration of the Church passed to the Holy Synod.

Mitrofan did not wait for the formation of the Synod, he saw the beginning of Peter's reforms, but did not assess their dual consequences for Russia. The archpastoral activity of St. Mitrofan in the Voronezh diocese lasted 20 years. During this time, 57 new ones were added to the existing 182 temples. Under Mitrofan a huge Annunciation Cathedral was built, decorated with a six-tier iconostasis. By the consecration of the Annunciation Cathedral in 1692, the sovereigns Peter and Ivan Alekseevich gave a 160-pound bell.

Among the archbishops of the Voronezh diocese, Anthony Smirnitsky (1773–1846) is quite famous. Hieromonk Anthony in January 1815 was appointed governor of the Kiev-Pechersk Lavra, and in 1817, he was elevated to the rank of archimandrite. According to the recommendation of Metropolitan of Kiev and Galitsky Evgeny Bolkhovitinov at the end of January 1826, Anthony Smirnitsky was transferred to the rank of bishop, and in December 1832, he was elevated to the rank of archbishop.

In the Voronezh diocese, Archbishop Anthony Smirnitsky created temples and arranged monastic monasteries. In 1841, he consecrated the Intercession Church in Voronezh. The remains of the Archbishop of Voronezh and Zadonsky Anthony Smirnitsky are located in the hierarchal necropolis of the Voronezh Aleksievo-Akatov Monastery and are called holy relics. In the Voronezh diocese, the memory of St. Anthony Smirnitsky is celebrated on the day of his death on December 20, 1846.

In 1849, the Voronezh Spiritual Consistory made an inventory of the property of the deceased Archbishop Anthony. He owned the following church utensils. These are, in particular, holy icons and other sacred things: the icon of the Forerunner and Baptist John, the icon of the Assumption of the Mother of God, the icon of St. Nicholas, the icon of the Mother of God of Smolensk in a silver massacre, crosses and other orders. In particular, the cross of the Order of St. Prince Vladimir, various things related to church use: these are two wooden candlesticks with two compartments for candles. Archbishop Ignatius Semenov significantly influenced the appearance of Russian Orthodoxy in the 19th century. Archbishop Olonets and Petrozavodsk Ignaty Semenov was born on August 5, 1791 from metric books, but recognized his birthday on August 2, 1790 as more correct. He was born in the Poksheng parish of the Pinega district of the Arkhangelsk province, where his father, priest Athanasius served. Ignatius Semenov (in the world of Matvey) from early childhood knew church service and loved it.

In July 1816, Matvey Semenov was transferred to the Arkhangelsk Seminary, where he taught Greek and French. In the Arkhangel'skiy monastery, the rector of the seminary, Archimandrite Paul, in June 1820, Matvey Semenov was tonsured a monk and was named Ignatius. In August 1820, the monk Ignatius was made a hieromonk. In November 1822, Ignatius was elevated to the rank of archimandrite, and in December 1827, he was named bishop of Starorussky, vicar of the Novgorod diocese. In February 1828, the consecration of Bishop Ignatius took place in St. Petersburg.

Bishop Ignatius at the Voronezh Department himself received petitioners, talked with each of them, made frequent trips to the diocese, thereby showing himself to be an energetic and experienced pastor. Ignatius Semenov died on January 20, 1850 in St. Petersburg, he was buried as a famous preacher in the Zlatoust church of the Alexander Nevsky Lavra.

In the XIX century, the discovery and glorification of the relics of St. Tikhon of Zadonsky and Voronezh took place. The memory of the virtuous archpastor grew and became convinced that Saint Tikhon is glorified by the Lord and is a holy man. Everyone revered it: those who heard about Tikhon's life, and those who read his works. After the death of Tikhon Zadonsky, his works were published, which, by their simplicity and clarity, were accessible for general understanding. Gradually, all places associated with the life of St. Tikhon gained fame, the main reason for this was that those who called on the help of the saint, in various cases, received gracious help from above. All people believed that Saint Tikhon was a great saint of God, since miracles were performed wherever the name of the saint was called. People went to the tomb of the saint with gratitude for the healing received, cases of miracles spread the glory of him.

Evgeny Bolkhovitinov, clergyman of the Voronezh diocese, who was born on December 18, 1767 in the family of a priest of the Voronezh diocese, should also be called here. Evgeny Bolkhovitinov studied at the Voronezh Theological Seminary and the Moscow Slavic-Greek-Latin Academy and attended lectures at Moscow University. Exploring churches, their libraries and archives, Evgeny Bolkhovitinov published historical documents ("The abbot of Hegumen Daniel to the Holy Land", "The Legend of Boris and Gleb"). E. Bolkhovitinov, widowed in 1799, takes monasticism, and then becomes the prefect of the Alexander Nevsky Academy. In 1804, Bishop Eugene was consecrated to the Bishop of Starorussky, Vicar of the Novgorod and St. Petersburg Metropolitan.

Since 1808, E. Bolkhovitinov headed the Vologda department, since 1813 - Kaluga, since 1816 - Pskov; and in 1822 it was approved by the Metropolitan of Kiev and Galitsky. His Grace Eugene in all dioceses manifested himself as a church historian of the region.

The reform of the system of spiritual education in Russia was based on the project for the construction of religious schools, drawn up by Bishop Evgeny on behalf of the Metropolitan of Novgorod Ambrose. Metropolitan Eugene suggested that church theological centers endowed with publishing functions from theological academies.

Studies on the Russian church history of Metropolitan Eugene were of great importance. In 1818, his work "Dictionary of Russian Writers" was published, which contains data on the life and work of 720 spiritual and secular writers. Of great importance are his books on the history of churches and monasteries. In 1799, he published a study of local history on the provincial and district centers of the Voronezh province - "Description of the Voronezh province in 1777." The basis of this work was archival materials, documents and rare sources, various documents of Lieutenant Colonel Kostrominov on the study of the province, "revision tales" of 1795. The author studied the archives of churches and monasteries, where there were decrees, letters, and scribe books. Metropolitan Eugene in the preparation of manuscripts began to use one of the first archival materials. His work is listed in the category of bibliographic rarities. Metropolitan Eugene died in February 1837. The last way he was escorted by the clergy of the Theological Seminary, to which he gave 23 years of his work (Zlatoverkhovnikov, 1902).

The replacement of the posts of white and black clergy in the middle of the 19th century was carried out in various ways: by means of elections, hereditary obtaining of a place and appointment as a local bishop. The clergy of the All Saints Cemetery Church asked to elect the Voronezh merchant Ivan Alekseevich Popov as the clerk of this church. Priest Mikhail Askochensky and Deacon Mikhail Nikitinsky signed the petition. Popov was approved as a clerk at the church in accordance with the decree of the Voronezh City Council of January 12, 1859. Ivan Popov proved himself to be a very honest man, observed the sacraments of worship. The Voronezh City Government decided on February 14, 1875, to promote Ivan Popov and confirm him as a church elder at the All-Saints Cemetery Church. In the Kursk province, it should be noted clergyman Ivan (Ioann) Vasilyevich Korensky, who was born in the village of Krupets in 1791 in the family of a priest. Ivan V. Korensky studied at the Kiev Theological Academy, after which in November 1814 he was appointed a teacher at the Kursk Theological Seminary, where he served until April 1819. Then, Ivan Vasilyevich Korensky was ordained a priest of the Transfiguration Church of the city of Rylsk, and in March 1835 he was ordained a priest. Since 1840, he began to serve in the Cathedral of the Assumption Church of Rylsk. Father Ioann, in addition to the theological work, was also engaged in social and religious activities. In Rylsk spiritual rule from 1822 to 1869, he was first a member, and then first present. In 1832, he becomes the dean of the Church of the city of Rylsk, and in 1835 - the caretaker of the county and parish Rylsk school, where he worked until 1850. St. John was a censor of sermons and catechisms. He led many people on the path of truth, he worked hard for the benefit of the Fatherland, the Church, and the people. Father («Svyatitel'») Ioann was awarded church awards for his work: a pectoral cross, a violet velvet skufu, a leg gait, and a velvet kamilavka. In 1858, he was awarded the cross "In memory of the war of 1853-56" and the Order of St. Anne of the III degree, and in 1864 - the Order of St. Anna of the II degree with the imperial crown. Saint John was hardworking, he did all the work himself. He received visitors at any time of the day, with all he was affectionate. In January 1870, in connection with the disease, he left the post of dean. Saint John died on March 12 and was buried near the St. John the Theological Church.

In the Kursk diocese, Archpriest Alexei Alekseevich Tankov, who was born on March 5, 1817 in the village of Volkovo in the family of a priest, was a famous archpastor. He graduated from the theological school in Kursk, and in 1833 entered the Kursk Theological Seminary. Even then, he read sermons in the Trinity Monastery of Belgorod. From 1839 to 1843 he studied at the Kiev Theological Academy. At the end of the Theological Academy, he is appointed inspector of the Rylsky Theological College, and then he becomes an inspector of the school in Belgorod, where the Master Cross marked him for his work. In 1850, he was transferred to the Kursk Gymnasium. There he taught the Law of God and served as a priest in the gymnasium of the Nikolaev Church. For more than fifty years, Alexy was engaged in pedagogical activities. Also A.A. Tanks made a great contribution to the historical description of the Kursk diocese. His works were published in the Kursk diocesan sheets. He was awarded church awards: a gold pectoral cross with diamonds, a violet skufu and a kamilavka, as well as the Holy Icon of St. Nicholas the Wonderworker. In April 1885, Alexy was elevated to the nobility. Saint Alexy showed confessional tolerance: during the funeral service of the teacher of the Catholic gymnasium, A.I. Miegera Alexy, together with the Catholics, entered the church, which made a favorable impression on everyone. As a member of the Kursk Committee of the Guardianship of the Poor, A.A. Tankov did a great job in the field of guardianship and charity. He participated in the work of other public organizations: he lectured on pedagogical courses, was a member of the Provincial Statistical Committee, and for 23 years he was a censor of sermons in the Kursk diocese. A.A. Tankov died on July 22, 1904 and was buried at the All Saints (Kherson) cemetery. Among the Kursk clergymen, Professor Alexander Mikhailovich Ivantsov-Platonov stands out. He was born in 1835 in the family of a priest. A.M. Ivantsov-Platonov studied at the county religious school of the city of Kursk, and since 1851 - at the Kursk Theological Seminary. He did not finish the seminary, as he was sent ahead of schedule to study in Moscow at the Moscow Theological Academy, which he graduated in 1860 as a second master. To his last name, he received an increase in "Platonov", as he was a scholarship holder to the Metropolitan of Moscow Plato. After graduating from the Moscow Academy, he served as a bachelor in the St. Petersburg Theological Academy. A.M. Platonov published his articles in the newspaper Den and in the journal Orthodox Review. In 1863, he was appointed the law teacher at the Alexander Military School in Moscow. In 1874, he rose to the rank of archpriest.

Of great interest among scientists was his research. In 1872, he became a professor of church history and lectured at Moscow Imperial University. He received his doctorate in theology in 1877 after defending a dissertation in which A.M. Platonov consecrated the issues of schism in the I-III centuries. Christianity. In the future, other significant works are published. For his labors, he was awarded the Prize of Metropolitan Macarius. For educated women, father Alexander in 1880-1886 in Moscow he conducted religious and moral conversations on church history. As a result of this, a special library was created on this topic. A.M. Ivantsov-Platonov led a great public work in church fraternities. For a long time, students used the Church history textbooks they wrote. His works on the history of the initial period of Christianity were also published. A.M. Ivantsov-Platonov died on November 12, 1894 at the age of 58 years.

In the Kursk province, among the theological scholars, Yakov Andreevich Novitsky stood out. Ya.A. Novitsky was born in the Kiev diocese in the family of a priest. He studied at the theological seminary, and after graduating from 1865, he worked as a teacher in the Kiev-Podolsk Theological College. In 1871, he graduated from the Kiev Theological Academy and began teaching at the Kiev Diocesan School, and then in the same year he was transferred to the Kursk Theological Seminary, where he taught philosophy until August 25, 1886.

In 1886, he was appointed rector of the Vitebsk Theological Seminary, where he did not serve long, since on January 20, 1868 he became rector of the Kursk Theological Seminary. Since 1891, he was chairman of the council of the diocesan brotherhood of the Monk Theodosius of the Caves in Kursk. Ya.A. Novitsky worked as an editor of the Kursk Diocesan Gazette, which published articles on the history of the Kursk diocese (Kovrigina, 2000).

The largest number of clergy at the beginning of the 20th century was in the Oryol diocese. The correlation of categories of clergy in 1910 was as follows: of the clergy - 0.05%, the deacons - 0.02%, the priests - 0.05%, the archpriests - 0.002%. Future Oryol hierarchs were natives of the Central Black Earth Region. Most bishops were children of the clergy. They were educated in theological schools located near the parental home, and then continued it in theological seminaries in the provincial city. A morally healthy province laid the foundations of Orthodoxy in the souls of future bishops and archbishops, shaped their character, fostered respect for the hierarchal rank. His Grace Apollos became the first Oryol-Sevsky bishop, and Dositheus became his successor. Under Bishop Jonah, the successor of Dositheus, significant changes occurred in the diocesan life. In 1803, the question arose of the need to transfer the bishop's chair from Sevsk to Orel. Dosipheus, by decree of the Synod of December 17, 1803, began to prepare for the relocation of the bishop's chair to Orel, but he hesitated because he wanted to stay in the Sevsky bishop's house, where he had life amenities and his own stud farm. By the decision of the Holy Synod of August 29, 1807, the stay of the bishop with the consistory was left in the county town of Sevsk. After 10 years, the Oryol diocesan authorities again raised the issue of the relocation of the Oryol bishop's chair, this happened during the service of Bishop Jonah. On February 25, 1820, he reported to the Holy Synod about his departure from Sevsk, but he could not wait for the final accomplishment of the Bishop's House and the Church, since July 17, 1821, Bishop Jonah was transferred to Tver to the Archbishop's Chair, and November 6, 1826 years from Tver was transferred to Kazan. In the Oryol province, the martyr Kuksha Pechersky was deeply revered and revered. The holy martyr Kuksha, the monk Monk of the Caves, spread Christianity between the Vyatichi, and thus glorified his name. First, he spread Christianity in the Kiev-Pechersk monastery, and then, around 1215, he began to preach Christianity to the Vyatichs who worshiped idols. Thanks to the miraculous power of Kuksha's words, the pagans began to be baptized, but the embittered priests of Vyatichi subjected the Monk Kuksha to cruel tortures and cut off his head. The significance of the feat of the Monk Kuksha was realized in the second half of the 19th century in the Orel diocese. Church historians of the 19th century called Kuksha "the apostle of the Vyatichi" and the "Equal-to-the-Apostles Enlightenment". The county town of Bryansk, Orel Province, has become a center of worship for Kuksha. In the Kiev Pechersk Lavra on the personal savings of the benefactor and merchant A.N. Komarov's icon in 1903 was made an icon of the holy martyr Kuksha, and the inhabitants of Bryansk asked the spiritual cathedral to put particles of the relics of the saint in the icon of his name. In August 23, 1903, Archpriest of the Intercession Cathedral of the city Bryansk V. Popov, M.G. Dobychin (Head of the city Bryansk), A.N. Komarov, a native of Bryansk district, professor of the Kiev Theological Academy, A.I. Bulgakov, having accepted the shrine, went by rail from Kiev to Bryansk. Along the route of the icon, many people flocked to it, wishing to worship the shrine. The icon was delivered to Bryansk on August 25, 1903. 20 thousand people from neighboring cities and villages greeted the icon with a procession, and on August 27 in Pokrovsky Cathedral, on the day of memory of St. Kuksha, a solemn service was held. One of the shrines of the Oryol province was the icon of St. Kuksha with a particle of his relics. Among the clergy in the Tambov province, the bishop of Tambov and Shatsky, Theophil Raev, should be named. Theophil Raev was born in the Chernihiv province in the Glukhovsky district. In early childhood, he lost his parents. Theophil Raev was educated at the seminary, and then at the Kiev Theological Academy. In 1762, he became a monk and was ordained to the rank of hierodeacon. At the same time, he teaches at the Novgorod Theological Seminary. Bishop Theophil revived the church life of the Tambov Region, did a great job of managing the diocese. He was distinguished by his generosity. In 1808, he allocated 1,000 rubles for the education of orphans in the Kiev Academy, in the Temnikovsky Sanaksarsky and Shatsky Cherneyev Monasteries, in the Sarov Desert and for orphans and widows of ministers of the bishop's house. Bishop Theophil was the founder of theological schools, and G.R. Derzhavin is the founder of city schools. Both of them played a large role in the education of the population in Tambov. In the Tambov region, neither among the black nor among the white clergy, there were people who wanted to take teaching positions, nor therefore, at the opening of the seminary, Bishop

Theophil invited the rector from the Vladimir diocese, and the teachers from Ryazan (Blokhina, 1997).

Theophil in his diocese made it a duty to educate all the children of the clergy. There was no desire to learn from the children, and therefore they did not go to the seminary, therefore, by order of Bishop Theophil, they were brought to Tambov. Bishop Theophil did not like the clergy, exceeding power, did not tolerate scammers, did not stand on ceremony with the guilty clergy. He loved his flock and tried to improve the material and moral life of the Tambov diocese. He looked like a stern man, he was accused of cruelty, but he defeated slander with his calmness and firmness.

Makarii Bulgakov played an important role in the establishment of the Tambov diocese. Makarii Bulgakov was born on September 19, 1816 in the Novooskolsky district of the Kursk province, in the village of Surkov, in the family of a priest. When Mikhail was 7 years old, his father died. In the mother's arms were six young children, so in childhood Michael experienced poverty, poverty and deprivation. However, his mother tried to educate all the children. First, his godfather taught Michael at home, and then he entered the parish theological school, which was located in Korochansky district. Since 1827, he continued his studies at the Belgorod Theological School at the Kursk Theological Seminary. During his training, Michael was not distinguished by his abilities, but was hardworking. Michael's clearing of mind appeared after a stone, accidentally thrown by a comrade, cut his head and a hemorrhage occurred. After treatment, Michael becomes the best pupil of the school. At the age of 15, His Grace Makarii served at the St. Petersburg Academy, and in May 1857 he became bishop of Tambovsky and Shatsky. In the Tambov diocese, Bishop Makarii did not serve long. He paid the main attention to church beautification and deanery, and put things in order in the secretary and clerical office work. Makarii Bulgakov played a large role in reducing the local schism and sectarianism. He also followed spiritual schools. His Grace Makarii published History of the Russian Church, and published articles in magazines. Macarius died on June 9, 1882, his body was first delivered to the Cathedral of Miracles Monastery, and then to the Trinity-Sergius Lavra. Theophanes, the Recluse («Zatvornik») of Vyshensky (1815–1894) can also be noted among of the Tambov saints. Georgy Vasilievich Govorov was born on January 10, 1815 in the Yelets district of the Oryol province, in the village of Chernavsk, in the family of a priest. Little Georgy often came to the temple of God and served there at the altar. At first, he studied at home, and in 1823 he entered the Livensky Theological College. On May 29, 1859, Father Theophanes was named bishop of Tambov and Shatsk, and on June

1, Metropolitan Gregory in the Trinity Cathedral of the Alexander Nevsky Lavra performed his ordination. He served in the Tambov diocese for four years, during which he earned sincere love for his great attention to the needs of parishioners. Saint Theophanes zealously served in all spheres of church life. Under the administration of the Tambov diocese, he worked hard and cared for the laity. The sermons of Bishop Theophanes came from the heart and breathed deep conviction, which attracted many people. Two volumes of his words of sermons to the flock were published (109 words in total). With the participation of St. Theophanes in the Tambov Seminary, the seminar church was renovated. Also, many Sunday schools, parochial schools, and a female diocesan school were opened. In 1861, by decision of the Holy Synod, Bishop Theophanes participated in the celebration of the opening of the relics of St. Tikhon of Zadonsky, which made a great impression on him. Bishop Theophan died on January 6, 1894 and was buried in the Kazan Cathedral of the Vyshenskaya Desert in the Vladimir chapel (Posternak, 2003). Towards the end of the 19th century, Russian society is beginning to change dramatically. Those who are only serving in the Church are attracted to the clergy estate. Persons of other classes could join the ranks of the clergy if there were not enough persons of a clergy rank for the corresponding position, provided there was a leave certificate from peasant or city society. The clergy, awarded orders, acquire noble rights: the white clergy receive the hereditary nobility, and the black clergy had the opportunity to transfer property by inheritance along with the order. Noble rights from 1825 to 1890 received 10 thousand clergy of the white and black clergy. Elected priests elders and dozens of priests were given fees from the white clergy. The new rules were formally fixed, and for a long time, there was a procedure for occupying church posts by inheritance, as other candidates did not have real opportunities to exercise their rights. In the works of the church historian P.V. Znamensky speaks about the conditions that developed in this period. The historian Znamensky wrote that "instead of destroying the relations of the heirs to the ownership of church places, they even had to officially recognize them, because it was possible to deprive the heir of his hereditary place in favor of another candidate only by buying up this place by assessment". The bishop officials were on the maintenance of the white clergy, the white clergy built and renovated the bishop's house, gave them fodder and carts for trips around the diocese. The position of the white clergy was aggravated by the fact that it was not exempted from payments and duties in favor of the state. From the black clergy, no obligations in favor of the state were required, and donations to monasteries were constantly increasing, which improved the life of the black clergy. The government hindered both the expansion of the clergy and the influx of outsiders into it, but it strictly demanded that those who chose the clergy should remain in it until the end. Children of the white clergy became priests, the black clergy replenished from them.

CONCLUSION

According to church law, the Orthodox clergy had personal immunity, privileged jurisdiction. The educational activities of prominent clergymen of the dioceses of the Central Chernozem region played a significant role in the development of Christian values of the population of the region under study by introducing the inhabitants of the provinces to the Orthodox culture and publishing.

REFERENCES

Blokhina, N. N. (1997). Moscow communities of sisters of mercy. Experimental curriculum of a special course for pedagogical secondary and higher educational institutions. *Moscow City Teachers' Seminary Scientific Collection*, 195–206.

Dobronravov, N. (1904). Patient care in ancient Christianity and in Russia. *Moscow Church Gazette*, (2), 14–18.

Efremov, L. V. (1874). The Life of Matrena Naumovna Popova, the first organizer of the strange house of the Zadonsky monastery. Academic Press.

Kovrigina, V. A. (2000). Health care. In Essays on Russian culture of the XIX century: Vol. 2. Power and culture. Academic Press.

Lapotnikov, V. A. (1998). *History of nursing in Russia*. Academic Press.

Lykoshina, P. I. (1901). *Charity Russia. History of state, public and private charity*. Academic Press.

Posternak, A. V. (2003). History of the Sisters of Charity communities. *Charity in Russia. Historical and social studies,* 312-320.

The memorial book of the Voronezh province. (1899). Printing house of Voronezh Lips.

Chapter 8
Spiritual Education System

ABSTRACT

The process of transformation in the theological school began in the late 19th-early 20th centuries. New opportunities were opened up for the church in the field of enlightenment and missionary activity, which required the clergy to be prepared for the new realities of church life. The churching of Russian society before the revolution was due to the fact that children from an early age introduced themselves to church life and assimilated the fundamental truths of Christianity. In the 19th century, the clergy were not sufficiently educated, not all priests had a seminary education, and graduates of theological seminaries were appointed deans. It was enough for church servants to be literate.

INTRODUCTION

Spiritual education in the Church was theological and included the upbringing and education of future clergymen, as well as Orthodox laity who worked in theological enlightenment. In order to live the church life fully, each Christian should determine value priorities. That is why they needed to study church traditions.

In the XIX century, the clergy were not sufficiently educated, not all priests had a seminary education, graduates of theological seminaries were appointed deans. It was enough for church servants to be literate. The bulk of the population was illiterate, and the activities of the clergy in organizing schools and in teaching children to read and write were useful. The way of

DOI: 10.4018/978-1-6684-4915-8.ch008

thinking of the clergy and Orthodox traditions in Russia were reflected in the specific framework of the educational activities of the representatives of the clergy. In the dioceses, the conditions for the functioning of schools were different, the quality of education was different, the personal qualities of the clergy influenced the arrangement of schools and the assimilation of knowledge. But church-educational activity did not always achieve the necessary goal - to provide priests with church parish schools with a permanent student body and with a curriculum. Efforts were also made to improve the well-being of citizens based on Christian commandments. This was necessary, as new trends were observed in society, as a result of which the attitude towards the clergy was skeptical.

The basics of Orthodoxy were taught at all levels of the pre-revolutionary education system: in gymnasiums and real schools, in secondary schools, in higher education. And that means those problems that modern spiritual education faces, and which we are called to overcome today, simply did not exist in those days.

In 1808, there were three theological Academies in Russia: Moscow, Kiev, St. Petersburg, 115 lower theological schools, 36 seminaries with almost 28,000 students. In 1842, the Kazan Academy was opened. Theological schools were of a mixed type: with special and general education courses. Children of the clergy were required to receive education in them. Under Alexander I, the number of students in theological schools was 46,000. The course of lower schools enrolled children of other classes. The seminar course consisted of three departments and lasted two years. Seminarists studied philosophy, rhetoric, theology. In the Academies, the course consisted of two biennial departments - a special theological and general education. At the end of the Academy, students were awarded the degree of candidate and master, and they received salaries depending on these degrees after they accepted the holy dignity. In 1814, several clergymen were awarded by the Commission of Theological Schools a doctorate in theology with special salaries. Masters and doctors with holy orders were awarded special crosses.

Since 1820, 1 674120 rubles have been issued for the maintenance of all theological schools. The life of theological schools revived: the reconstruction of buildings and the construction of new schools began, the maintenance of teachers and students became better. In theological schools, new subjects began to be studied: universal and church history, mathematics, German, French and Hebrew, as well as Greek, along with Latin. In 1822, detailed

Draft Charters were published for Academies, Seminaries, and Schools. In the specific villages and settlements of state peasants, schools received the greatest development. In the landowner villages, there were obstacles to the opening of schools, since only members of local parish clergy could teach in them.

The Russian state has traditionally provided comprehensive support to religious education through the public education system. This was promoted by the active in 1812-1824 in Russia, the Bible Society, which had 57 branches and 232 "partnerships" in the provincial and district cities. The purpose of the society was the distribution of religious books in Russian, Slavic and other languages of the peoples of Russia. The Tambov branch of the Russian Bible Society was opened no earlier than 1814. The director led the committee, which was the governing body. According to the report of the committee in 1821, funds were received in the Tambov branch of the Russian Bible Society from the sale of scripture books in the amount of 220 rubles. In Shatsky district, 120 rubles and in Elatom district, 100 rubles. At least two branches of the Russian Bible Society existed in the Voronezh diocese - in Ostrogozhsk and Olkhovatka. "Olkhovatsky Auxiliary Partnership" in 1818–1819 led by the priest Stefan Chekhov.

November 5, 1804 in the Russian state adopted a new "Charter of educational institutions subordinate to universities." According to this Charter, small public schools were replaced by district schools, and the main public schools were transformed into gymnasiums. Educational institutions of the Voronezh province in 1824 were annexed to the Moscow school district, and in 1831 they were transferred to the Kharkov school district. To create a parish school, the priest's written consent to conduct religious classes in the newly opened school becomes necessary. The study of religion becomes mandatory in all schools and is on the first line in the list of subjects (Ershov, 2011).

Less time was spent on teaching religion in county schools than in parish schools. Only ecclesiastical persons could hold the position of a law teacher in schools. The law considers the teaching of religion as the basis of moral education. The rights of the law teacher were equalized with other teachers of the county school. Changes appeared in the synodal system that influenced the spiritual censorship formed in 1808 at theological academies. The Commission of Theological Schools under the Synod was its supreme executive body; it united all theological schools under its supervision. The academies supervised the secondary and lower ecclesiastical institutions. The department was divided into three districts in which there were uniform charters. Pupils who graduated from seminaries received higher education in the Academies. There was one seminary for each diocese, it was a secondary spiritual educational institution. In each diocese, there were 10 county lower schools, where the children received primary education.

The materials of our study showed that in total, 300 schools were opened in the Central Black Earth provinces. Epiphanius, Bishop of Voronezh, by decree of the Synod of November 19, 1816 "on the opening of parish and district religious schools in the dioceses" worked energetically in this direction. In 1817, theological schools were opened in Voronezh, Zadonsk, Pavlovsk. On the occasion of the opening on January 26, 1819 of the parish theological school in the Zadonsky Monastery, a moleben was served by the rector Archimandrite Samuel. In 1821, the Zadonsk School became full-time. In 1846, all theological schools were converted into county schools, and several more rooms were transferred from the cells to the Zadonsky spiritual district school. This school was subordinated, together with other district schools of the diocese, to the Voronezh seminary government. On October 20, 1818, the Biryuchensky Theological Parish School opened. The fundraising for the opening of which was begun by Anthony Sokolov in 1814 Olkhovatsky Theological School operated from 1819 to 1822.

At the beginning of the 19th century, female theological schools appeared. They were housed in buildings suitable for training sessions, and were kept on monastery funds. In 1822, at the council of the Voronezh diocesan school for women, the issue of a more accurate distribution of monetary contributions between the churches of the diocese was discussed, since the school did not regularly report to the council of the school. In the year 12,000 rubles were required to maintain the school. The rate of contributions from churches depended on the number of people in the diocese. From the monasteries 5000 rubles were supposed to come, 7000 thousand rubles were decided to be distributed according to the number of population, collecting 4 kopeks from each parish soul. The school council also spoke about the lack of facilities in the school. The Council of the Voronezh Diocesan Women's College, applying to the Voronezh Spiritual Consistory, asked for money for the construction of new buildings, and the Voronezh Spiritual Consistory allocated 16,170 rubles for this. Archpriest Evlampy Svyatozarov signed this decree.

The quality of instruction was high at the children's women's school at the Tikhvin Borisovskaya Maiden Desert in the Kursk province. The school was founded on July 5, 1870, it was kept for the salary of Abbot Margarita - 131 rubles 62 kopecks, which she gave each year for the maintenance of the school and the student fees. "The maiden is the daughter of a deacon", who graduated from the Kursk Gymnasium, was engaged in teaching pupils various subjects and received 150 rubles a year. She was assisted by the daughter of a deceased priest, who was studying at the Greyvoron female gymnasium. For her work, she received 50 rubles a year. Priest Alexei Trukhmanov taught the law of God to girls for free, and Anna Fedorovna Martanskaya, widow of a court counselor, taught children needlework for free. There were no nuns among teachers, since qualified specialists taught the children. So, the responsibilities of the monastery included only the organization of educational activities and the maintenance of pupils who lived at the monastery school. In 1882, 19 girls studied at the school, including 6 clergy, 8 of the merchants, 5 of the peasants.

Some clergy in the Voronezh province gave their homes to parish schools. Residents of the settlement of Zakotnaya, Starobelsky district, wished to have their parish school. Since there was no room, the priest Stefan Rodkovsky gave his own house to the parish school. Residents of Zakotnaya settlement contributed 210 rubles every year to maintain the school. According to the decree of the Voronezh Spiritual Consistory, approved on November 1, 1823, the priest Stefan Rodkovsky was in charge and taught in it.

Under Alexander I, there were many priests in the villages who completed the seminary. Large funds were allocated for them, however, the situation in the seminaries was not easy. Since the clergy were poor, many students studied at public expense. Seminar funds were required to provide assistance to lower schools. In 1836, new changes took place in the programs of the ecclesiastical institutions: the Highest Government Decree obliged, under churches and monasteries, to open public schools and colleges. The clergy enthusiastically began to open parish schools and colleges at their own expense.

Minister of Education of Russia Count S.S. Uvarov said on January 31, 1846:

Then the first class received 22 students. The caretaker of the Ostrogozhsky school N.I. Podolsky opened a county school. G. Yarmolenko taught arithmetic and geometry. G. Ozerov taught history and geography (Karpova, 2015).

In 1880, this school was transformed into the "Alexander City Three-Class School." From 1848 to 1857 338 students graduated from the school. In teaching theology, they were guided by the "Statement of the Orthodox Faith" compiled by the Eastern Patriarchs and the "Orthodox Confession of Faith" written by Peter Mogila.

In 1843, a school was established in Tsarskoye Selo under the authority of Empress Maria to educate the daughters of the clergy. Gradually, such schools began to open in other cities.

In 1860, at the suggestion of Archbishop Joseph II, a shelter school was opened in Voronezh for orphans and daughters of the poorest members of the clergy. Vladyka donated 1,000 rubles to the shelter, ordered the Zadonsky Monastery to allocate amounts annually, and the Mitrofanovsky Monastery of the Annunciation was supposed to contribute 20 thousand rubles to the school. So the material support of the Diocesan Women's College was created. The head of the school was N.A. Kolodkina is a pupil of the Smolny Institute. The opening of the school took place on October 1, 1865 under Bishop Seraphim of Arethinsky. 506 pupils studied in it according to the data of 1900.

The reform of the 60s of the XIX century in the Russian theological school was a turning point, it included the administrative, military, judicial, socio-economic and other transformations that were carried out under Alexander II.

The "Regulation on elementary public schools" in 1864 outlined the measures that Russian education had turned on the way of the mass school. The purpose of primary education was the dissemination of useful knowledge and the acquisition by people of religious and moral concepts. Elementary schools became accessible to all classes, peasant children could study in them. Priests taught literacy to peasant children before, but such students he could have no more than four or five, which was too few for a large village. Only parish schools could change this situation. Such a school was founded in 1826 in the Voronezh province in the village of Kozlovka with the participation of priest Fyodor Gerasimovich Merkhalev, who served in the Assumption Church of this village from 1842 to 1859. Unselfish father Fedor built a room for the school on his own money and constantly cared for the improvement of the school. Then parish schools began to form at each of the churches. There were libraries at the churches, where in addition to church service books, there were "everyday", spiritual and historical works. In 1889, another parish school was formed at the Assumption Church of the Voronezh province. In 1911, 23 girls and 49 boys studied in it, and there were 450 volumes of books in the church library. In the opening of educational institutions, private and zemstvo initiative was welcomed, which contributed to the development of women's out-of-school education. Reading Russian and Church Slavonic books, arithmetic, writing, church singing, the Law of God became the main subjects.

In 1860, a special committee was formed under the Synod to consider the reviews and materials received from the field. It was decided that theological subjects should be distinguished and concentrated in one higher cycle, which was in the spirit of the old school system. The school was twelve years old, the first eight classes were in line with the plans of the general school. Theological subjects have been studied in the last four years. Ancient languages were proposed to be made an optional subject; only those who wanted to continue their education in higher education should study them. However, the committee considered it impossible to lower the general educational level of the theological school. In the seminar course, the Greek language, as the language of the Holy Scriptures and the Holy Fathers, was supposed to remain untouched, and Latin had to be studied as a classical language. The math course was shortened. Schools from the government received 1.5 million rubles.

By the highest order, approved in 1862, the parish schools were to remain in the department of the clergy, and the Ministry had the right to manage the schools that it itself would open.

In 1864, provincial and district school councils were created, representing departments and zemstvos under the supervision of bishops to unite the activities of public schools. Many of these councils did not sympathize with the activities of the clergy, and therefore church schools in these councils did not even receive moral support.

Zemstvo dreamed of non-religious schools, with new methods, a cultural direction and new teachers, and therefore in 1864 they opposed clergy schools. Parish schools began to come under the jurisdiction of the Zemstvos, since the clergy did not have the means to support them. The number of schools under the clergy has declined sharply.

The Spiritual-Educational Committee in May 1867 became the central supreme administration of theological schools. New charters for seminaries and schools were approved, and in 1869 a new charter for academies. Academies were freed from administrative worries, districts were abolished. According to the academic charter of 1869, the scientific character of a higher theological school was firmly defined. On the reform of the spiritual education of 1867–1869 access to theological schools was open to representatives of all classes, and seminarians could continue their education in secular higher educational institutions. But in the 1870s, the graduation of seminaries into secular careers and universities was so great that there weren't enough candidates for priests. "The clergy tried to provide their sons with a secular career and save them from the low financial situation of a priest or teacher of a theological seminary and school, and therefore sought to educate their children in high schools. There was no such choice before," - wrote historian I.K. Smolich.

Alexander II considered the main task of his government "to protect the Russian people from harmful false doctrines" and in 1866 gave instructions on the education of young men in the spirit of Orthodoxy. In 1874, the Ministry of Education issued an "Explanatory Note to the Rules for Students," which states that "All schools should educate children in a patriotic spirit, in the spirit of devotion to the Emperor, his people, in respect for the past history of his Fatherland and faith in his future". The fundamental principle of education for the reform of the 60s of the XIX century affirmed equality of public estates in rights (vsesoslovnost').

The features of the state-public education management system were first identified.

At the Holy Synod in 1867, an Education Committee was formed. The Synod appointed the Chairman and nine members of the study committee from clergy, and members from the clergy and secular. The chairman, with the knowledge of the Synod or chief prosecutor, was invited to participate in the work and other persons from scientists and teachers who lived in St. Petersburg. The Educational Committee carried out the methodical guidance of theological schools and seminaries.

In 1869, a reform of theological academies was carried out, this reform reproduced the university charters of 1863, which caused indignation of the clergy. The dependence of theological schools on the chief prosecutor increased. The relationship between seminaries and theological academies was weakened, but, nevertheless, the academies could nominate candidates for school positions, but in fact this created confusion. The academic committees of secular officials with an academic background, who represented the head of the public prosecutor, created the institution of auditor members, which strengthened the influence of state power in theological schools. In 1874, the bishops ceased to chair the school councils, and nobles began to take their place. In provincial and district school councils, the clergy had the right to have only one deputy. In such circumstances, the clergy ceased to open new schools and began to abandon law teaching in secular schools.

Since 1871, the Synod allowed to occupy law-teaching vacancies for secular persons. The connection between the public school and the church was weakening. When the post of Minister of Education and Chief Prosecutor was taken by Count D. Tolstoy, who pursued a unified policy on public schools, an improvement came. In the church administration the rights of the parish clergy were expanded, the procedure for removing the priest from his dignity was simplified. The number of parochial schools increased, and the teaching level in these schools increased. Seminar graduates were allowed to enter universities, the material position of the clergy was improved. In theological schools, officials, except for rectors, began to be selected. The local clergy was involved in seminary affairs; it had representatives in the boards of educational institutions.

Special and general education courses in seminary and college programs were clearly distributed. The seminar program was shortened: the doctrine of liturgical books and patristics, as well as biblical history, were excluded from it. Teaching philosophy was expanded. The seminaries began to teach pedagogy.

The board at the seminaries began to elect the rector. But the candidates were selected by the general pedagogical meeting, the diocesan bishop represented the selected candidates to the Synod. The synod could appoint its candidate or approve one of the elected. In most cases, representatives of the white clergy or laity were elected to the rectors of the seminaries, who agreed to take the priesthood. The post of inspector also became selective. Teachers began to take part in the management of the seminary; this was a departure from the previous system.

Deputies from the clergy who were members of the seminary boards began to take an active part in the life of theological schools. Theological schools were under the care of the local clergy. Clergy from local funds provided financial support to schools. Since 1867, "diocesan congresses" began to take place, the purpose of which was the organization of estate cash assistance. According to the Highest Command of March 20, 1879, seminarians could enter universities only after graduating from high schools, which affected the change in the composition of students.

Big changes in public education occurred during the reign of Alexander III. He attached great importance in educating religious foundations. Parish schools began to revive in 1882. From the funds of the Ministry of Public Education at the Highest Command, 55500 rubles were transferred to the Synod for the establishment and maintenance of the clergy of public education schools. In 1884, under Alexander III, a new charter of seminaries and theological academies was published. The Ministry of Education increased the salaries and pensions of teachers under the new Charter. Church historian I.K. Smolich wrote that the Charter of 1884 set the task only on a local Russian scale. This consisted in the training of trustworthy church-administrative personnel, who were supposed to appoint teachers to theological schools of middle and lower level.

Scientist's historians V. Skalon, F. Blagovidov, I.V. Preobrazhensky in his writings investigated the role of parish clergy in Russian public education in the 19th and early 20th centuries. These scholars positively evaluated the centralized network of religious educational institutions created under Alexander I, and the changes made in these educational institutions under Emperor Nicholas I negatively. Historians believed that the clergy did not come close to parishioners, and the training of priests worsened.

In 1884, religious rules on parish schools were published. Parish and literacy schools passed under the control of the clergy. The schools were managed by the created diocesan councils, and the School Council, established under the Synod in 1885.

The Chairman of the School Council was appointed by the Synod. The council consisted of 9 permanent members, a school supervisor and his assistant. The composition of the diocesan council was the same, but the council included a representative from the Ministry of Education. Temples and parish schools in the late XIX - early XX centuries. were educational and cultural centers that have a huge impact on the moral and spiritual development of Orthodox people. The richness of the Christian religion and Orthodox culture was received by the population in parish schools, which were under the leadership of the Russian Orthodox Church, as clergymen or secular people who graduated from religious schools taught at parish schools. Primary subjects and arithmetic were taught in parish schools, and church and Russian history in four-year-olds. The priest carried out general supervision of the schools. The number of parochial schools grew, and from 4,500 by 1890 it reached 24,600.

Since 1883, small amounts were annually received from the state treasury for maintaining schools, and in 1895 the state treasury allocated 700,000 rubles for maintaining parish schools, and since 1896 this amount was raised to 3279,145 rubles, due to which the parish education gained decent support state. Parish schools played a large role in the moral education of future generations.

In the years 1891-1892 in the Kursk diocese there were only 405 church schools, of which 202 were parochial schools, and 206 were literacy schools. In 1893, there were 486 schools, of which 221 were parochial schools and 265 were literacy schools. The primary public schools belonging to other departments in the region were 592. The primary education of the ecclesiastical department took a strong position in the region.

Later in the Kursk province, church schools continued to spread, especially parish schools. Theological schools at the beginning of the 20th century were subordinate to the Kursk Diocesan College Council, the curricula of these schools were divided into three types: two-class church schools of the highest group, the most massive one-class church-parish schools, and literacy schools. Parish schools were of two types: two-class and ordinary one-class schools. Particularly common in the Kursk province were one-class parish schools. In 1904, parish schools numbered 626, accounting for 64.7% of the total number of elementary public schools, literacy schools were 336, or 34.7%, which confirms the qualitative changes in the structure of primary education. 866 schools were located in rural areas, and there were 77 schools in the city. In 1900, the Chief Prosecutor of the Synod noted in his report that theological elementary schools were mainly located in rural areas, and in the city there were 5% of the total number, which was an all-Russian trend.

The clergy provided great support to parochial schools and took a responsible attitude to the education and upbringing of young people. For zealous service, clergymen received various awards from the authorities, the main of which was the medal "25th anniversary of the formation of parish schools". Here is what can be said about the deacon of the village of Gavrilovka, Tambov province A.V. Alekseev: "For 10 years he was a trustee of a local parish school, and taught there for 22 years. For his work with students, the Holy Synod thanked him, awarded him with a diploma and a silver medal "for diligence".

At the end of the XIX century, Chief Prosecutor of the Holy Synod Konstantin Petrovich Pobedonostsev became interested in the school experience of S.A. Rachinsky. In this school, teaching science was interconnected with teaching religion. K.P. Pobedonostsev wrote: "the school teaches not only to write, count and read, but also teaches to know and love God, to respect parents, to love the Fatherland. This sum of knowledge and skills forms a conscience in a person and gives him moral strength to fight the evil temptations of thought, and helps maintain peace of mind in life.

The development of public education and upbringing in Russia was initiated by theological schools; they laid the foundations of secular science. The contribution of theological schools is of great importance in the development of the cultural and scientific potential of the Voronezh province. In the Voronezh province at the end of the 19th century, there were 7 parish schools; the diocesan Teachers Council and the Holy Synod paid for their maintenance, and 790 rubles were allocated for this. In 1890, 270 children attended these schools.

In 1898, the Office of the Ministry of Public Education, "in memory of the coronation of Emperor Nikolai Alexandrovich and Empress Alexandra Fedorovna", approved the Charter of the Society for Student Assistance in Primary Public Schools of the Voronezh Province. Princess Oldenburg patronized this Society, which was of great importance in the education of students of loyal feelings. The Voronezh governor, who embodied the highest authority in the province, was the chairman of this Society. In the activities of the Company he owned the main management, which was stipulated in the Charter. Education charities were affiliated with a religious department that was involved in the religious education of children. Therefore, the Voronezh diocesan bishop was an honorary member of the Society, and the trustee of the Kharkov school district and those who made impressive donations or provided significant services to the community were honorary members. The Council, chaired by the Governor, managed the affairs of the Company. The council consisted of eight members, which were power structures: the director of public schools, the provincial leader of the nobility, the chairman of the provincial zemstvo council, and the chairman of the diocesan school council. The council also included four people elected by the general meeting, who were approved by the Princess of Oldenburg.

The charity had connections with all counties in the province. The Society Council included the chairmen of the county branches of the diocesan Council and the chairmen of the county school councils, which had the right to vote.

The Council monitored the receipt of cash at the cash desk of the Company, kept receipts and books, made reports and reports on the activities of the company, analyzed applications in which students asked for financial assistance. The Chairman of the Society sent all the reports to the Princess of Oldenburg, Minister of Public Education, Minister of Internal Affairs and Chief Prosecutor of the Holy Synod. This indicates tight control over the activities of the charity. The purpose of the Society was not only to provide financial support to students, but also to implement educational tasks. The society helped students not only financially, but also provided students with study books and reading books, tried to improve the conditions of students and encouraged hardworking students (Kolupaev, 2019).

Much attention was paid to the preservation of manuscripts and ancient texts. On November 18, 1891, a decree of the Holy Synod was sent to the Voronezh Spiritual Consistory, which stated that in churches, in no case, the correction of antiquities was allowed without the permission of the Holy Synod. All monasteries and churches should have inventories that will contain an accurate description of their sacristy, manuscripts, ancient acts, letters, valuable in historical terms. The clergy of the Voronezh diocese had to follow this decree of the Holy Synod steadily.

The masses of the people had many books of spiritual content, and there were few popular science and fiction books. In 1889, the peasants of the four districts of the Voronezh province had 28,728 books and brochures, among which 14,482 books (50.6%) turned out to be books of spiritual content. On July 12, 1875, the Holy Synod notified the Voronezh Archpriest Mikhail Scriabin that the Ministry of Education was recommended to publish the book "Study of Christian Orthodox Teaching". The book consisted mainly of the sayings of the Holy Fathers, mainly - Tikhon Zadonsky. The book was supposed to serve as a teaching tool for teachers of grammar schools and public schools. The church also assisted the clergy for their diligent fulfillment of pastoral duties in spiritual education.

In 1911, in the Voronezh province, priest Ivan Mikhailovsky worked as a teacher at a local parish school. Ivan Mikhailovsky received his education at the Voronezh Theological Seminary, having completed the first-class course. For the diligent performance of his pastoral duties in teaching children, Ivan Mikhailovsky received a salary from the state treasury of 300 rubles a year. Bishop of Voronezh and Cherkassky Anthony Sokolov at the beginning of the 19th century began to revive the seminary in the Voronezh province. The theological school was located in one of the buildings of the bishop's courtyard. Its situation was disastrous. Therefore, Vladyka Anthony decided to build a new seminary room, for which, in 1811, with the permission of the Holy Synod, a collection of donations was organized among Voronezh residents for these purposes. Bishop Anthony turned to the inhabitants of the province and to the Don Army with a request to donate to the construction of the seminary.

In 1812, 30 thousand rubles were raised for the construction of the Voronezh seminary. The bishop himself contributed 500 rubles, and Countess A.A. each contributed 5 thousand rubles. Orlova-Chesmenskaya and the merchant Samuel Meshcheryakov. In 1812, the estate of state adviser Nikolai Lazarev-Stanishchev was bought on Bolshaya Dvoryanskaya Street, for which 8 thousand rubles were paid.

On February 17, 1813, the Holy Synod considered a plan for the construction of a seminary. "It was proposed to build two stone buildings in which classrooms should be located, a library, a church in the name of St. John the Evangelist, apartments for bosses and teachers, a kitchen, a bakery, a dining room, cellars, and pantries for bread." On November 13, 1813, the Synod blessed this construction. The author of the project for this building was supposedly the Voronezh city architect Timofei Kondratyev.

A special role in the development of the Voronezh Theological School in the 19th century is given to St. Tikhon Zadonsky, Bishop of Voronezh and Yelets, personally supervising the Voronezh Theological School, and Archbishop of Voronezh and Zadonsky Anthony Smirnitsky, who paid great attention to enlightenment.

Thousands of clergy of the Russian Orthodox Church and famous figures of the Russian state left the walls of the Voronezh seminary. Ten of its pupils were glorified by the Russian Orthodox Church as saints, thirty-five representatives of the Voronezh Theological Seminary became bishops: Archpriest Tikhon Popov, rector of the Moscow Theological Academy, professor N.N. Glubokovsky, Archpriest Stefan Zverev, Bishop Methodius Smirnov, Metropolitan Evgeny Bolkhovitinov, Bishop Lavrenty Nekrasov, historian P.V. Nikolsky.

We should also mention Metropolitan Pyotr Polyansky, who was born on June 28, 1862 in the Korotoyak district of the Voronezh province in the village of Storozhevoy. The father of Metropolitan Pyotr Polyansky was a parish priest. In 1885, Peter Polyansky graduated from the Voronezh Theological Seminary in the first category, and in 1892 he graduated from the Moscow Theological Academy with a degree of candidate of theology, which he received for his work "Explanation of the First Epistle of St. Paul to Timothy." Pyotr Polyansky was by nature compliant, complacent, benevolent. While studying at the academy, he was friends with the future patriarch Sergius of Stragorodsky. From 1885 to 1887, Pyotr Polyansky served as a psalmist in the Church of the village of Maidens of Korotoyak Uyezd, and in 1892 he taught the Law of God to students of the Sergiev Posad Women's School, and was an assistant inspector of the Moscow Theological Academy. In 1895, in the village of Storozhevoy of the Voronezh diocese, he served as the church elder. Pyotr Fedorovich Polyansky was a member of the Guardianship of National Sobriety, was a magistrate of the Slonim District, and participated in the first All-Russian population census. For diligent service he was awarded the Order of St. Stanislav 3rd and 2nd degree. At this time, he met with the future patriarch, Bishop Tikhon Belavin. In 1997, Pyotr Fedorovich Polyansky was canonized.

Noteworthy is the fairly well-known archbishop Nikander Pokrovsky (in the world Pokrovsky Nikolai Ivanovich). N.I. Pokrovsky was born on May 17, 1816 in the village of Dvuluchi of the Valuysky district of Voronezh province in the family of a priest. At the Voronezh Theological School, he received his initial education. Then he began to study at the Voronezh Theological Seminary, and graduated in Kiev. In 1886 he was awarded a diamond cross on the hood. Honorary member of the Kiev Theological Academy. Nikander Pokrovsky died on June 27, 1893 in Tula and was buried there. Here is what church researcher S. Vvedensky tells about the death of the archbishop:

To prepare clergymen, the program of the Voronezh seminary, in addition to special disciplines, included general educational subjects: rhetoric, philosophy, agricultural business, ancient languages, mathematics, and medicine. Voronezh seminary was the only one who trained educated cadres for the needs of the Church. The historian Pavel Vasilievich Nikolsky noted that during extracurricular time, upper-class students composed speeches on theological topics in Russian and Latin and composed sermons, the best of which were defended at public debates. Each year, students had to memorize three of their own sermons, one of which was delivered in a private debate, the second in a public debate, and the third in a temple. Seminarists should be able to speak Latin, be able to read and translate theological books. In solemn occasions, the best students composed speeches and poetic odes, which indicated the level of knowledge of the students, this happened in the presence of the diocesan bishop in a ceremonial setting for Christmas or Easter. Sometimes seminarians wrote speeches for the bishop, which were combined into one book, and then were stored in the seminary library. There were cases of dismissal of priests from the seminary and their placement in church service. The student of the Voronezh Theological Seminary Nikolay Zelenov was assigned to the position of clerk in the Varvarovka settlement of the Voronezh province. When one church was supposed to be a priest, deacon, sexton.

Many students in a theological seminary could not always count on a church position (sexton, deacon). On December 5, 1811, a student at the Voronezh Theological Seminary, Luka Markov, asked him to approve the position of deacon in the settlement of Petropavlovka, Bogucharsky Uyezd. Voronezh seminary asked his Grace to appoint Luka Markov at the Peter and Paul Church as a deacon. Luka Markov, studying at the seminary, was distinguished by good behavior, studied Latin and Greek. According to the certificate of the Voronezh Spiritual Consistory, it turned out that there was no deacon or Ponomar place in the Peter and Paul Church.

Since the mid-19th century, the Voronezh seminary has become the center of the cultural and spiritual life of the province. At the initiative of the seminary, the Voronezh literary collection began to be published, together with the theological schools of the Moscow Patriarchate, the Voronezh seminary is pursuing a course towards the revival of the traditions of theological science, and is improving curricula. Voronezh seminary under the leadership of its rectors, Archpriest Alexei Spassky and Archimandrite Seraphim Sobolev, was able to defend the independence of church education from secular and revolutionary trends.

Another important center was the Kursk Theological Seminary. It was formed in 1787 at the Belgorod Bishop's House. In it, as in the Voronezh seminary, children of the clergy class were trained. He founded the seminary Feoktist (Mochulsky), Bishop of Belgorod and Kursk. The first rector of the Kursk seminary was Justin, hegumen of the Belgorod Nikolsky Monastery, and during the entire existence of the seminary, 13 rectors led it. The seminary was not limited to the spiritual sphere; Kursk seminarians were patriots of their country, as shown by the Patriotic War of 1812. Many students in the Kursk seminary volunteered to join the militia.

A noticeable trace in the history of the Kursk Theological Seminary from 1832 to 1860 the rectors of archimandrite Varlaam and Nicodemus left. Lecturer Matvey Arkhangelsky under the leadership of the rector of the seminary Archimandrite Flavian in 1854-1856 created a historical and statistical description of the Kursk diocese and the Kursk seminary.

The Kursk seminary supplied honest, hardworking and energetic figures in various areas of public service for the whole of Russia, among them - well-known publicists, theologians, and doctors. Kursk seminary was completed by Bishop Vladimir (Nikolsky), Metropolitan of Moscow Makarii (Bulgakov), Archbishop Nathanael (Savchenko), Archbishop Eusebius (Ilyinsky). The seminary began in 1879, it moved to Kursk in 1883. Seminarians, in addition to basic education, also received secular education, and therefore the level of knowledge of seminarians was very high.

In 1888, Archpriest Jacob Novitsky led the seminary and worked in it until its closure. The seminary was engaged in educational activities among the residents of Kursk. In the parish school, in the public school of the Yamskaya and Streletskaya Sloboda, in the school of Semenovskaya Sloboda, in 1891, they began to conduct moral and religious conversations with the assistance of St. Theodosius of the Caves. The seminary held on Sunday and holidays religious and moral Palestinian readings. The future rector of the Leningrad Theological Academy and Seminary Ivan Epiphany and the future archbishop of Kursk and Oboyansk Dmitry Voskresensky at the end of the XIX century graduated from the Kursk Theological Seminary.

In 1817, when Bishop Jonah took office, there were changes in the Oryol Theological Seminary. It had three departments - lower, middle and higher; the lower classes were county and parish schools. The seminary was transferred from Sevsk to Oryol in the spring of 1827. It becomes among the population a distributor of faith and enlightenment. Metropolitans taught in it: Feognost, Isidore, Arseny, Plato. Oryol seminary was completed by Archbishop Seraphim and Holy Bishop Theophan the Recluse.

Among the population of the Oryol province, the highest percentage of literate people gave the clergy: men - 83.1% and women - 68.1%. Higher university education had 0.4% of the total clergy. Technical higher education institutions completed 0.03%, special secondary schools - 0.3%. Most of the clergy studied in secondary schools - 49.2% of people: men - 76.8%, women - 23.2%. In higher secondary military educational institutions, the Oryol clergy did not study. From 1883 to 1893 the number of church schools increased by more than five times from 5,516 to 29,944. And the number of schools in the Oryol diocese at the same time increased 50 times, from 10 to 550 schools. Similar indicators characterized the Voronezh, Kursk and Tambov dioceses (Ershov, 2017).

On September 22, 1779, by decision of Empress Catherine II, a theological seminary was opened in Tambov, which was located in the Kazan Monastery. In the seminary building in 1847, the St. Nicholas Church began to operate. In the years 1867-1870. at the seminary, a Sunday school began to work, where high school students taught. Priests needed to know the languages of the local population, so since 1818, the Mordovian and Tatar languages were included in the curriculum. In addition to theological subjects, in the middle of the 19th century Tambov seminarians studied Mordovian, Tatar, French, German and ancient languages, physics and mathematics, church and universal history, natural history, agriculture, medicine, there was an icon painting class. Any resident of Tambov could attend lectures on carpentry, gardening, beekeeping, gardening.

Great importance in the Tambov seminary was given to music education and choral singing: there were 14 liturgical choirs in it. In the XIX - early XX centuries the educational center of the Tambov province was a seminary. The seminary library collected the best book editions of the time. By the beginning of the 20th century, the Tambov Seminary was a large educational institution in Russia. About 30 people studied at the Tambov seminary at the beginning of the 19th century, and 600 at the end of the 19th century. Metropolitan Vladimir Bogoyavlensky, Metropolitan Veniamin (Fedchenkov), Ambrose Optinsky, Anthony (Vadkovsky) graduated from the Tambov seminary. The seminarians could go for walks without permission until 5 pm, and in the evening, ask the inspector for help.

Seminarians of all classes, starting from 3, with the permission of the rector, had the right to leave for 2 hours for private lessons from five to seven in the evening, upon returning to the hostel they should be noted at the guard on duty. Students living in apartments noted their arrival and departure time in special journals. Such tutors by 1901 there were up to 100 people. Rector of the seminary in 1900-1902 was Archimandrite Athanasius, in 1902-1904. - Archimandrite Nathanael, 1904-1906 Archimandrite Theodore, 1906-1907 - Archimandrite Simeon and from August 23, 1907 Archpriest Panormov. A large number of students dropped out of seminary and entered mainly higher secular educational institutions. In 1905-1906 after the seminary, 25 people entered higher education institutions, and seven people entered the theological academies. In 1861, in the Kirsanovsky district of the Tambov province there were 109 clergymen, 58 people - deacons, 205 people - clerks. All priests and two deacons graduated from the seminary. 35 deacons and 1 clerk received incomplete seminary education, so half of the deacons and all clerks of the systematic education did not.

In 1894, there were 118 priests, 61 deacon and 124 psalmists in this county. 79 priests completed the seminary; four priests had incomplete seminary education. Three deacons and eight psalmists graduated from the seminary, and three deacons did not have a seminary education.

In 1911, there were 123 priests in the Tambov province, six of them had no seminary education. There were cases of petitioning students from the Tambov Theological Seminary to transfer them to the state corps. The 1897 clergy reporting journal of the Tambov diocese contains a humble petition from Alexey Lebedev, a pupil of the Tambov Theological Seminary, asking that Alexey Lebedev request that he be released from residence fees in the Tambov seminary board. He explained that his father was extremely poor and had no opportunity to pay for the stay of his son in the seminary board. The general diocesan congress of the clergy examined the request of Alexey Lebedev and decided to allocate a vacant place in the state corps to Alexey Lebedev.

Thus, the process of transformation in the theological school began in the late XIX - early XX centuries. New opportunities were opened up for the Church in the field of enlightenment and missionary activity, which required the clergy to be prepared for the new realities of church life. The churching of Russian society before the revolution was due to the fact that children from an early age introduced themselves to church life and assimilated the fundamental truths of Christianity.

CONCLUSION

In conclusion, it should be noted that the rapid rise of theological science in the middle of the 19th century suggests that Christian devotees influenced the system of spiritual education in the Russian province, among which Metropolitan Pyotr Polyansky, Timofey Sluchevsky, Tikhon Zadonsky and Voronezh were worth mentioning. The organizational and pedagogical aspects of the activity of the bishops of the Central Black Earth Region contributed to the opening of theological schools. The educational activities of the theological seminaries of the Central Black Earth Region significantly increased the level of education of clergymen. The clergy invariably showed steadfastness, defending their views on public education, its unity in their religious beliefs.

REFERENCES

Ershov, B. A. (2011). Church charitable societies and institutions of the Voronezh province in the 19th century. *Bulletin of the Tambov University. Series: Humanities, 1*(93), 276-282.

Ershov, B. A., & Drobyshev, A.V. (2017). The emergence and role of church charitable institutions in the provinces of the Central Chernozem region in the XIX-early XX centuries. *History: Facts and symbols, 2*(11), 103-109.

Karpova, V. V. (2015). Everyday life of participants of student labor detachments in Russia (1915-1916). *Bulletin of the Tomsk State University. Leningrad State high fur boots named after A. S. Pushkin*, (2), 48–55.

Kolupaev, A. A. (2019). Organization of assistance to refugees during the First World War (on the example of the Kursk province). *Izvestiya Yugo-Zapadnogo gosudarstvennogo universiteta. Series. History and Law, 9*(6), 201–208.

Kozyrev, E. E. (2015). Charity of the Royal family during the First World War. *Church and Medicine, 1*(13), 101-104.

Chapter 9
Family Basics of the Life of Clerics

ABSTRACT

The position of the husband in the church ranks determined the legal status of a woman from the clergy, since after marriage the woman became a representative of the church department. Women from other classes, having married a priest, assumed the duties of "representative of the church department." The spouses of the archpriests and rectors of the parishes occupied the upper step in the church hierarchy, then the deacons and psalm-followers followed – they should not be confused with the priests. The rhythm of life of members of the spiritual family was different from the rhythm of the life of the parish priest, so it was very important to perform family prayers and services at home led by the father-priest.

INTRODUCTION

The importance of studying the field of family life in Orthodox theology is very great. The Orthodox had different views on the life of the clergy, since the family life of clergy is also Christian work. Family life is blessed with a series of church ordinances and prayers. A Christian family cannot be created without a joint religious life, without spiritual experiences, without common prayer, therefore, prayer plays a big role in the life of the priest: in addition to morning and evening prayers, the priest reads prayers daily before the liturgy, prayers to the saints, in the church and at home - prayers about spiritual

DOI: 10.4018/978-1-6684-4915-8.ch009

children. The rhythm of life of members of the spiritual family was different from the rhythm of the life of the parish priest, so it was very important to perform family prayers and services at home, led by the father-priest. The spiritual family was a part of the Church, and therefore, it had to pray not only for its near and dear ones, but also for the whole church and its leaders.

The role of the spiritual family is the spiritual and moral education of children. In such families, children are perceived as a gift of God, and parents should protect their child and reveal his talents, which will lead him to a virtuous life. In the Trebnik, which is the liturgical book of an Orthodox priest, there are prayers for the mother and the born baby, prayer for the name of the child and his baptism, prayer for housewarming and consecration of the house, prayer for the dying. Thus, the Church takes care of its children throughout life. Orthodoxy not only allows, but also encourages a married clergy. Orthodoxy welcomes the married clergy. The marriage of persons of a clergy could only be before initiation into the priesthood, then the priest cannot marry. The time for finding a companion of life for a person in the spiritual estate was extremely short, since at the end of his studies he became a deacon. Either he found a future mother for years of study, or he was lonely all his life. Marriages were most often between representatives of the spiritual estate. Divorce was not possible for the priest.

Christian morality was the norm in family-marriage relations in the families of priests in the 19th century. Initiation to the dignity separated the worldly from the spiritual, the priest should not have been interested in worldly interests and vanity. The priest, bound by a vow of celibacy, could fully devote himself to serving God, since there is no family between him and God, and he is not bound by the interests of the family. After the priest devoted himself to serving God, his marriage was impossible.

Acceptance of monasticism is an exceptional way, and it is absolutely wrong to think that monasticism in Orthodoxy is an easier way to advance along the hierarchical ladder. They went to monasticism exclusively by calling to a solitary life. In 1898, two boys from several villages in the Oryol province went to pray to God at the Monastery Belye Berega. There, they liked it so much that they wanted to enter the monastery, but their parents did not allow it. Another teenager planned to go to the monastery on Mount Athos. Since his parents did not want to let him go, seventeen-year-old Jacob took a vow of silence and stopped eating. And then his parents promised to let him go after two years, when his strength will grow stronger. More insistent was the girl who "against the desire of her parents who wanted to marry her, entered the Bolkhovsky (Bolhovskij) Monastery (Veselovsky, 1876).

"Another nun, her mother's only daughter, was from a wealthy family. While studying at a rural school, she came across a book about Pechersk saints, and she decided to follow suit. Mother wanted to marry her and had already prepared a good dowry for her, but Aksinya, contrary to her mother, fled to leave for the monastery. However, without a contribution to the monasteries they did not take, and the father, seeing her sincere desire to enter the monastery, promised to make a contribution for her. She entered the Klyuev monastery of the Kromsky district of the Oryol province. The monastery was far from the city and villages, the nuns were engaged in the cultivation of land that belonged to the monastery. Aksinya liked this monastery, and she stayed there. Her father contributed 80 rubles to the monastery". The children belonged to the clergy, but if the children under 15 remained without education or were expelled from theological schools, did not inherit the clergy and were assigned to the bourgeois or peasant class, and could also be registered as merchants.

Until 1860, the "excess" children of the clergy, whom they could not identify anywhere, were surrendered to the soldiers. When entering civil service, children of clergymen, on a par with noble children, enjoyed the same rights. Children of clergy who graduated from the secondary department of the seminary, upon admission to military service, had freedoms. For priests who wished to enter the civil service and retired the priesthood, such entry was forbidden (for priests — for 10 years after the removal of the rank, and for deacons — for 6 years).

In 1864, the heads of departments of the Voronezh provincial government were mostly children from the clergy and bureaucratic children. The children of clergymen most often held the leading positions of the county level. In 1879–1880, 12 district police officers and their assistants served in the Voronezh province, among whom 4 were from the clergy, 4 from the bureaucracy, 2 from the nobility, 28 from the military estate. Of the 6 district judges, 3 were children of clergy, 1 - a tradesman, 1 - a nobleman and 1 - an official. One of the functions of priestly families was to take care of disabled relatives. This function persisted for a century and decreased only by the end of the 19th century, when trusteeship and pension funds were established. Throughout the 19th century, an older representative from the clergy clan took care of elderly parents, minor brothers and sisters, orphans who were left without parents. If this was not the case, the place of the deceased breadwinner was assigned to the man who was being sued. The widow was supposed to help the man who entered the place of her deceased husband; he had to give her half of his income. The mother-in-law was supposed to contain the son-in-law who took the place of her husband. In 1852, in the city of Morshansk in the Tambov province, 4 of the suspects lived with funds of guardianship of the poor clergy, 15 people were kept by relatives (Ershov, 2020).

In the Voronezh province, facts of the care of the children of the clergy about their parents were also discovered. In 1822, the humble petition of the bishop of Tambov and Shatsky was sent to the Voronezh ecclesiastical consistency to accept priest Vasily Dmitriev, priest of the Tambov diocese, to serve in the Voronezh diocese. The petition stated that, in old age, the priest of the Tambov diocese, Vasily Dmitriev, was dismissed from the Nikolaev Church, and the priest was allowed to stay in Starobelsk with his son, Archpriest Pokrovsky Cathedral Mikhail Dmitriev. Due to the difficulties of moving to another region, the priest asked about the possibility of being registered with the Voronezh diocese and living in the house of his son Mikhail Dmitriev. The Voronezh Spiritual Consistory decided that it allows the priest Vasily Dmitriev and his wife to live in the Voronezh diocese in the city of Starobelsk. In addition, it is said that the priest must notify himself in writing to the Tambov diocese. Requirements of a canonical nature in Orthodoxy were presented to the marriage of a priest, the fulfillment of which was mandatory. The priest could not marry an infidel, his children should not have been married to heretics, his house should be Orthodox. The widow or actress could not be the wife of the priest. If the priest's wife was seen to be in a vicious behavior, he should have divorced her or be tidied up. Priests could not marry again, as church authorities forbade it. "Priests and deacons were allowed to marry only once; a second marriage was forbidden to the widowed priest. However, many of the widowed priests violated this law, and such priests were not allowed to serve dinners or perform sacraments, they were only allowed to perform the duties of clerks. So among the priests there were those who were married a second time, or a third time, although there were not so many of them. For example, in 1877, in the village of Sosnovets of the Kozlovsky district of the Tambov province, there lived a 27-year-old sexton (ponomar') who was married three times. The theme of the bride's choice was traditional. This was reflected in the textbooks of pastoral theology of the 19th century. Life itself contributed to this problem, firstly, the hereditary priesthood. The son of the priest received the inheritance or as a dowry for the bride. In any case, he remained in a spiritual environment. The centuries-old customs and wise policies of the great Russian hierarchs spiritually prepared priest candidates and their wives. The future priest went through 10 years of training, and then could enter a higher spiritual school. In many dioceses of Russia for the daughters of priests, "diocesan schools" were created with a special program adapted for future wives of priests. In these schools, the daughters of priests studied general subjects, church history, theological sciences, Church Slavonic languages, church singing and liturgical regulations. The school paid great attention to the preparation of housekeeping and parenting, as well as to education in the spirit of strict morality and secular decency. The church tried in family life to give the correct concepts about marriage. Divorces were allowed in the case when the husband or wife was tonsured as a monk, the remaining half of the world could enter into a new marriage. The views on marriage and on women were ascetic. At the end of the 19th century, the priesthood ceased to be an estate, there were no normal theological schools, the tradition of the priesthood and everyday life died out, diocesan women's schools ceased to function. Therefore, the whole issue now had to be resolved in a new way. Many girls were embarrassed by the question of becoming the wife of a priest, "becoming a mother". There were various internal psychological obstacles, and therefore were unequally assessed, both by the women who faced this question, and by the young people who were going to take the priesthood. It is difficult to trace the life path of women from the spiritual estate. Sons of priests from childhood were trained to receive a profession in the church department, from six to seven years of age they were sent to theological schools. Later, vivid childhood memories from them were associated with their mother. There were few recollections on the pages of diaries about the wives of persons of the clerical class. The memoirs are supplemented by official documents: priests' track records, information about girls of women's educational institutions, the level of education and family affiliation of women, legislative acts, and protocols for interrogation of seminarians. In their memoirs, the priests talked about their mothers and sisters, mostly they talked about priests and clerks, about "deacons" and "psalm-goers" - the information is scarce. The position of the husband in the church ranks determined the legal status of a woman from the clergy, since after marriage the woman became a representative of the church department. Women from other classes, having married a priest, assumed the duties of "representative of the church department". The spouses of the archpriests and rectors of the parishes occupied the upper step in the church hierarchy, then the deacons and psalm-followers followed - they should not be confused with the priests. The fate of the rural Orthodox priest before the revolution in Russia was unenviable. It was especially difficult for his wife, procreation and raising children was her main function. She also had to do household work and help her husband. The priest was the sole breadwinner of his family, and after the death of her husband, tragedies occurred. After the death of priest Andrei Pavlov, the guardianship of his daughter, the priest Lev Panteleimonov, could not be issued due to the fact that the daughter of the deceased priest was married, and there were no other children left. In 1811, the deacon of the Barannikovka settlement of Starobelsky County, Porfiry Makarovsky, died. After his death, his wife Tatyana Kirilova and the children of Evdokia, Pelageya, Mikhail remained. The Voronezh Spiritual Consistory decided to identify children for upbringing with the relatives of the deceased. Epiphanius, Bishop of Voronezh and Cherkassky supported this decision. In Russia of the 19th century, the inheritance of the profession and the reproduction of estates usually went along the male line. For the clergy, the order was different. The woman played a large role in the inheritance of the spiritual position: the eldest daughter of the priest for the future husband was assigned the place of her late father. They tried to marry the youngest daughters "to the side", if they remained in the house, then as implants. The place could go to the nearest unmarried relative in the event that the family did not have an heiress. In the event of the death of the clergyman, the land and the house, from which there was little income, became the property of the successor in office, and even the parish priest could not postpone the savings for retirement. The family of the priest, as a rule, was large. In this regard, difficulties arose in determining the children of priests in church service. Deacon Vladimir Todorsky addressed the bishop of Voronezh Epiphanius with a humble petition. It says that in connection with the constant moving from apartment to apartment (apparently there was no own housing), Vladimir Todorsky requested that his son Nikolai be assigned a proper place after the seminary. According to the certificate of the Voronezh Spiritual Consistory, it turned out that there was no approved place (Kalinin, 1975). By the beginning of the 20th century, the birth rate in priestly families began to be inferior to the peasant families in terms of the birth rate, whereas earlier the birth rate in spiritual families was ahead of all other classes. Wealthy noblewomen or merchants in urban families could invite a nanny, and rural mothers raised and taught children to read and write, read the Gospel and the Lives of Saints. The male version of education, based on the principle: "the rod is not an archangel, but will do a lot," existed in rare families. The religious nature of the home way was given most often by the wives of priests. The prayer ritual was strictly observed thanks to mothers: before each meal they read a prayer, ate in silence, treated bread as a gift of God. The posts were very strictly enforced. Fasting can be moral, spiritual, churchly and natural. Spiritual fasting is the removal of oneself from sins; it calls for abstinence from unrighteousness and from all evil deeds. All people should observe such a post on the biggest holidays. Moral fasting is the moderate use of potion and food for a righteous life. The natural fast is not to drink or eat anything, this fast was observed before the acceptance of the Body and Blood of Christ for the grace and holiness that are contained in the Holy Mysteries of Christ. Church fasting is abstinence from food according to the law established by the Church itself. When considering church fasting, there are discrepancies with opponents of the Orthodox faith. For those wishing to obtain the highest moral perfection, it is necessary to observe the "spiritual fasting" and "bodily fasting". The position of the woman in the church family determined the attitude of those around her. Respect was given to those who taught children church singing and reading and writing, were in charge of the funeral homes, and were engaged in other trustee affairs. By the middle of the 19th century, the daughters of the clergy were not only taught at home the basics of reading and writing, but were also brought up in shelters and convents, where they mastered various needlework. The difference in the level and content of the education of husband and wife in the family of the priest influenced the relations between members of the families of the clergy. The church authorities seriously took care of this problem and considered it necessary for girls from clergy families to give secondary education. Since 1843, female diocesan schools began to open. In 1869, such a school was opened at the Kursk Holy Trinity Nunnery, where 30 girls from clergy families studied; all teachers in this school had higher education.

The school was 2-4 grades. In 1888, it was ranked as a parish school, and in 1890, 15 pupils studied in the 1st grade. The training of the pupils was free. They paid 10 rubles a month for the premises and for their care. The abbess of the monastery, Mother Superior Sofia, supervised the school, and the nun Alevtina, who was brought up in the Moscow educational house, observed the pupils and taught the children about needlework. In 1890, 465 rubles were spent on the maintenance of the school. Later, this school was transformed into a parish church classroom with three departments, where monastery priests and sisters of the monastery began to teach. The poor population of Kursk from all classes tried to identify their children to study at this school. In addition to good general education, this school paid great attention to the upbringing and development of mental qualities of children, tried to give children moral and religious education; therefore, the number of applicants to enroll in this school was huge. From the middle of the 19th century, women's private educational institutions began to emerge, which became very popular. They competed with other educational institutions, therefore, the directorate of these schools, taking care of their reputation, influenced all aspects of the life of their wards. The social situation of the woman was difficult, she was weary of early marriage, frequent childbirth, domestic work, illness, and family turmoil. If a woman remained a widow, then she had to worry about official maintenance, about the possibility of bringing up children and preserving the right to reside in a priest's house. Assistance to widows was insignificant and irregular, despite the fact that there was a fund to support clergy families, and in 1866 there was a special collection in all dioceses for its replenishment. In a year, the widow could receive from 65 to 90 rubles, but the pension payment period was short, so I had to bother to renew it. The synodal administration strictly monitored the provision of material assistance and inheritance rights. The regular priests and psalmists dismissed from the service, and after their death widows and children, were entitled to receive pensions. The size of the pension depended on the status of the spiritual institution, on the spiritual rank, on the size of the salary for the position held. The widow of a deceased priest or psalmist received 50% of her husband's pension for each year, and children - 1/3 of the other half for each son or daughter. Widows with three young children received a full pension. Each of the 4 young children left without a mother and father received 1/4 of the salary. If there were more, then the pension was divided into parts by the number of children. The legal system was imperfect and incapable of providing good living conditions for wives and children of clerical rank. The whole life of the priest's wife is the real ministry of the Church. She took care of her husband and children, helped him in everything, built his family life so that the priest in his house could draw strength for his various church services, the priest's wife should help with advice to everyone who came for help. Mother took an active part in the ministry of her husband, which showed their unanimity. The daughters of the priests were great toilers. Women from the clerical class sought to exercise their civil rights and showed interest in self-employment. Many women in religion found the main value orientations, and God was an interlocutor for them, they turned to him in an internal dialogue (Marru, 2003).

The church and communities influenced the individual religiosity of women and their social behavior. According to statistics contained in the "Reference book for the clergy of the Voronezh diocese for 1900", it is said that in 1857 in the Voronezh province there were a total of white clergy of clergy of full-time and family 8514, state and orphaned 1769. Family clergy belonged to 11228 souls of both sexes. With churches in the province there were 750 family priests, including in cities 49 and 701 in villages. In 1911, there were 4060 Orthodox nuns in the Tambov province, and 2797 in the

Kursk province. Of the 83.4% of novices, only 16.6% passed into the official status of nuns. Each of the novices at any time could change their belonging to one or another class of the population, which made it possible to feel the freedom of the individual.

The family life of the clergy was supposed to be a model for others, provoking a desire to imitate a cleric. The priest was the "standard" of the Christian in everything. An important duty of the priest was to raise children in love for the temple of God and for the ministry of the Church. The family life of the priest was to be built so that all members of the family were involved in the liturgical life of the priest and, imbued with a prayerful spirit, participated in the church service. The Orthodox priest had to lead the church parish as his family, since he was guided in his family life by Christian ideals [189]. The priest in relation to himself should be firm and strict, despite the soft attitude towards others. The "life" of a priest is what the Old Testament called "walking before God." He had to live in such a way that every business, every inner movement, every thought took place in the face of God (Khavin, 1979).

Summing up, it can be noted that the family status of clergy in the provinces of the Central Chernozem Region changed with the development of the Russian family, but there were some peculiarities. Spiritual and moral education of children, where readings of prayers and liturgical charters played a crucial role, these are the main functions of the spiritual family - the "home Church". The main task of clergymen in our time is to surround the family with attention, love, advice, sympathy and understanding of modern needs.

CONCLUSION

Thus, it can be noted that in the XIX - early XX centuries the clergy in the provinces of the Central Black Earth Region was a significant socio-political force. The fundamental areas of clergy participation were educational and moral activities aimed at raising children in the spirit of Orthodox ideals. This was done through sermons, opening libraries, shelters. Monasteries and churches played the role of spiritual centers for the surrounding population. They contributed to the formation of a system of life values and moral education of the people.

REFERENCES

Ershov, B. A., & Lubkin, Y. Y. (2016). The activities of the Russian Orthodox Church in countering extremism and terrorism in modern Russia. Historical, philosophical, political and legal sciences, cultural studies and art history. *Questions of Theory and Practice, 11*(73), 97–99.

Ershov, B. A., Nebolsin, V. A., & Solovieva, S. R. (2020). Higher education in technical universities of Russia. *7th International Conference on Education and Social Sciences. Abstracts & Proceedings,* 55-58.

Ershov, B. A., Perepelitsyn, A., Glazkov, E., Volkov, I., & Volkov, S. (2019). Church and state in Russia: management issues. *5th International Conference on Advances in Education and Social Sciences. Abstracts & Proceedings,* 26-29.

Ershov, B. A., Zhdanova, T. A., Kashirsky, S. N., & Monko, T. (2020). Education in the university as an important factor in the socialization of students in Russia. *6th International Conference on Advances in Education. Abstracts & Proceedings,* 517-520.

Kalinin, M. I. (1975). *About youth: Selected speeches and articles.* Young Guard.

Khavin, B. N. (1979). *All about the Olympic Games.* Physical Culture and Sport.

Kuhn, L. (1982). *Universal history of physical culture and sports.* Raduga.

Marru, A. I. (2003). *History of education in antiquity.* Academic Press.

The Code of Laws of the Russian Empire. (1912). St. Petersburg: Russian Book Partnership "The Worker". Collection of information on public charity. SPb. 1880–1886. T. 1-7. Archive Raven. spirit. Consistory, Cases Divnogor. Monastery, N°. 450.

The Holy Righteous John of Kronstadt. (1997). The Soul-Christian. *The Ladder.*

Veselovsky, G. M. (1876). *Cities of the Voronezh province, their history and current state, with a brief outline of the entire Voronezh province.* Voronezh: Veselovsky Publishing House.

Chapter 10
Church Charities
and Institutions

ABSTRACT

The Russian Orthodox Church before the revolution paid much attention to issues of mercy and social service in the 19th-early 20th centuries. Charity is reinforced by the charity of individuals, unions, the church, and the state through the charity of orphans, widows, poor, crippled. The concepts of morality and spirituality were rooted in the popular consciousness. The centuries-old traditions of Russian charity were being revived. The materials of the Code of Laws of the Russian Empire include reports that in imperial Russia there was a well-defined system of social assistance and public charity.

INTRODUCTION

The development of charity in the Russian province in the 19th century took place in line with the all-Russian process, but local characteristics left an imprint on the practice of charity. In the 19th century, about 100 communities in the form of almshouses, which existed thanks to the alms of the parishioners, were created at the parish churches. In most cases, these communities were elevated to the rank of monasteries, without fail engaged in charity work. The materials of the Code of Laws of the Russian Empire include reports that in imperial Russia there was a well-defined system of social assistance and public charity. The types of this help were diverse - this is children's charity, free medical care, the charity of the poor from different walks of life,

DOI: 10.4018/978-1-6684-4915-8.ch010

caring for old people. The spiritual department played a big role in this help. Donations and charity were associated with religious feeling. Orthodoxy proclaimed obligatory donations, and wealth was declared sinful.

The main reason for the prosperity of church charity was the desire to live in good conscience, to avoid inner spiritual discord, this was helped by strict education and a religious idea of the soul in the other world. Carrying out charity, the laity tried to combine their life affairs and the desire to save their soul. With the priority position of the nobility in the estate state, church charity could receive public recognition, but the main force was the internal motivation, desire and need to create good, good, understanding of their responsibility to society. In very difficult conditions, the Church made its way, recreating the forms of ministry typical of it in full, one of which was mercy and charity. This church sphere was multifaceted and multifaceted, it included material assistance to the poor, work with the elderly and convicts, assistance to victims of natural disasters, medical patronage in hospitals.

These areas of the clergy's diaconal ministry made it possible to study the motivational aspects of the charitable activities of the Russian Orthodox Church in the context of the spiritual organization of society.

Many societies that functioned in the 19th century had an Orthodox character; from 20 to 40% of all charitable societies that emerged during 1856–1875 provided assistance only to people of the Orthodox faith. More than a third of all societies established in the 60s. XIX century and continued to exist, in 1899 were under the jurisdiction of the "Departments of Orthodox Confession".

Under Alexander II, in 1864, legislation was issued on parish trusteeship and on the Church Brotherhoods, this legislation regulated church charity. Since 1866, each newly discovered monastery was obliged to establish educational and charitable institutions at the monasteries. April 6, 1866 Chief Prosecutor of the Synod Count L.A. Tolstoy issued a decree according to which the founders of the monasteries had to combine the conveniences of monastic life with a charitable or educational purpose; and from 1866 to 1869, 10 monasteries with almshouses, schools and shelters were created.

In the XIX century, a large number of works devoted to church charity came out. A unique publication on church charity in Russia in the 19th century was a collection in seven volumes, which was edited by I.E. Andrievsky and P.P. Semenov from 1880 to 1886. The collection contains information on church charity in different dioceses and provides statistics on charity. This is the most complete description of charitable activities from 1855 to 1880. Such a review from 1881 to 1917 was not carried out. From 1855 to 1880 according to this collection, 37 monasteries were founded that were engaged in charity work. In 1903, 480 hospitals and 660 almshouses were established at parish churches. The provincial and regional cities accounted for 5270 charitable institutions, that is, 35.5% of the total, the remaining 64.5%, which were 9584 institutions, were located in county towns and other settlements.

The authors of the clergy often turned to the internal motives of charity, to the origins of this ministry. Archpriest G. Smirnov-Platonov praised charity as charity, a virtue of the heart. He suggested that Christian society cannot exist without private and public charity, and the priest's task is to lead it. Church historians said that the Church should be an important link in the system of social assistance.

At the end of the XIX century, scientists I.K. Labutin, E. Nikitin, G. Ulgorn noted in their writings that in the pre-Christian world, charity did not have a system and moral justification, because of which it was spontaneous, and, in most cases, pursued selfish goals. However, with the advent of Christianity, charity acquired a moral foundation and became the center of social activity of every Christian, community and Church.

Scientists attached key importance to the Christian commandments of love and non-possessiveness in the development of the institution of charity and considered the service of neighbor as an obligatory duty of any Christian.

The emergence of charitable societies and institutions dates back to different times, but the largest number of them in the national framework arose in 1889-1899. Until 1861–1870, the founding of charities went slowly. From 1870–1880 the formation of charitable societies took place intensively. It should be noted that the most important events in the reigning family or in the external and internal life of Russia have always been reflected in the number of charitable institutions that have arisen.

In the provinces of the Central Black Earth Region, the Church was in charge of a large group of charitable institutions. A special group of subjects of charitable activity included private individuals, these were representatives of commercial and industrial sectors who had significant financial resources. In the provinces of the Central Black Earth Region, most of the almshouses and shelters were created on the initiative of private charitable organizations (Shmeleva, 1999).

In the late XIX - early XX centuries, in Voronezh province, the most typical charity institution was an almshouse. In 1883, in the Ostrogozhsky district, the Liskinsky rural public almshouse was opened, where 21 women were kept. It existed on interest on capital (capital of 62,000 rubles), which was donated by testament priest Peter Kozmin. In 1891, a rural public almshouse was opened in Buturlinovka settlement of Bobrovsky district (uyezd), which saw 38 men, 3 living children and 48 women coming. This almshouse was maintained by Buturlin volost on public funds.

The owner of the estate G.A. Chertkov in the village of Rossosh, Ostrogozhsky district, also organized a rural public almshouse. For this purpose, the founder donated a house with a manor, where 13 people lived. Near the poorhouse in 1834 the Holy Cross Exaltation Church was built. It was a massive building crowned by a large dome. Forty years later, according to the project of the architect of Burenin, Moscow, a bell tower was built near the Church, whose height was 60 meters, and the throne was consecrated in 1876 and dedicated to St. Alexander Nevsky. The Rossoshanskaya bell tower was remarkable in its construction, in height it was only slightly inferior to the bell tower of the Mitrofanievsky monastery in Voronezh.

In 1865, a rural public almshouse was opened in the Vorontsovka settlement of Pavlovsky uyezd, which existed at the expense of society, and where there were 5 children and 16 adults. In 1858–1871 at the Mitrofanovskaya Annunciation and Assumption churches, three rural public almshouses were founded, which were supported by local volost funds. Merchant V.O. Ukhin in 1867 donated funds for the construction of an almshouse at the Intercession Church of the city of Voronezh, which gave shelter to the poor and single women. In 1904, there were 1282 parishioners in the Intercession Church. The staff of the Church included two priests, one deacon, and two psalm-worshipers. The clergy kept on interest from the donated capital of 8 thousand rubles.

The local merchant Klochkov, at his own expense, arranged an almshouse for women at the Epiphany Church of Voronezh. In 1825, Nikolai Bogdanov, a Voronezh merchant, at his own expense established an almshouse for several people at the Jerusalem Church. In 1893, in the city of Boguchar, a local merchant P.M. Kuranov opened an almshouse for 40 people, which was kept on his money. A stone one-store building worth 23,500 rubles was allocated under the almshouse.

Russian merchants donated their money, except for almshouses, for the construction and improvement of churches and monasteries. The Voronezh Spiritual Consistory Fund contains information on interest-bearing securities belonging to the Ascension Cemetery Church of the city of Voronezh, deposited with the Voronezh City Public Bank from 1870 to 1883. The archival documents said that the bank accepted from Voronezh merchant Ivan Yegorovich Bezrukov 200 rubles in silver for eternal storage with the right to use interest. It was said that Ivan Yegorovich Bezrukov contributed 200 rubles in silver to the clergy (clergy) of the Ascension Cemetery Church of the city of Voronezh on the basis of a spiritual testament. Merchant Alexander Avdeev contributed 100 rubles in silver for perpetual storage with the right to use interest in the name of the clergy of the Ascension Cemetery Church in Voronezh in order to remember the deceased sister Anna. In 1876 a spiritual testament was drawn up by the merchant merchant E.V. Nazarova on the issue of money for the decoration of the Vvedensky church in the city of Voronezh. 400 rubles were issued with interest-bearing securities to decorate the Vvedensky church in the city of Voronezh at face value. 300 rubles were invested in the Voronezh Bank, and percent of this capital by will should be given to the clergy of the Vvedensky church. In addition, the will instructed to donate the image of the icon of the Kazan Mother of God with two diamonds to the church in which the widow E.V. Nazarova will be buried.

It can be noted that the Voronezh Divnogorsk Monastery experienced great material needs. The pilgrims were amazed at the poverty of the monastery, and wealthy people donated funds for the needs of the monks. In 1836, Maria Isaeva, seeing the extreme poverty of the monks, with their hard work, and not having the opportunity to dress properly, respectively, to their dignity, donated 1000 rubles. In the same year, another 1,000 rubles were donated by an unknown person. At the Kursk Theological School merchant F.V. Taranov built the house of the Cyril and Methodius Church with his own money, which cost him 9,000 rubles. At the request of the school leadership for this construction, the merchant F.V. Taranov was awarded the medal.

Famous major donors for the construction of monasteries were Rylsky merchants, for example, the merchant I.V. Lavrov gave to Panteleimonovsky monastery and Andreyevsky monastery on Mount Athos 2 thousand rubles.

Not only merchants were engaged in charity, but also rich people from other classes. Hereditary honorary citizen Ya.I. Nechayev, at his own expense, opened a church parish almshouse in Voronezh in 1864, and captain Khabarov in 1862 founded a church parish almshouse in the village of Olshanka in the Biryuchensky Uyezd, in which 4 women lived, and its capital amounted to 5700 rubles. In 1873, with the money of the collegiate assessor Antonov at the Mitrofanov Cemetery Church, a church parish almshouse was built, in which 13 women lived, and its capital was 16,700 rubles. In 1878, a real state councilor Vasilinin, using personal funds in a suburban settlement of Dubovskaya, opened a shelter for the poor and the elderly. There were three houses in this shelter, 2 of which were stone, a manor, a house church, a parish school, 22 tithes of land worth 20,700 rubles (Lykoshina, 1901).

In the middle of the 19th century, state adviser Anna Ivanovna Scelle (1792–1877) was the owner of one of the estates in Ramon', she constantly cared for the Church and was engaged in charity work. During the liberation of the peasants from serfdom, the landowner had from 3 to 4 thousand acres of land. Her estate in Ramoni included the villages of Zabolotnoye, Parinovo and Salmanovo, according to the census of 1858, there were 72 yards in the villages, 993 people lived in them, 501 of them were men, 492 were women. According to the information from the Voronezh priest D.I. Sambikina in Ramoni was built stone Orthodox Church of St. Nicholas with donations from A.I. Schelle. At this church in 1884, pop Sidor Prokofiev served.

Church parish guardianship in the city of Usman knew the almshouse for the elderly with an orphanage, as well as a plot of land in 100 acres. This almshouse was founded by M. Okhotnikov in 1875. The county zemstvo also took part in its maintenance, for which 600 rubles were allocated annually. In 1896, in the Voronezh province there were 20 church parish almshouses. Directly in the provincial center, there were 19 almshouses.

In the late XIX - early XX centuries, in the Tambov province for city funds there was in Elatma, the Strizhevsky women's almshouse for 14 people. In Kursk at the Vsesvyatsky cemetery there was a city almshouse for 56 people. In the Oryol province there was an almshouse for women of advanced age for 50 people at the Sergeevskoye cemetery Church. Merchant Gudilin donated interest on capital in the amount of 32703 rubles to this almshouse. In the provinces of the Central Black Earth Region there were other charitable institutions created at monasteries, for example, strange houses and houses of industriousness, of which there were several in the Voronezh province. Only in the city of Voronezh there were two strange houses. In 1856, at the Mitrofanovo-Blagoveshchensky monastery, a strange house was founded for the shelter of pilgrims, up to 15 thousand people visited the monastery annually. In 1861, a strange reception house was created at the Tolshevsky Spaso-Preobrazhensky Monastery, whose visitors received shelter and food for free, up to 6 thousand people received this help annually. At the Valuy Uspensky Monastery, in 1865, a strange reception house was also opened for the reception of pilgrims, which was kept at the expense of the monastery, annually providing charitable assistance to 2500 people in need. At Zadonsky Holy Trinity Nunnery, a stranger-reception house («strannopriimnyj» house) was operating. 3 thousand pilgrims and poor urban residents used the services of that house. In 1882, Ioann Kronshtadskij built the so-called "House of Hard Work". This "House" gave everyone the opportunity to receive help as a reward for work. The purpose of this "House of Hard Work" was to stimulate labor activity.

In Kronstadt Ioann Kronshtadskij placed charitable institutions where the poor were not only employed, but also treated, rested, studied, received benefits and an overnight shelter. Here they tried to replace alms with labor of the needy themselves, to change the feeling of pity for compassion.

Ioann Kronshtadskij watched the events taking place in the church and public life of the Oryol province. In 1901, a congress of the clergy was held in Oryol, to which Ioann Kronshtadskij drew attention. At this congress, the provincial leader of the nobility M.A. Stakhovich, who made a speech that made a lot of noise about freedom of conscience, in which he expressed the idea of freedom of transition from one religion to another one.

The preaching and social activities of Father John took place in Kronstadt and in the capital, and he was often invited to other cities. The great prayer book and philanthropist visited Orel more than once, however, almost nothing is known about these visits, except for his visit in 1901. The charitable society at the Voronezh House of industriousness arose in 1891 and was under the jurisdiction of the Ministry of Internal Affairs, it was established before the formation of the Guardianship for Industrial Homes and Workers' Homes.

Gradually, in the provinces of the Central Black Soil donations from industrialists and the scale of donations from private individuals are declining. Mainly charities were engaged in city administrations, this phenomenon spoke about the process of modernization of the charitable sphere. The Tambov province was an exception, as merchant capital continued to play the main role in urban charity. During the 1860-90s in the counties of the Central Black Earth region, there was an increase in the number of charitable institutions and the number of those hired in them. In the Oryol province, the number of almshouses increased by 3 times during this period, the number of people suspected by them increased by 2.5 times, and shelters by approximately 5 times. The number of almshouses in the Kursk province has increased approximately 2 times, the number of people being hijacked by 1.5, and shelters by 4.5 times.

In addition to the almshouses, which belonged to the spiritual department and the Ministry of Internal Affairs, and strange houses, new types of charitable institutions were founded. In the 1890s, a house of cheap apartments was created in Voronezh, which was managed by the Imperial Philanthropic Society and which was maintained at the expense of a female charity. The house had 24 apartments, where about 60 people lived. The local branch of this Society was in charge of cheap apartments for high school students.

It must be said here that charitable assistance was rendered to the participants and invalids of the war, as well as their families. The clergy of the Tambov province during the war, responding to patriotic appeals, participated in collecting donations for the needs of the army, for the wounded and sick soldiers, provided assistance to the families of the drafted. In the Tambov province during the Russian-Turkish war of 1877-1878 guardianships were organized to assist families, of which reserve lower ranks were called up for war. Along with the board of trustees, ladies' committees and other charitable organizations, the Tambov clergy played an important role in collecting voluntary donations. The growth of the sacrificial activity of the inhabitants of the Tambov province was facilitated by solemn services, circle gatherings, sermons in churches and a personal example of clergymen (Lapotnikov, 1998).

The daughter of the clerk Pelageya Grigoryevna Popova, who lives in the city of Kozlov, Tambov province, donated 500 rubles in favor of the wounded and sick soldiers. The report of the bishop of Tambov and Shatsky Palladium on the situation of the Tambov diocese in 1877 stated the following. Male and female Orthodox monasteries, in spite of their various means, were ready to respond to the call of charitable societies to help the Slavs of the Balkan Peninsula and to donate to Russian Orthodox soldiers who shed their blood for the holy cause of liberation from the Muslim yoke.

The Sarovsky Monastery donated 500 rubles and 3 different things, the Vyshinsky Monastery - 300 rubles in money and 175 rubles in things, Treguliaevsky - 100 rubles, Bishop Palladium - 150 rubles. The Sukhotinsky Nunnery donated 124 rubles and 6 pounds of things with money, Kozlovsky - 135 rubles with money and 8 pounds of things. Thus, thanks to the patriotic activities of the Tambov clergy, the inhabitants of the Tambov province during the Russian-Turkish war of 1877-1878 made a feasible contribution to the collection of donations. The Voronezh clergy also did not remain indifferent to that war. The archive fund of the Voronezh Spiritual Consistory contains documents related to charitable assistance to the Orthodox Slavic population of the Balkan states.

In particular, it was said that the St. Petersburg department of the Slavic charity committee received permission to send, through the rectors of the churches of the Voronezh diocese, donations. There was a permission to collect church donations («tarelochnyj sbor») in the churches in favor of the Orthodox Slavic families. They suffered from the Turkish aggression in Bosnia and Herzegovina. This was reported to the Voronezh Spiritual Consistory on December 1, 1875.

The Russian Orthodox Church did not disregard socially vulnerable layers of society - orphans, unemployed, illiterate, poor, starving and other victims of disasters, as well as prisoners and alcoholics.

At the beginning of the 20th century, the Russian Orthodox Church took part in the charity movement for sobriety, as evidenced by the "coupon stamps" "Alcohol - Poison" of the Annunciation sobriety society, which were signed by the chairman of the society, Archpriest Peter Vozdvizhensky.

The merciful activities of the Church should have been financially supported and well organized, which was carried out by charitable societies, trusteeships, and assistance committees located in parish communities. If charitable societies were in secular organizations or under municipal government, the Church actively participated in their work. Under the Russian Orthodox Church, as part of charitable societies, hospitals and hospitals were created for the mentally ill, seriously ill, and disabled, where mercy sisters from among the nuns and laity took care of them. In the tea and dining rooms, all those in need could get free food.

In addition, the Church allocated money in the event of crop failure and famine. In 1891, the Holy Synod decided on the failure of grain in the Voronezh province. The definition said that the population of the province lacked food. In this regard, the Holy Synod prescribed: to establish in all dioceses the reading of the liturgy and a special petition, to perform prayer songs to God and the Blessed Virgin Mary. To instruct the diocesan elders to organize special committees from clergy and secular persons who would collect the necessary amounts of donations and immediately send them to provincial committees. Archpriest of the Voronezh Spiritual Consistory Mikhail Nekrasov signed this decree.

Before the revolution in Russia, with the assistance of the Church, one of the types of donations from ordinary citizens was the sale of special charitable stamps, which are receipts that attest to the fact of beneficence. Charity checks, coupons, credit marks, receipts served as control and reporting of the expenditure of funds. These charitable bonds in agreement with the owners of tea, canteens, shops, shops were accepted as payment for services, goods, products. It is noteworthy that for substitutes for banknotes that were distributed through the sobriety struggle society, it was impossible to buy vodka products. One of the important social functions of the cloisters was their charity work. Shelters and hospitals were organized at monasteries, assistance was provided in arranging chapels and temples, and funds were donated to charity funds. Another important area of the charitable activities of the monasteries was the financing of projects that ensured the presence of the Russian Orthodox Church in the places of residence of global Christian shrines. The Imperial Orthodox Palestinian Society was the main vehicle for Russian politics. This society in February 1909 made a plate gathering to maintain Orthodoxy in the Holy Land and the needs of Russian pilgrims. The Voronezh department of the company in 1911 participated in the distribution of the prefabricated sheet for donations and for the needs of the Orthodox in Jerusalem. The monasteries in 1911 collected feasible donations for the erection of the church in the name of St. Nicholas the Pleasant for Russian pilgrims in the city of Bari, where the relics of the saint are located.

Another area of the Church's charitable activity was donations from parishioners for the construction of Orthodox churches. The construction of the Church of the Nativity of Christ of the Lushnikovskaya settlement of the Voronezh province began in 1872. It was built by parishioners of the Epiphany Church in the Lushnikovskaya settlement, the construction of this Church was led by Stepan Ivanovich Minaev. The Church of the Nativity of Christ was built for 19 years due to a lack of material resources. The completion of the Church and its consecration was completed in 1891, and a monument to Alexander III was erected near this Church.

Residents of Ostrogozhsk built on their donations a wooden Preobrazhenskaya Church, which belonged to the courtyard of the Divnogorsky monastery. In material terms, it was the poorest church in the city. In 1819, two side altars were added to the temple, next to the main altar, but because of financial difficulties, the decoration of the chapels was delayed for seven years, and only on October 9, 1826, they were consecrated. Pious parishioners were able to fulfill their divine aspirations in 1834. The Temple of God with three thrones was renewed and in all parts consecrated, the main of which was the throne in the name of the Transfiguration of the Lord, attached to the right in the name of the Sign of the Mother of God, and to the left in the name of the holy prophet Elijah.

In this form, the Church lasted until 1896, until again it was required to renew the iconostases and the internal state of the Church with domes, an altar, walls and arches. All these works were completed in 1897.

For more than 60 years, the ostrogozhskij family Strel'covy served under the Preobrazhenskaya Church, one of which was the merchant S.T. Strel'cov, who served as the headman of this Church for over 25 years. The Preobrazhenskaya Church exists in this form today. In Voronezh province in 1802 with personal funds of Natalya Fedorovna Sinelnikova, with the help of residents, was built the Exaltation of the Cross Church. Grieving for her dead son Alexei, N.F. Sinelnikova thought about the construction of this

Church. She and her husband Dmitry Petrovich began the construction of this temple back in 1780. And only in 1802, after 22 years, the Holy Cross Exaltation Church was completed and consecrated. On the wall in the narthex of the Church was a portrait of N.F. Sinelnikova, the temple founder of this cemetery Church, in memory of the benefactor of the Holy Cross Church. This Church accommodated many parishioners, as it was spacious inside, it had a large bell tower and a closed connecting corridor. The walls were decorated with magnificent icon painting, and the beautiful iconostasis was painted by the local famous artist Velichkovsky, who also painted the Trinity Cathedral. For the Holy Cross Exaltation Church, he painted six icons: the icon of the Mother of God, the Savior talking to the apostles, the icon of the Prophet David, the Exaltation of the Honest Cross, King Solomon, and the Nativity of Christ. These icons, made at a high artistic level, were of great value, since in other churches of Ostrogozhsk this was not. In the Voronezh diocese there was a book for voluntary donations for the construction and decoration of churches. The book at the beginning of each year was opened for recordings, offerings were received from private individuals of secular and spiritual rank.

In 1823, proxies petitioned Bishop Epiphanius for blessing for the issuance of the "Collection Book" to the merchant I.F. Vyakhirev.

In 1836, the city church of the Annunciation lost its parish, as it turned out to be in the center of the Mitrofanovsky monastery. The authority of the cathedral church passed to the Smolensk church, which was distinguished by its greatness and wealth among the Voronezh churches. The throne icon of the Mother of God, written in the 17th century, was especially revered, before this icon was in the sacristy of Bishop Mitrofan. Anna Orlova – Chesmenskaya, the merchant Anton Mikhailov, the merchant woman Alexander Andronov, the sister of the poet Alexei Koltsov donated to maintain the splendor of this cathedral. Among the parishioners was the Nikitin family.

In the Voronezh province, great importance was attached to the veneration of saints, among them Nikolai the Miracle Worker stood out. In the village of Nikolskoye-on-Emanche of the Khokholsky district of the Voronezh province, a church was built in honor of Nikolai the Wonderworker. This church was located in the center of the village, its construction was carried out with donations from rural residents. The church in the Nikolsky' village, on Emancha, was stone, had a bell tower. Its construction was completed in 1878. The church owned 34 tithes of arable fields and hayfields.

Parishioners of the church had to contribute 750 rubles each year. In the village of Kozlovka, Voronezh province, there was a dilapidated St. Nicholas

Church, and therefore, in 1821, parishioners of this Church Ivan Zolotilin and Mikhail Sustretov turned to the Voronezh Bishop Epiphanius for permission to build a new stone church in the name of the Assumption of the Blessed Virgin Mary. February 17, 1822 they were given permission to build the Church, and in the same year the construction began.

In 1827, the old Church was dismantled, and in the new Church, the chapel was consecrated in the name of the miracle worker Nicholas and began to perform services in it. The new church was built in the center of the village; it had the shape of an oblong cross with a large dome. It had three chapels of the altar - in the name of Panteleimon, in the name of Nicholas the Wonderworker, in the name of Mitrofan, the saint of Voronezh. Behind the refectory there was a bell tower, the spire which was above the dome. Porfiry Serebryansky held services in the church.

It should be noted the request of the landowner Sukhanova in the name of Bishop Epiphanius of Voronezh and Cherkassky to donate money for the new iconostasis to the church of the Smolyaninova village of Starobelsky district in the amount of 15 rubles. From the Voronezh Spiritual Consistory, permission was granted to put on a new iconostasis, as reported by the pious Archpriest Kirill Mikhailovsky on June 24, 1822.

In 1884, in the village of Nikolsky, Oryol province, Livensky district, the landowner Maria Magdalena was built with the money of landowner Maria Okhotnikova, which was located on the outskirts of the village on a flat open area. At the beginning of the XX century, the main part of the monastery was the huge Mary-Magdalene Cathedral, built in 1884-1886. Since 1887, a school for girls began to exist at the monastery. In the St. Nicholas Church of the city of Voronezh, it was necessary to update the iconostasis. In 1839, the merchants of Lyapina donated funds for this charitable cause. In 1864, wall painting was restored. The last pre-revolutionary repair in St. Nicholas Church was carried out in 1900: steam heating appeared in the church, iconostases and frescoes acquired a new look. Particularly revered and revered Russian believers St. Nicholas. Since ancient times, the Russian believing people have known the glory of the miracles performed by the Prelate on land and at sea.

The image of Saint Nicholas was especially expensive for a Russian person, they pray to him, believing and hoping for his help and comfort, since the whole life of the saint passed in the affairs of kindness and love. And his posthumous life serves people.

In 1886, a petition was received from the residents of the village of Sredny Karachan, Novokhopersky district, who wanted to build a church, for which they had 8,000 thousand rubles, which is enough to build a church. For service in the church there are enough male souls in the amount of 794 people to provide a one-time clergy. The Voronezh ecclesiastical consistory allowed the construction of a stone church, which she informed the peasant Artyom Filatov, the authorized representative of the village of Sredny Karachan. The approved plan for the construction of the church was approved by the construction department of the provincial government. The track record of the clergy of the Bobrovsky district of the Voronezh province contains a sheet of the Church of the Nativity of Christ, which states that the church was built in 1895 in honor of the Nativity of Christ at the expense of Prince Vladimir Anatolyevich Bagryanskiy. The church is stone, utensils in the church are enough. According to the state, it is supposed to be two priests and two psalm-goers. 4000 rubles are spent on a church a year. In addition, one can note the book of the record of the collection of alms for the construction of the church in the settlement of Makaryk of the Voronezh district from 1863. This book was compiled at the request of the Archbishop of Voronezh and Zadonsk Joseph on the basis of the charter of the Voronezh Spiritual Consistory. Three rubles in silver came from the peasant Victor Kasharin to this church. It is said that funds for the church also came from other counties, in particular, Bobrov - 12 rubles in silver. Received 30 rubles in silver from the landowner Peter Golubinsky. With the money raised, a wooden church was built in the name of the Kazan Mother of God.

On October 20, 1875, the Decree of the Holy Synod was announced on the opening everywhere in the empire of collecting donations for the construction of a cathedral church in the city of Orenburg. It was reported that the Orenburg Chief Prosecutor filed a petition with the Voronezh Spiritual Consistory for the construction of a temple that is consistent with the significance and population of this city.

The Voronezh ecclesiastical consistory considered such an application deserving of respect, and requires that personally from monastic and clergy of the white clergy such donations be presented to the consistory. In 1884, in the settlement of Rossosh, Ostrogozhsky district, a magnificent stone church was built in honor of the Ascension of the Holy and Life-Giving Cross of the Lord. This temple was unlike ordinary rural churches. The temple was five-domed and accommodated up to 3 thousand praying people. But as a result of the increasing population, the temple could not accommodate one third of the parishioners. In this regard, parishioners turned to the diocesan authorities to build a new church. The new church needs 7,000 thousand rubles. Parishioners participated in fundraising with their offerings. In 1890, a new Holy Cross Church was built (Ershov, 2020).

In the late XIX - early XX centuries the construction of the largest churches, including the Vladimir Cathedral in Voronezh, was carried out with private donations. Merchants and manufacturers expanded the network of charitable institutions in the Voronezh province, which was a consequence of a sufficient degree of churching in Russian society. Only a large number of people in the world with a gracious heart could create and maintain church charity institutions. In the Voronezh province, the spiritual department had 36 charitable institutions, 7 times more than in the Tambov province. Nevertheless, it can be noted that in some districts of the Tambov province church charity was well developed. In particular, in the 5th deanery district of the Morshansk district of the Tambov province in 1895, there were 22 churches. All the churches were well-maintained and clean enough.

All building material at the church was donated by a representative of the parish guardianship Victor Yermolaev. A total of 6,000 rubles were spent on a church in Morshansk district. Some of these funds were collected by simple peasants.

The activities of many ascetics and saints took place in the Orel-Sevsk diocese in the second half of the XIX century. Bishop Polycarp was highly respected among believers; he was distinguished by humility and charity. At the cemetery Baptist Church, which was housed in a two-story stone house, in 1862, on his initiative, a shelter for 40 girls was organized for orphans of a clerical rank. Subsequently, the Bishop of Oryol and Sevsk, His Grace Macarius transformed this shelter into the Women's Diocesan School. All these facts indicate that private church charity in the provinces of the Central Black Earth Region was widely developed, and church parish charity was a priority. In a special section, the Church highlighted the issues of charity of poor clergy. Sources of funding for this category of people were voluntary and charitable donations, cemetery, penalties collected by the ecclesiastical department, circle fees, income from the sale of candles. In 1823, the Voronezh Theological Seminary provided medical assistance to the priest of the settlement of Berezova, Starobelsky district, John Lokhnitsky, which he received for his sick son. Due to the serious illness of his son Daniil Lokhnitsky, as well as the poverty of the priest, the seminary allocated 125 rubles 25 kopecks, it was decided to give this amount to the priest from the state sum allocated to the hospital where the priest's son was treated. The track record of the clergy of Bobrovsky uyezd for 1911 states that the widow of the deceased psalmist Tamar Kuzmina received 20 rubles from guardianship and 10 rubles from the diocesan cash register. Moreover, the collection of donations, charitable contributions should be carried out in conditions of strict reporting. In 1814, with the blessing of the diocesan archpastors, in memory of His Grace Tikhon, the Zadonsky Monastery should contain from 10 to 12 poor students who were considered to be pupils of St. Tikhon. Since 1780, the monastery with the tomb of St. Tikhon, with the miraculous icon of the Mother of God, attracted many pilgrims. The number of buildings of the monastery increased, but there were difficulties in the timely conduct of worship at the request of the faithful, due to the fact that the number of religious workers was limited. To eliminate such a shortcoming in the brethren and to maintain excellent services in the monastery, the widow (headquarters captain) Ekaterina Semenova of the city of Chebyshev asked the Holy Synod to increase the number of monks, promising to pay 15,714 rubles in silver to the Moscow Guardian Council in favor of the Zadonsky Monastery. The Ober-Prosecutor of the Holy Synod proposed to build the Zadonsky Monastery of the third class in the first class, without increasing the maintenance from the treasury. On February 3, 1851, the Sovereign Emperor approved this decision of the Holy Synod. A solemn prayer for this was made on March 24, 1851, on the eve of the Annunciation, under Parthenius, Archbishop of Voronezh and Zadonsky, and under Archimandrite Seraphim, rector of the monastery. The priests of the monastery did not receive any benefits, although some priors had personal rights, which they served in other monasteries. The local abbot had a staff with apples, a red mantle, and he passed to the altar before the liturgy of the liturgy by the royal gates (Ershov, 2018).

In 1848, from an honorary resident of the city of Livna, Avdotya Fedorova Nebuchenova, a ticket of the Board of Trustees was issued for the maintenance of the 12 poorest students. According to the decision of the Moscow Board of Trustees, no interest was paid out on this ticket until the expiration of 15 years, and only after the expiration of the term on interest from the accumulated capital could clothes and shoes be bought. The second ticket of the Moscow State Treasury in 1851 was allocated by the benefactor E.S. Chebyshev. Pupils were grateful that they had the opportunity to use the free premises, clothes, and in gratitude on Sundays and holidays took part in worship. The specially established Guardianships under the supervision of the Diocesan Bishops disposed of allowances for the charity of the poor clergy. In each diocese, such guardianships were formed, consisting of 3–6 trustees, who were elected from the white clergy, or, if necessary, from among the monks. The trustees had to be experienced, philanthropic and enjoy the trust of society. Among such trustees can be identified Alexander Ivanovich Bunin. Alexander Ivanovich Bunin was born in the Voronezh province in the village of Verkhny Karachan, Novokhopersky district on August 30, 1792 in the family of a priest. He graduated from the Voronezh seminary and remained there to teach, and then was transferred by the teacher to the district school of the city of Voronezh. From December 20, 1818 he became a priest of the Church of the Nativity of the Virgin Mary of the city of Boguchar. From 1821 he was appointed present in the Ecclesiastical Board of Boguchar, from July 1822 - deanery, and in July 1827 he was ordained archpriest. A.I. Bunin did a lot of charity work, thanks to him, churches were erected in the settlements of Shurinovka, Grekovka, Dubovikova, Dyachenkova, and Grushevoy. For charitable deeds, he was awarded many awards and encouragements: in 1847 he was awarded a pectoral cross, in 1853 - the Order of St. Anna of the 3rd degree, in 1857 - the Order of St. Anna of the 2nd degree. "Pray and work" — these words were the motto of all his life. Each year, the trusteeship, under the authority of the departments of local bishops, had to draw up reports and send them to the economic department under the Holy Synod. So a centralized management system was formed. The forms of assistance to the distressed were different, which was enshrined in the law: 1) determination of the widows and orphans of women in churches; 2) official maintenance of orphans in schools; 3) the receipt of pensions by elderly clergy from interest on capital from the income of the Synodal Printing House. Advantages by definition in the almshouse had orphans and widows of the clergy of cathedral and city churches. The military and naval clergy, and their families, lump sums and pensions received from the state treasury. The Orthodox clergy also received help in special situations, for example, in the event of a fire. In the Voronezh province on May 6, 1891, a fire occurred in the St. Andrew's church in the village of Mikhailovka of the Bobrovsky district, the cause of which was the careless handling of the fire of a church watchman, who was instructed to extinguish the candles after the evening service. The fire was discovered to start from a box of cinder, which had been thrown by the guard. Due to the fact that cases of candle fires in churches are not uncommon, clergy of the diocese and church elders were instructed to conduct vigilant supervision of church watchmen who were responsible for extinguishing candles after the service. This decree was signed by Archpriest of the Voronezh Spiritual Consistory Pavel Orlov. The behavior of the petitioner, the composition of his family, and the damage from the fire were also taken into account. The synod appointed allowance, which was sent to places. Independently through guardianship, those dioceses, whose income each year was more than 5 thousand rubles, helped in fire cases, these included the Tambov, Voronezh, Kursk, and Orel dioceses. The Holy Synod annually compiled a report to the Emperor on the distribution of cash benefits. So, the Russian Orthodox

Church before the revolution paid much attention to issues of mercy and social service. In the XIX - early XX centuries. charity is reinforced by the charity of individuals, unions, the church and the state through the charity of orphans, widows, poor, crippled.

Churches and monasteries in the provinces of the Central Chernozem Region especially tried to provide assistance to orphans. At the Kursk Znamensky Monastery in 1854, an Alexander Shelter was created for young orphans - boys from the clergy of the Kursk diocese, which was opened in memory of Alexander II in 1879 by order of the Diocesan Congress of the Clergy. The shelter was designed for 10 orphans. A separate house was allocated for the shelter, provided free of charge and contained at the expense of the clergy, Znamensky Monastery took an active part in this. The monastery at its own expense repaired the building of the shelter every year. In Kursk in 1884, a female diocesan orphanage was opened in the school building, in which there were 15 orphaned girls. These shelters, male and female, were the responsibility of the Council of the Women's Diocesan School, and the head of the school, Mother Superior Sofia, was their guardian. The priest of the Kursk Convent, John Shkorbatov, who served for free, was a caretaker in a men's shelter. Teacher M. Volobueva worked immediately, and in 1886 she graduated from the Kursk Diocesan School for Women. The widow of the priest, Maria Chefranova, was the caretaker at the women's shelter; she graduated from the Kharkov Diocesan School of Women in 1875, and the teacher was the widow of the priest, Lydia Karpinskaya, who graduated from the Kursk Diocesan School of Women. Thus, it is clear that educated people worked for the time in shelters (Ershov, 2019).

The combination of state and public principles in the activities of institutions "under special rights of the governed" was the optimal condition for organizing charity in pre-revolutionary Russia. The state principle in the activity of this type of public institutions was manifested in the patronage of institutions by members of imperial families, certain state funding, organizational and methodological support for the functioning of church charitable societies and institutions. Such an organization was significantly supplemented by public participation in the development of socially-helping activities, expressed in both attracting additional material resources and an active role of the public in carrying out specific charitable events on the ground. Before the October Revolution, charity activities of the Church were financed: from contributions of public organizations; from donations from individuals; due to government subsidies. Large donations to help those in need, to organize and maintain hospitals, shelters, schools, were made by the Russian Orthodox Church itself.

Addressing the parishioners, Orthodox priests in their sermons spoke about the need for their participation in charity work. According to the researcher P.I. Lykoshina, in the Russian Empire the total number of charitable institutions by January 1, 1899 was 14854, of which 7349 were charitable associations and 7505 were charitable institutions.

CONCLUSION

It should be noted that charitable societies provided assistance only to those who came; in charitable institutions, except for this category, in need of help, those who lived in them permanently received shelter and food. In the XIX - early XX centuries the role of the Orthodox Church was growing in the life of Russian society. The concepts of morality and spirituality were rooted in the popular consciousness. The centuries-old traditions of Russian charity were being revived. Church charity formed in people feelings of nobility, solidarity and spiritual generosity, made them real citizens of their Fatherland. Before the revolution, the charity of the Russian Orthodox Church was an integral part of its social life in the country and in the provinces of the Central Black Earth Region. Parish trusteeships, which were created with the participation of the clergy, together with state bodies, zemstvos and other social forces contributed to the organization of the social protection system, the development of literacy and culture among the population. The historical experience of charity, which was based on the state and church-public foundation, remains in demand. Today, church charity is becoming more relevant than ever, since it allows us to determine the feasibility of developing church and public organizations, the activities of which were carried out by various subjects of socially-assisting labor.

REFERENCES

Ashmarov, I.A., Ershov, B.A., Bulavin, R.V., Shkarubo, S.N., & Danilchenko, S.L. (2020). The Material and Financial Situation of the Russian Orthodox Church in the XIX - Early XX Centuries. *Smart Innovation, Systems and Technologies*, 149-158.

Ershov, B. A., & Ashmarov, I. A. (2018). Interaction Of The Orthodox Church And The State In Russia At The Present Stage. *Bulletin Social-Economic and Humanitarian Research*, *2*, 19–24.

Ershov, B. A., Perepelitsyn, A., Glazkov, E., Volkov, I., & Volkov, S. (2019). Church and state in Russia: management issues. *5th International Conference on Advances in Education and Social Sciences. Abstracts & Proceedings*, 26-29.

GAKO (State Archives of Kursk Region) F. 20. Op. 2. D. 174.L. 7.

Lapotnikov, V. A. (1998). *History of nursing in Russia*. Academic Press.

Lykoshina, P. I. (1901). *Charity Russia. History of state, public and private charity*. Academic Press.

Shmeleva, M. N. (1999). *Public life of the middle of the XIX - beginning XX centuries*. Ecsmo.

Chapter 11

Communities of the Sisters of Mercy and the Orthodox Church

ABSTRACT

The main thing in the work of charitable institutions was caring for the sick; therefore, professional medical workers were required, which was facilitated by the community of charity nurses. They contributed to the development of medical education, science, and healthcare in the Central Black Earth Region. Compassionate patients took turns caring for patients in hospitals and private homes. After 10 years of service, they received a pension, which, like the sign of compassion, remained with them until the end of their lives. High moral demands were placed on a woman who decided to devote herself to a charitable cause – to help the poor, defenseless, sick. Moral requirements were recorded in special documents – the oath, oath and instructions.

INTRODUCTION

The value of the charitable activities of the Orthodox Church in the 19th - early 20th centuries grew with the growth of social consciousness. In the 19th century, charitable brotherhoods and sisterhoods were created in Russia, and until the 19th century in Russia, there were no special institutions that would care for the sick. In 1803, in St. Petersburg and Moscow, so-called "widow houses" were created at the Educational Houses. They were governed by

DOI: 10.4018/978-1-6684-4915-8.ch011

honorary guardians, and the abbots monitored the suspects. At these houses, compartments of compassionate widows were organized, which went through a trial period during the year, and then took the oath, and they were entrusted with a golden cross on a green ribbon, which is a sign of compassion, they wore this cross all their lives, even leaving the department, but staying in widowed house. Compassionate patients took turns caring for patients in hospitals and private homes. After ten years of service, they received a pension, which, like the sign of compassion, remained with them until the end of their lives.

Educated representatives of the Russian state, using the experience of Europe and taking into account the problems of Russia, took part in the development of training programs for nurses, compassionate widows, midwives and in the implementation of care for the poor, wounded, sick and pregnant. High moral demands were placed on a woman who decided to devote herself to a charitable cause - to help the poor, defenseless, sick. Moral requirements were recorded in special documents - the oath, oath and instructions. The emergence of communities of sisters of mercy was important in the development of Russian medicine. For women the opportunity opened up to acquire new knowledge and bring it to life. Russian society, having an excellent example of the work of the sisters of mercy, made an important step - it opened schools for paramedics. Researchers A.A. Shibkova, I.V. Zimina and V.A. Kovrigina devoted his work to this topic.

The history of charity in Russia is associated with the activities of communities of sisters of mercy. Priest N. Dobronravov devoted his essay to the care of the sick and described all the available types of his organization. The author also spoke about the first communities of sisters of mercy, talked about the principles of their work, based on the rules for sisters of mercy and statistics for 1899-1900. The spiritual component of nursing ministry was studied by L.A. Karpycheva, who determined the status of the first Russian communities of sisters of mercy, tried to determine their Western prototypes and show the degree of their participation in the life of the Russian Orthodox Church. Orthodoxy in Russia was the state religion, and therefore in the Russian communities of the Sisters of Charity, which are institutions of private and public charity in the country, there was a church component. In 1844 Grand Duchess (Knyaginya) Alexandra Nikolaevna and Princess Teresa Ol'denburgskaya founded the first community of sisters of mercy in Russia (in the capital of Russia, in the city St. Petersburg).

This community since 1873/74 became known as the Svyato-Troickaya (Holy Trinity) community. The community was led by ladies committee, and it contained interest from the income of Knyaginya Alexandra Nikolaevna from private donations and from the imperial family, but there were no other means. Unmarried women and widows from 18 to 40 years old, and only literate ones could be in the community. In cases where the sister got married, she was expelled from the community. The probationary period of the sisters lasted from one year to three years, the duties of the sisters were on duty in hospitals and in apartments, the reception came to the community of patients. The sisters should have known some medical procedures and sanitary-hygienic rules for patient care. In the middle of 70-ies of the XIX century in the community there were five departments: test sisters, sisters of mercy, educational, medical and female schools of four classes. Also, there was a women's hospital in the community, designed for 52 patients: 38 adults and 16 children.

The most comfortable in the Voronezh province was the hospital located in Ramon', Voronezh district, and the Nikolaevskij hospital of the community of sisters of mercy, which was patronized by Princess E.M. Ol'denburgskaya. These hospitals were in charge of the Voronezh Department of the Red Cross Society.

The hospital in the village of Ramon' was run by two doctors. About 400 people were treated at the hospital. 16,000 rubles were allocated for its maintenance, of which 11,740 rubles were spent on patients, and 4,260 rubles on medical personnel. There was also an outpatient clinic where drugs were given to outpatients for free. The community of sisters of mercy was in charge of the hospital of the Red Cross Society, which also had an outpatient department. Local public institutions and individuals paid 15 of the 20 beds available. In 1898, 6832 rubles 17 kopecks were spent on the maintenance of this hospital. Communities of sisters of mercy in the Voronezh province were created on the initiative of the main military medical department in 1893.

The Sisters of Mercy studied anatomy, surgery, physiology, therapy, hygiene, the Law of God for one year. The rules of the Ministry of Internal Affairs and the program of the Main Directorate of the Russian Red Cross Society established the course and practical exercises on February 19, 1882.

In 1817, the Board of Trustees of the Imperial Philanthropic Society was established in Voronezh Province, which cared for the poor. This committee provided assistance to victims of accidents and natural disasters, redeemed debtors from prisons, assisted in acquiring dowry for poor girls, assisted in the funeral of the poor, incapable, in educating children, in finding jobs for

162

the unemployed, and in paying benefits during epidemics. In the activities of the Poor Guardianship, the Women's Charity Department was of great importance, which paid special attention to the organization of female labor and the marketing of finished products.

The prototype of the first communities of sisters of mercy in Russia were "novice monasteries" that existed for decades and had Orthodox traditions to provide various kinds of charity. The inhabitants of the novice monasteries did not give monastic vows, but had a monastery charter. They opened hospitals and almshouses, where they cared for the sick and elderly, welfare homes, orphanages, schools and nurseries for children. Civil and church authorities ignored these communities, their number grew due to private donations and a large number of people wishing to enter them.

The Orthodox community, located in the city of Zadonsk, Voronezh province since the 20s XIX century, in 1851 sent a petition to Metropolitan of Moscow Filaret Drozdov to help them legally be called the Tihonovskoe Society of Sisters of Charity.

Metropolitan Filaret approved this idea and said that it was good that Tihonovskoe society arose in the simplicity of the Russian Orthodox spirit. Ascetic Matrona Naumovna Popova (1769–1851) founded that female monastic community.

The good deed, in connection with the death of the old woman, was continued by the cathedral archpriest Peter Alekseevsky of the city of Zadonsk, who was the executor of Matrona Naumovna, and her spiritual heirs (Dmitrievsky, 2008).

With the money of Naumova, according to her will, they built the Church in honor of the icon of the Mother of God "All Who Sorrow of Joy", as well as household and living quarters. Bishop of Voronezh Joseph the Theological, on the day of the Assumption of the Virgin, in 1860 consecrated the newly built Church. The community that existed with her began to be called the "Tikhon Community of Sisters of Mercy," nuns of this community helped the sick and poor wanderers who arrived in Zadonsk to worship shrines. And on April 20, 1868, the ryasophore novice Porfiriya Alisova was officially approved as the head of the Tihonovskoe Society of Sisters of Charity.

On February 27, 1868, preosvyashchennyj Seraphim Aretinskij, Bishop of Voronezh, sent the following proposal to the spiritual consistory.

The body of the founder Matrona Popova on September 3, 1869, with the permission of the Holy Synod, was transferred to the church of the community and buried to the right of the Skorbyashchenskaya Church in a special crypt. Archpriest Peter Alekseevsky was also buried there in March 11, 1875.

The House of Sisters of Mercy, formerly known as the strannopriimnyj house, received the status of an independent Tikhonovskaya community by order of the Holy Synod on March 29, 1880. On this occasion, on August 17, 1880, on the day of memory of the old woman Matrona, a solemn service was performed. The sisters of the Tikhonovsky hospice had no other means of livelihood than donations from private benefactors. So, the Yelets landowner Palitsina bought a house for the community with a fruit garden, located near the monastery, where the head of the community lived until 1873. The landowner Korovkina, as promised, transferred 50 acres of land to the sisters of the community in eternal possession. So the good deed ended, which began 30 years earlier, with the request of Matrona Naumovna's employees for a government approval of the strange house she founded.

In the rules drawn up by the diocesan authorities for the newly approved female community, the following text can be read.

In 1884, in the name of the Life-Giving Trinity, they laid down a new cathedral church, which was a five-domed tented temple, the project of which was executed by the provincial architect of the city of Voronezh A.A. Kyui. Anastasius (Dobradin), Archbishop of Voronezh and Zadonsky, consecrated the cathedral, built on August 12, 1897, in the name of the Holy Trinity.

In May 1888, by decision of the Holy Synod, the Tikhonovskaya community was erected in a monastery and became known as the Holy Trinity Tikhon Zadonsky Nunnery, which had a strange house. The number of nuns was allowed to have such a quantity that the monastery could support at its own expense. The decision of the Holy Synod was announced on June 19, 1888. In this temple and gathered for the services of the inhabitants of the monastery. By the beginning of the 20th century, there were only 200 of them permanent. So, in 1901, "the Holy Trinity Convent lists 50 nuns, 54 novices and 79 living under trial, 183 in total." The completion of the cathedral was the last major contribution of Mother Porfiry to the strengthening and improvement of the monastery she created.

In September 1901, she, according to her own petition, was fired retired with the right to reside in Holy Trinity Monastery. Nun Angelina was soon chosen to replace her, with the abbess Porfiry continuing to help all the meager physical forces to help guide the monastery. On March 25, 1902, mother Porfiry was tonsured into a schema with the same name, and she died on March 25, 1906. The porch of the Scorpion of Porfiry was buried in the tomb at the Church of the Holy Trinity Monastery near Matrona Naumovna Popova and Archpriest Peter Alekseevsky. Replacing Abbess Porfiry as abbot of the monastery, nun Angelina, in the world Alexandra Afanasyevna

Artyomova, was born on April 20, 1838 in the family of a tradesman in the city of Zadonsk. From a young age, she was under the care of her cousin Matrona Naumovna Popova and in 1860 entered her community of sisters of mercy, and on July 31, 1888, the first of the sisters of the newly opened monastery received monastic tonsure in the name of Angelina. In the community, she passed the obedience of a choir singer, reader and statutress, and from 1887 to 1899, treasurers. Dismissed to retire in 1899, mother («matushka») Angelina was unanimously elected in 1901 by the nuns of the monastery to the place of Mother Superior Porfiry, and as she did not refuse this position due to her extraordinary meekness and humility, she was forced to agree only on monastery obedience.

On April 29, 1902, mother («matushka») Angelina was approved as the trustee of the women's monastery parish school, which had been operating at the monastery since 1891. On May 26, 1903, nun Angelina was elevated to the rank of hegumen. But already the next year, on June 9, mother Angelina died after a serious and prolonged illness, and on June 11, 1904 her body was buried on the southeastern side of Trinity Cathedral near the Assumption chapel.

The new abbess of the Holy Trinity Tikhonovskij Monastery by decree of the Holy Synod of September 10, 1904 approved the nun Vitaliya. Erected as abbess in 1906, she led the sisters of the Tikhonovskij monastery until the post-revolutionary ruin. In any case, it is well known that in 1915 it was she who nourished the sisterhood of the Trinity (Troickij) Monastery. In 1908, in the Orthodox holy monastery there were "1 abbess, 51 nuns, 128 novices".

In the same year, 70 girls attended the monastery parish school. There was also a separate class for 12 girls at the school, where nuns taught them various handicrafts, which, according to the recollections of Zadonsky old-timers, were perfect in themselves. The monastery carried out gold embroidery, engaged in embroidery and weaved carpets. According to 1910, 49 nuns and 161 novices were saved in the monastery. The number of nuns by the year 1914 remains the same, but the number of novices is somewhat reduced - to 148. The monastery operated safely until 1917, the number of nuns at the beginning of the 20th century was 50, and the novices were 150. Among the mercy communities of the provinces of the Central Black Earth Region, the Kursko-Znamenskaya community of sisters of mercy, so named in the name of the miraculous icon of the Sign of the Mother of God, which was organized in 1893. The General Directorate of the Russian Red Cross Society, which had long been operating in Russia, approved the charter of the community on April 7, 1893.

The widow of the cavalry general, Nadezhda Fedorovna Montresor, was the head of the Board of Trustees, and for her dedicated work for the benefit of the Russian Red Cross Society, she was elected May 16, 1910, Honorary Member of the Russian Red Cross Society. The elder sister of the community in 1902 was M.A. Orlova, and on January 14, 1910, N.K. was invited from St. Petersburg to perform the duties of a sister abbess. Zolotareva, sister of mercy of the Community named after Adjutant M.P. von Kaufmann. Archpriest I.F. Puzanov throughout the time was a law teacher, a confessor of the community and a mentor of the sisters of mercy (Lisovoy, 2009).

According to the Charter, women of all Christian confessions with good health, aged 20 to 45 years, who could read and write in Russian and knew the four rules of arithmetic, were accepted as sisters of mercy. Moreover, they had to meet the conditions that were determined by the rules on the Red Cross sisters (that rules were approved on January 31, 1875).

Persons more mentally and morally developed took advantage of admission to the community. When entering the community, it was necessary to file with the guardianship a petition, birth certificate, police certificate of trustworthiness and permission of the husband for the married or permission of the parents or guardians for women under 21 years of age, as well as a medical certificate. The probationary period passed for 3 months, during which time it was possible to find out whether the subjects had the necessary qualities for such an activity and whether the sisters of mercy satisfied their activities. The training lasted a year and a half, during which time studied surgery, anatomy, hygiene, therapy, physiology, the Law of God. The subjects were on duty near seriously ill, operated patients, were present during operations, and when receiving patients, under the guidance of doctors they worked in the dressing room and outpatient clinic. The sisters of mercy received their title after passing the exam.

In 1902, a community report stated that excellent success was shown in the exam, and the subjects answered the questions correctly, they knew the human anatomy and physiology well, pharmacology, medical hygiene, knew how to care for patients, prepare materials for dressings and operations, and the law of God was well known. N.F. Montresor, Trustee of the community, blessed everyone with the holy Gospel, prayer book and gilded image of the Mother of God. According to the Charter, there were eight cross sisters in the community. That number was kept constant. Under the community, there was a house of the Skorbyashchenskaya Church, which was consecrated on January 8, 1898. That church was supported by N.F. Montresor. In the Church on holidays and Sundays and on the eve of them, services were held that brought comfort to the free sisters who were present at them, subjects, patients and parishioners. At Christmas, for the sick they put a tree decorated with donated things.

On September 1, 1902, Emperor Nicholas II, who arrived at the Kursk military maneuvers, visited the community. Emperor Nicholas II was together with Prince Mikhail Alexandrovich and Princes Nikolai Nikolaevich, Vladimir Alexandrovich, and Mikhail Nikolaevich. Chair of the Board of Trustees of the community N.F. Montresor, her daughter, older sister, head doctor honored their meeting.

Emperor Nicholas II looked at the wards for the sick, a new bright room for operations. Distinguished guests signed the Community Honor Book. Everyone who had the good fortune to see the emperor, to see his gracious attention to everyone, to hear his pleasant conversation, was seized with a joyful feeling, as described in the 1902 report. This report reported the following information:

Daughter P.G. Oldenburg, Grand Duchess Alexandra Petrovna, on November 1, 1858 created the Intercession Community of Sisters of Mercy. The community had a department of nurses and test subjects, a female gymnasium and a paramedic school, a maternity shelter, a department for infants and young children, a surgical hut for 12 beds, a hospital, an outpatient clinic and a pharmacy. The church was consecrated on November 10 in the name of the Protection of the Blessed Virgin Mary, which gave the name to the community. Founder with spouse and capital merchants in 1865–1868 donated funds for the construction of a two-story extension for the hospital and consecrated the house church of St. Mitrofan of Voronezh, which was located on the top floor.

Church charitable women's communities in the second half of the 19th century are becoming more widespread, already with the approval or at the initiative of church authorities. In Russian monasticism, "feminization" begins: the number of women's monasteries is growing, and the number of nuns and novices is increasing. The novices, entering the female community, were in no hurry to take the tonsure; they wanted to take part in charity affairs. Many scholars have studied these features of female monasticism of the 19th-20th centuries, caused by socio-political, economic and ascetic reasons.

Despite the fact that the number of sisters from 1853 to 1876 amounted to only 23 people, they provided care for 103,758 patients. At the beginning of the Crimean War in St. Petersburg, with the assistance of Grand Duchess Elena Pavlovna, the Krestovozdvizhenskaya Community was organized on November 5, 1854, which occupies a special place in the activities of the sisters of mercy communities. The day of the creation of the community coincided with the symbol of the Christian faith - the Orthodox holiday of the Exaltation of the Holy Cross. This female community of sisters of mercy provided medical assistance to the wounded on the battlefield, it became the prototype of the Red Cross Society. The Russian society, which cared for the wounded soldiers, was created in 1867; and in 1879, this society became known as the Red Cross Society. In all Russian provinces, there were 232 committees of this Society and 62 communities of sisters of mercy. These Societies had hospitals. From the 70s of the XIX century, the Red Cross Societies began to be established in the provinces of the Central Chernozem Region and finally formed in the 90s of the XIX century. In the Voronezh province in the county town of Boguchar, a local committee was created in 1894, in Bobrov in 1898, in Nizhnedevitsk and Pavlovsk in 1894. At this time, the Biryuchensky, Novokhopersky, Valuysky, Zemlyansky, Ostrogozhsky, Zadonsky, Korotoyak committees were formed.

The clergy in the Voronezh branch of the Red Cross Society performed various duties. In 1898, the priest Semyon Koshelev served as an accountant at the local branch of the Red Cross. In the Voronezh province, special institutions of the Red Cross Society were created. So, in 1893 the Nikolaevskaya community of sisters of mercy was organized in Voronezh, its capital amounted to 26590 rubles, and in 1898 they spent 10973 rubles on current funds, and the total expense amounted to 14995 rubles. Under the Nikolaevskaya community of sisters of mercy, a shelter was established in a specially purchased estate for chronic patients. The philanthropist Yagupova donated 50 thousand rubles to this shelter. The guardian of the shelter was the wife of the Voronezh governor Golikov. There was a hospital for 20 people in this community, but a much larger number of patients were treated there. There were 12 children on permanent treatment at the hospital, and 460 children were treated on an outpatient basis. Men were treated - 3,772 people, and women - 3,228. The Community kept the hospital at its own expense.

In 1894, the Elizabethan orphan shelter for 100 people opened at the Red Cross Society in Voronezh. In 1898, it assisted 129 children.

In Voronezh province, there were cases of typhoid fever. Measures were taken to end this epidemic, doctors and nurses of the Red Cross Society took part in this, as well as a medical inspector and chairman of the provincial zemstvo council. First, 9,000 pounds of bread were sent to the canteens, and then another 3,000 pounds were sent to improve the activity of these canteens. These departments and societies were organized at the expense of private individuals and persons of the imperial family. These Societies were state institutions, they performed the functions of public charity. The Kursk local government of the Red Cross Society was formed in 1875, it was headed by the Bishop of Kursk and Belgorod Lawrence. The members of the board were Governor Count A.D. Milyutin, Vice-Governor N.G. Von Bunting, Head of the Kursk branch of the State Bank A.I. Svetlitsky, Privy Advisor to the Zhavoronkov. In Kursk province, local committees of the Russian Red Cross Society were formed in Belgorod in 1893, in Sudzha, Dmitriev, and Grayvoron in 1894, in Fatezh in 1895. In the Tambov province, committees of the Red Cross Society began to form in the late 70s of the XIX century. The capital of the Tambov Red Cross Society amounted to 160846 rubles, in 1898 it received 102347 rubles, and the expense amounted to 86,233 rubles. In 1874, a committee was created in Usman. In 1877, the Committees were formed in Borisoglebsk, Elatma, and Lipetsk. In 1898, the Committee of the Red Cross Society was formed in Shatsk. In 1896, the Pitirim (Pitirimovskaya) Community of Sisters of Charity of the Russian Red Cross Society was established in Tambov, the outpatient clinic functioning under it assisted men in the amount of 12,104 people and women - 6,084 people. The Red Cross Society supported the clinic (Blokhin, 2009).

In the Tambov province, the material capabilities of the local committees of the Red Cross Society were more significant than in the Kursk province. In 1890, the creation of Red Cross Society committees in the Kursk and Voronezh provinces was facilitated by difficult circumstances such as epidemics, famine, and crop failures. In the provinces of the Central Black Earth Region, the committees of the Red Cross Society considered the development of a charitable movement in the region an integral part of their activities.

Archimandrite Mitrofan Srebryansky, a monk Sergius, who was born in the family of a clergyman on July 31, 1870, made a significant contribution to the education of communities of sisters of mercy in the provinces of the Central Black Earth Region. At first he studied at the veterinarian, then at the seminary, after which he married Olga Vladimirovna. Mother was a friend and assistant to him. Father Mitrofan served as a deacon in the village of Lizinovka, in 1894 he was a regimental priest in the 47th Dragoon Tatar regiment in Rypin of the Polotsk province, and since 1896 he served in Orel in the Dragoon Chernigov regiment.

The founder of the Martha-Mariinsky monastery of mercy, Elizaveta Fedorovna, glorified by the church in the guise of the Martyr, was the patroness of the regiment. The Grand Duchess knew Mitrofan and mother before the war. In 1905, after the assassination of Grand Duke Sergei Alexandrovich, Elizaveta Fedorovna began to engage in mercy. She wanted to create a secular community of sisters of mercy, which was to be based on monastic obedience and Father Mitrofan proposed selflessness, the draft charter of the future monastery. The Grand Duchess invited Mitrofan to the post of confessor of the Martha-Mariinsky monastery of mercy, as she highly appreciated him as a priest (Afanasyev, 2008). At that time, Father Mitrofan again served in Orel. He treated his parish with love. And he was highly respected by the townspeople. So, Father Mitrofan became the confessor of the Martha-Mariinsky monastery, mentor and assistant of the abbess. Having studied the experience of the communities of sisters of mercy, we can say that there were no significant differences in their activities. Mercy, morality, love for one's neighbor, selflessness, industriousness, discipline and unquestioning obedience to superiors were necessary qualities of the sisters of mercy. The charters of the communities differed from the conventions in that the community members retained some freedom: the sisters could own their own property and had the right to inherit. They could marry or return to their parents of their own free will. Girls and women of noble descent entered the sisters of mercy, but the charter did not give them any privileges, they all endured difficulties and hardships in peacetime and wartime. The medical, obstetric and nursing care in Russia was socially oriented, which was provided to the poor, pregnant, children, the elderly, the sick, the wounded, those who suffered from natural disasters, epidemics, and wars. The sick, wounded, orphan was provided not only care and physical assistance, but also shelters and schools were established in the community, i.e. organized "social rehabilitation and adaptation". Nursing assistance was economically effective. For example, in Voronezh province, educational institutions with the money they earned had the opportunity to open hospitals for the poor. Society and the state supported the development of nursing and midwifery care. The main functions of the communities were charitable: the main tasks of the Trinity and Pokrovskaya communities were raising children, charity of the poor, care for the sick (Surova, 2008).

The Krestovozdvizhenskaya and Georgievskaya Communities helped the wounded and sick soldiers; but these areas of activity among the communities were not strictly delimited. At the end of the 19th century, a peculiar structure was formed in Russia that provided medical and charitable assistance to the population, which made it possible to use the work of sisters of mercy, paramedics, midwives and compassionate widows. In addition to public health institutions, charitable institutions operated. At the beginning of the 20th century, all communities of sisters of mercy belonged to the Red Cross Society. Empress Maria Fedorovna patronized the communities. Therefore, the core of the first Russian communities was the religious foundation. Now, nursing is becoming a profession divorced from religion. Priests in large communities could not have a decisive significance, such as chief physicians, since their activities could not go beyond certain official boundaries. The main thing in the work of charitable institutions was caring for the sick; therefore, professional medical workers were required, which was facilitated by the community of charity nurses. They contributed to the development of medical education, science and healthcare in the Central Black Earth Region.

CONCLUSION

In the late XIX - early XX centuries. in the Russian Orthodox Church there was a certain institute of mercy, which had specially trained personnel — the sisters of mercy who worked "in the world" with the sick and disabled, orphans, the elderly, and the wounded on the battlefield, which shows a high level of social activity of the Russian Orthodox Church.

In the XIX - early XX centuries, in Russia, charitable and medical assistance to the population was provided by 30 thousand state, private and public institutions, among which the communities of charity sisters took their rightful place.

REFERENCES

Afanasyev, V. V. (2008). *Optinsky were: Essays and stories from the history of the Vvedensky Optina desert.* Siberian Invertebrate.

Blokhin, V. F. (2009). "Gubernskie vedomosti" as a mirror of the Russian province (XIX - early XX century). *Bulletin of the Russian State University, 17*, 20–31.

Dmitrievsky, A. A. (2008). *The Imperial Orthodox Palestinian Society and its activities over the past quarter century: 1882–1907.* Publishing House of Oleg Abyshko.

Lisovoy, N. N. (2009). *Mission in Jerusalem.* St. Petersburg: Publishing House of Oleg Abyshko.

Metropolitan Lemeshevsky Manuel. (2003). *Russian Orthodox hierarchs 992-1892, 2*, 87–88.

Rybakova, S. N. (2009). *Russian monasteries and temples. Traveling to holy places.* Astrel.

Surova, L. V. (2008). Way to heaven. *Pilgrimage to the holy places.* Edition of the Church of St. John Chrysostom of the Moscow Diocese.

Chapter 12

Folk Tradition of Orthodox Pilgrimage in the Sphere of Church and State Relations

ABSTRACT

The materials of the study show that the church in the 19th-early 20th centuries was an influential spiritual and moral force. The merit of the church consisted in the fact that it was actually the only institution conducting social work. In the 19th-early 20th centuries, the church was an ally of the autocracy, pursuing a pro-government policy to disseminate loyal ideas in Russian society, which was expressed in exercising control over the education system, as well as the all of public life. These scholars were of the opinion that a pilgrimage, even to a nearby monastery, is not rest and entertainment, but self-denial and bodily labor, which believers use to save the soul. The purpose of the pilgrims was not a cognitive goal (i.e., receiving information) although during the pilgrimage they acquired new knowledge.

INTRODUCTION

The tradition of pilgrimage in the XIX century can be traced according to documents. Pilgrimage reaches its peak by the beginning of the XX century. Thousands of pilgrims who worshiped icons, relics and other church relics visited the monasteries. Prayer books of the Russian Church and simple monks of the cloisters also attracted believers of all classes. However, among

DOI: 10.4018/978-1-6684-4915-8.ch012

the pilgrims were mainly tradesmen and peasants, who made up 80% of the population of Russia. The attitude towards pilgrims and wanderers was respectful, there were widespread customs of a good attitude to wanderers («strannopriimstvo»).

In modern Fatherland, interest in the origins of holy Orthodoxy is reviving, which led to the appearance of works on the history of the Russian pilgrimage movement, the activities of the Orthodox Imperial Palestinian Society and the Russian spiritual mission. Church leaders together with the Patriarch of Moscow and All Russia Alexy and Archimandrite Theodosius Vasnev, as well as historians E.S. Evseev, V.G. Solodovnikov, O.G. Peresypkin, studied this issue. These scholars were of the opinion that a pilgrimage, even to a nearby monastery, is not rest and entertainment, but self-denial and bodily labor, which believers went to save the soul. The purpose of the pilgrims was not a cognitive goal, i.e. receiving information, although during the pilgrimage they acquired new knowledge.

When visiting the shrines, the pilgrims received spiritual benefit, being present at the place consecrated by the abode of the Lord or His saints, the petrified heart softened, and the soul ascended from the earth to heaven. The Orthodox man in contact with the shrine experienced a feeling of tenderness, which differed from sentimentality in that the person in front of the shrine forgot himself and humbled himself in heart.

A Russian pilgrim of the 19th century, Abraham Norov, traveling in the Holy Land in 1835, said that one of the bright nights, they, along with a Russian monk, gathered to worship the sacred places of the Passion Road of the Savior. When they reached the place where, according to legend, the Blessed Virgin Mary met with Her Son, exhausted under the burden of the Cross, he told the monk about this tradition, and Abraham Norov saw how suddenly tears spilled from the monk's eyes.

Russian people often made a pilgrimage to repent before God in order to be cleansed of sin. Sometimes vowed pilgrimages took place, i.e. according to the vow that was given to God in everyday sorrow or illness. In 1898, according to archival data from the Oryol province, vowed pilgrimages made as a result of recovery from the disease or getting rid of any trouble, other people went in the hope of solving personal problems or recovering. Often, among ordinary pilgrims who made one-time trips, there were professional pilgrims who traveled to the Trinity-Sergius Lavra near Moscow in the fall, spent the winter in Jerusalem, went to Mount Athos in the summer, and repeated their travels the following year.

The social composition of the pilgrims of the distant pilgrimage was 95% peasants, the main contingent was women of different ages, due to the sincerity of their religious feelings. Some women even founded monasteries, for example, a native of the Oryol province, the daughter of a clerk, M. Popova, who came to the monastery for a prayer in Zadonsk for "healing at the sepulcher of the miracle worker Tikhon" and created a female monastery there. Peasant G.F. Khaleev, a resident of the Tambov province, finding himself outside of Russia, reached Greece, where at the age of twenty-five he became a monk in the Russian Panteleimon monastery on Mount Athos. There were pilgrimages by calling when the Lord or a saint in a dream or visions suggested that a person go to some holy place.

Members of the imperial family and all sovereigns of the XIX century took part in the pilgrimage, which was very important for the national consciousness. The phenomenon of Russian life - a pilgrimage - deep in its worldview value, attracted a large number of believers from near and far places to the processions. Pilgrims solemnly, with prayers, brought the shrine to those cities and villages whose residents had requested this in advance. At the request of the parishioners, prayers were held. This initiative belonged to the community or to individual laity, although the prayer was performed by a priest. Such prayers took place quite often and were spread throughout Russia, the reasons for them were church holidays or circumstances, such as the beginning or end of agricultural work, epidemics, continuous rains, the first cattle pasture, drought, the need to consecrate certain places, for example, wells, intersections etc. It was believed that the prayers that took place during the processions of the Cross have tremendous power to purify and sanctify people and lands, houses and sources. Prayers were held both in a simple hut and in a rich mansion, since the Russian people knew that a visit to their home by a priest with icons and a prayer service cleaned and sanctified their house.

These church sacraments gave people the opportunity to partake of grace and therefore embraced a large number of believers and doubters. Large territories were subject to consecration. For example, religious processions from the Valdai Monastery with the Iveron Icon of the Mother of God lasted almost half a year and covered numerous counties of the Voronezh province, along the composition of pilgrims could change, only those who accompanied the icon from the monastery remained constantly.

In 1813, the merchant wife Lyubov Andreevna Grigoryeva from the Bobrovsky district of the Voronezh province with her two-year-old son visited the Valdai Monastery. Lyubov Grigoryeva told in the presence of extraneous witnesses and elders of the monastery that her son was cured of a serious illness after some revelations that appeared to her in a dream, that she arrived in this monastery and served prayer singing with an akathist in front of the Holy Iveron Icon of the Mother of God.

Written by order of believers, hundreds of thousands of icons entered the public sphere and the personal lives of people of that time — schools, soldier's barracks, hospitals, special educational institutions, state institutions, private offices and homes (Belyakov, 2002).

It was believed that the icon can be healed. An example is the case that occurred in the Voronezh province, in the Bobrovsky district, in the settlement of Buturlinovka, with the peasant Evdokia Ivanovna Semerina. After marriage, Evdokia Semerin fell ill with a fever, which lasted 15 years. The disease manifested itself in thirst. The woman could not eat anything. Then she decided to resort to the help of the Mother of God and prayed for a long time to the Queen of Heaven to rid her of her illness. In a dream, Evdokia Semerina saw that she was in the Chalk Mountains, in a cave from which she was taken out and pointed to the door. Opening the door, in the room she saw a radiant icon of the Mother of God, the Divnogorsk Lady. Looking for this icon, she began to go to different places and finally came to Divnogorsky monastery. Arriving there, she saw there the very icon that appeared to her in a dream. A moleben was served to the Queen of Heaven, after which the patient kissed the icon, and immediately there was a severe pain in the head, the tinnitus ceased, her eyes began to see clearly, she could speak freely, the fever passed, her face was corrected, her thirst stopped, she became eating. The disease went away completely.

In the Voronezh province, in the settlement of Fedorovka, another incident occurred. The seventeen-year-old Matron, according to the stories of her parents, the whole Great Lent of 1885 and the feast of Easter was sick; on Sunday of Fomina week, having left the house in the evening, Matrona, with a severe headache, returned home late at night, and in the morning she screamed in a strange voice and tore her clothes. The patient could not sleep and eat for seven weeks, on this occasion, the parents turned to the Zemstvo doctors for the treatment of Matron, but did not receive any result.

Then the parents decided to take Matron to the Valuysky monastery and to serve a prayer service to the Miracle-working icon of St. Nicholas; when a prayer service was served in front of the Icon of the Prelate in the Church, the patient at the same moment became easier, and this happened on May 19, 1885. Upon arrival home, the patient began to recover, in the fall, during field work she was able to help her parents; in October, mother and Matrona came to the monastery on foot to serve a thanksgiving prayer, and happily talked about getting recovery from the icon of St. Nicholas. The inhabitants of the settlement of Fedorovka, as well as the local priest Stefan Koshelev confirmed the reliability of this information.

In 1889, in the Voronezh province, in the Bogucharsky district, the wife of priest Andrei Komarov, Elizaveta, said that for six years she suffered from bleeding, was treated in the Voronezh hospital and by private doctors, but this did not bring her any benefit. She was advised to go to Moscow for surgery, but due to poor health she could not follow their advice. It seemed that the hope of recovery was lost, but the Lord showed mercy. Elizabeth in the pamphlet "The Kozelshchansky Image of the Mother of God" read about the miracles that came from the miraculous icon of the Most Holy One, and decided to travel to the Kozelshchina, hoping for the mercy of the Lord. Before the trip, she acquired the Kozelshchansky image of the Mother of God and began to pray in front of the icon, and also wrote to the Kozelshchina with a request to pray for her. Prayer was heard, the disease passed, and she recovered.

In Voronezh province, miraculous healings took place in front of the icon of "All Who Sorrow of Joy". In 1866, in the city of Pavlovsk in the Transfiguration Church layman A.I. Shaposhnikov before death asked to serve a prayer service in front of this icon, but he died without waiting for the prayer service; and when the prayer service began, he returned to life and lived another 2 days.

Numerous healings of people in the Voronezh province came from the icon of the Tolga Mother of God. In 1831, during the cholera epidemic, the merchant Dyakova had a revelation in a dream to serve a prayer service to the Tolga Icon of the Mother of God; with this icon they made a procession in the city of Voronezh, and most of the faithful, including the Dyakov family, were healed. In 1836, in the St. Nicholas Church of Voronezh, according to the vow of the merchant Dyakova, a chapel was built in honor of the Tolga Icon of the Mother of God, and since that time this icon was especially revered in the Voronezh province.

In the Tambov province, the icon of the Kazan Vyshenskaya Mother of God was especially revered, which was brought to Tambov from the Ryazan Diocese, from the Uspensky Vyshensky Monastery. The story associated with this image dates back to the beginning of the 19th century. During the war of 1812, nun Miropia Adenkova, fleeing the French, went from Moscow to the Tambov Ascension Convent, carrying the Kazan Icon of the Mother of God. On the way, the coachman attacked her and wanted to kill her, but the nun began to pray, turning to the Mother of God for help, as a result of which the coachman unexpectedly went blind, and the nun was saved. The coachman repented, after which his vision returned.

The nun Miropia, before her death, bequeathed the Kazan icon of the Mother of God of the Vyshenskaya pustyn' of the Tambov province of the Shatsky district. On March 7, 1827, a holy image was delivered there, where many healings and miracles came from the icon, and at night, the icon glowed unusually. The fame of this image quickly spread throughout the Tambov province.

To pray before the icon, a pilgrimage to the Vyshensky monastery began, and this Image became known as Vyshensky. The icon of the Mother of God in 1871 saved the inhabitants of Tambov from a terrible cholera. By procession, the miraculous icon was delivered to Tambov, after which the number of dying people decreased. In Tambov, the icon was a whole month.

Theodosius Shapovalenko, bishop of Tambov and Shatsky, in 1871 turned to the Holy Synod with a request to bless the arrival of the miraculous Vyshensky image for worship every year in Tambov. For many years, thousands of believers in Tambov greeted this icon as an expensive shrine. Every year on May 26 in the Tambov diocese religious processions from the city's churches were held to meet the miraculous icon, all city churches rang the bells. Religious procession wore an icon in the cities and villages of the Tambov province until July 8, prayers from the deliverance of various diseases and about the harvest served before it.

In 1858, in the Oryol province, the miracle-working icon of the Mother of God Balykinskaya, which became famous for its miracles, became the main shrine of the Vvedensky-Christ Nativity monastery. The image of the Virgin of Three Hands was also revered, which was stored in the Mother of God-All Saints Monastery in the city of Bolkhov, Orel Province.

The relics of St. Tikhon of Zadonsky and Mitrofan of Voronezh - the main shrines of the Central Black Earth provinces - attracted pilgrims from different regions of Russia with great force. The pilgrimage to the tomb of St. Tikhon and the service of the requiem began long before his glorification, which happened in 1861. Places associated with the life of the saint began to be widely known at the beginning of the 19th century.

When the Synod unveiled the decision to glorify and discover the relics, the number of pilgrims in Zadonsk reached 300 thousand people. Those people were accommodated in tents and wooden barracks, set in advance around the monastery and the city. In tents and barracks, the saint's mantle was laid on the sick person, they were anointed with oil from the grave lamp, and pilgrims were applied to the tomb, which hid the holy relics of St. Tikhon, funeral services were performed with repentance and communion of the Holy Mysteries of Christ at the grave of God's Grace. Many believers avoided danger by prayer calling for the help of the Saint. From the miraculous icon of the Mother of God of Vladimir and the honest relics of St. Tikhon, grace poured out, which caused zeal for the Zadonsky monastery. The influx of pilgrims to Zadonsk required an increase in the number of active priests and provided funds for the improvement of the monastery.

In 1814, Bishop Anthony I notified the Holy Synod that from remote places of Russia a huge number of pilgrims of various ranks flock to the Zadonsky monastery to bow to the miraculous icon of Bogomater' Vladimirskaya and to the memory of St. Tikhon. Therefore, on the part of the abbot, friendly courtesy with the pilgrims and observation of the order and care for the magnificent appearance of the monastery are required (Srebryansky, 1995).

This message of the diocesan lord positively influenced the position of the Zadonsky monastery, the hierarchical degree of the monastery was changed. Residents of Ryazan, Kursk, Tula and other provinces left their notes on healing.

Zadonsky monastery until 1810 in the complete list of monasteries of the third class was 130th. In 1815 and 1816 rector's cells, fraternal refectory and other buildings were redone.

In 1817, a stone building with two floors was built for the Voznesenskaya Church on the east side of the two-story stone building, and hospital cells were built below. In 1818, on the western side of the same building, a three-story stone building was erected for a religious school, on the lower and middle floors of which there were rooms for students, and on the upper - for mentors.

The ascetic and pious life of the recluse Georgij Mashurin from 1820 attracted attention to the Zadonsky monastery. Georgij Mashurin was born into a noble family in 1789 in Vologda. His parents already had a daughter. Before the birth of George in the family, the greatest misfortune occurred; his father was killed. Mother, deprived of support in life, turned to Heavenly Father for protection. As a child, George was quiet and obedient, and from his youth, teachers and mentors educated him.

Georgij prayed earnestly, attended the Church, was merciful to the poor. When he was 18 years old, he entered the military service as a cunker in the Lubinsky Hussar Regiment. Georgij, having received the rank of lieutenant, did not want to seek higher ranks in the future, but began to think about a complete renunciation of military service and filed a letter of resignation, which was approved on Christmas Eve, September 7, 1818. Voronezh Bishop Epiphanius identified Georgij as a novice in the Zadonsky monastery, Georgij was then only 29 years old. In obedience, Georgij spent less than a year, after which he became a recluse. He lived in a stone cell, which was closed on all sides, a cell that did not have access to air, and therefore the air in it was very heavy. Spiritually and bodily, only God's grace warmed him. Sometimes he heated his house in order to avoid various perverse human opinions.

Constantly fulfilling his vows, Georgij lived in this cell for 5 years, after which Archimandrite Samuel, the rector of the monastery, persuaded Georgij to move to a wooden, spacious and ventilated cell. By the will of the abbot, he moved to a new home, but regretted the underground cave and his former cell.

With the blessing of the abbot, Georgij brought from the church in the cell an icon of the Mother of God of God, to which he showed particular zeal, performing liturgical singing with an akathist, which was his greatest event. Georgij possessed the gift of insight, and with the help of God's grace he subtly and wisely understood human hearts. Without notice from the outside, he knew which of the brethren wore only the image of monasticism, and who really led a pious life, who had a high opinion of himself and who was prone to pride. To such people, Georgij answered the following:

He told the visitors who came to the elder Georgij, by the grace of God, what kind of life they lead, named the reasons why people came to him, and knew what they wanted to talk with him about. He saw people who came to him because of vanity, and he told them that they do not know themselves, whose will they do, that they are accompanied by a spirit of guile. Until Georgij's death, there were few people who knew that he was a monk, not a novice. He was tonsured a monk and secretly named Stratonik, but he did not change the name given to him at birth until the end of his days, since the name of Georgij Pobedonosec, his Guardian Angel, was so dear to him that until the end of his life he signed in his letters with this by name. In 1836, in connection with the discovery of the relics of St. Mitrofan, the Voronezh Annunciation Mitrofanov Monastery was established. Each year, up to 40 thousand pilgrims visited the monastery (according to the mid-19th century).

Famous Russian traveller and geographer P.P. Semenov-Tyan-Shansky recalled his childhood trip when his family went to Voronezh with his children from his estate in Ranenburg district of Ryazan province.

Several proxies from the Voronezh clergy carried out a detailed examination of the tomb of St. Mitrofan and concluded that the body of the saint is undoubtedly holy. Believers arrived in Voronezh in order to express feelings of gratitude for the grace of God before the cancer of Saint Mitrofan, through the prayers of the newly appeared saint, which poured out on everyone. With the patronage of Mitrofan was also associated the fate of Metropolitan

Veniamin Fedchenkov. When the child became seriously ill with pneumonia, his mother vowed to God: if he recovered, then she and him would go to prayer to Saint Mitrofan. When mother in the church stood St. Mitrofan, an old man passed by. He blessed them, and said about the child that he will be a saint. And in the future, with the name of St. Mitrofan, people not only linked the memories of Peter I, but also revered the saint as an intercessor of the common people from oppression.

In the Voronezh province, one of the revered pilgrimage centers was the Aleksievo-Akatov Monastery. The oldest monastery of Aleksievo-Akatov in the Voronezh diocese was founded in 1620 according to the vow of citizens, in appreciation of the victory over the army of the Circassians and Lithuanians. The monastery's temple was dedicated to Metropolitan of Moscow Saint Alexy, since the battle took place on the day of his memory. Until the beginning of the 19th century, the only man's monastery in the city was the Aleksievo-Akatov Monastery, and its abbots had the rank of archimandrite.

The appearance of the miraculous icon of the Mother of God "Troeruchica", the main shrine of the Aleksievo-Akatov Monastery, is associated with the name of Archimandrite Nikanor, who brought the icon from the New Jerusalem Voskresenskij Monastery, where Archimandrite Nikanor was a monk and then rector. This icon was written off from an ancient image, it was very loved by Voronezh people who believed in its miraculous power. The monastery consisted of 17 people. The monastery owned eight acres of land and a lake for fishing. Among the inhabitants of the Aleksievsky monastery was skhimnyy monk Agapit (Hieromonk Avvakum), who later became a particularly revered Zadonsky old man («starec»).

We have information about the official side of the life of the Aleksievo-Akatov Monastery of the 19th century. The works of the abbots concerned the construction and decoration of the monastery. In 1859, Archimandrite Illarion Bogolyubov compiled the most complete description of the Voronezh Akatov Alekseevsky Monastery. At the end of the 19th century, enlightenment activity flourished within the walls of the monastery thanks to the work of its rector, His Grace Vladimir Sokolovsky, who had extensive pedagogical and missionary experience. At that time, the Committee of the Orthodox Missionary Society and the Diocesan School Council worked at the monastery, there was a regent school and a teacher's school, religious readings were held on Sundays with light paintings of a moral content, a choir of boys was formed, the training of which was greatly paid by Vladyka Vladimir.

During the XIX century, the monastery was built and decorated. In 1804–1819 a stone two-storey church was erected, which has survived to the present. In 1812, the lower church was consecrated in the name of St. Alexis, in 1819 the upper church was consecrated in honor of Christ's Resurrection. The construction was carried out with funds donated by the merchant widow Evdokia Anikeeva, and designed by I. Volkov, the provincial architect. The old temple collapsed in the 70s of the XIX century, and the bell tower, which remained of it, currently exists as the oldest building in Voronezh.

1840s became a decisive time and factor in the formation of pilgrimage in the modern system of church Russian-Palestinian ties. At this time, Western countries are fixing their sights on the Middle East and Jerusalem, disguising their political intentions with religious interests.

The earl N.A. Protasov, Chief Prosecutor of the Holy Synod, on March 1, 1841, informed Emperor Nicholas I the following information.

"Bishop of Voronezh, Archbishop Anthony of Smirnitsky informed that pilgrims returning from Jerusalem speak of the plight of the shrine, of the difficult stay of our compatriots in Jerusalem, since there is no refuge there". Anthony Smirnitsky suggested organizing a strannopriimnyj house for Russian pilgrims in Jerusalem, for which you could use the Krestnyj Monastery, where there would be a Russian Orthodox archimandrite with two or three monks to conduct Slavic worship for pilgrims. Archimandrite, in addition to worship, could transfer offerings that were delivered from Russia in favor of the Holy Sepulcher, and which could be converted into benefits for Russian pilgrims arriving there. From May 21 to May 31, 1881, Emperor Alexander III made a pilgrimage to the Holy Land. During the reign of Alexander III, the Orthodox Palestinian Society was opened, whose charter was approved by the emperor on May 8, 1882. On May 21, after a prayer service in the house Church, in the palace of Prince Nikolai Nikolayevich, the grand opening of this Society took place, which was attended by members of the imperial family, scholars and diplomats, Russian and Greek clergy. The day of celebration was specially determined, since the Church on this day honors the memory of Saints Constantine and Helena, and the mother of Constantine, Empress Helen, did much to restore Christianity in Jerusalem and Palestine. Under her auspices, archaeological excavations in Jerusalem began. According to the Charter, the society organized and equipped Russian pilgrims in Palestine, supported and assisted Orthodoxy in the Middle East, conducting charity and educational work among the Arab population. By the means of the Society, in Lebanon, Palestine and Syria, by the beginning of the 20th century, 113 schools, teacher's seminaries and colleges were kept. Throughout its history, the state has provided attention and support to the Society. Until 1905, from the moment of the founding of the Society, it was headed by Prince Sergey

Alexandrovich, and after his death, Princess Elizabeth Fedorovna, currently ranked by the Orthodox Church as a saint. In 1891, a department of the Orthodox Palestinian Society was opened in the Voronezh diocese. In 1891, a letter was sent to the Voronezh Spiritual Consistory from Prince Sergey Alexandrovich stating that the Holy Synod authorized the Imperial Orthodox Palestinian Society under his auspices to collect annually donations in all the churches of the empire on the day the Lord entered Jerusalem. Public funds from donations were spent exclusively on the needs of the Orthodox population of the holy land. The Holy Synod also entrusted the society with the care of satisfying the material and spiritual needs of Russian pilgrims who visited the Church of the Holy Sepulcher in Jerusalem. Archpriest Evlampy Svyatozarov signed this decree in the Voronezh Spiritual Consistory.

In the provinces of the Central Chernozem region, one of the revered pilgrimage centers was the Kursk (Kurskaya) Glinckaya Rozhdectvo-Bogopodickaya pustyn', in which church life was concentrated, it was a real school of monasticism, the school of Christ. The bishops in their reports on the Kursk diocese to the Holy Synod spoke of the Glinskaya pustyn' as the best monastery, and its elders were called the decoration of monasticism. The internal way of life of the desert was distinguished by rigor, spirituality and asceticism, therefore the Glinskaya pustyn' earned the high praise of the elders who were there. The pustyn' elders exerted their influence on the whole of society. Pilgrims from all over Russia traveled to the Glinskaya pustyn' in order to get advice and strengthen their spiritual strength. It spiritually healed people from different layers of Russian society. The Glinskaya pustyn' is on a par with such famous centers of Orthodoxy, such as the majestic Trinity-Sergius Lavra, Kiev-Pechersk Lavra, Optina Pustyn', pustyn' Valaam. Famous missionaries came out of the Glinsky monastery, thanks to which the glory of the Glinskaya pustyn' spread not only throughout Russia, but also far beyond its borders. At the end of the 19th century, up to 45 thousand pilgrims flocked to the Glinskaya pustyn' annually, and at the beginning of the 20th century - over 60 thousand. The pilgrims were located in the special room «strannopriimnica» of the monastery, the maintenance of which cost the monastery 6,000 rubles, the wanderers used clothes, shoes, monastery meals, housing, medicines, and sometimes they could receive cash assistance. Needy residents of neighboring villages used free bread from the pustyn', and in cases of starvation, death of cattle, fires, they received free cash allowance from the pustyn. The beginning of the twentieth century was a time of mass pilgrimages to the holy places of Russia. At the beginning of the XX century, the most visited pilgrimage centers were the Sarov and Optina pustyn's. In

Optina pustyn' there were no incorrupt relics, there were no miraculous icons, pilgrims sought to communicate with the elders. At the beginning of the 20th century, Nicholas II made a trip to Sarov, where the monastery of the revered Russian saint Seraphim of Sarov was located. In the celebrations of glorification of Seraphim of Sarov in July 1903 took part up to 500 thousand pilgrims. It was an amazing coincidence that the contemporary of the Monk Seraphim of Sarov was the holy ascetic of the Voronezh province, Elena, who was born only three years earlier than the future All-Russian saint. The spiritual paths of the Monks Seraphim and Helen crossed at the Florovsky Kiev monastery, where the ascetic Seraphim was told about the Monk Dosifei from the Kitaevskaya pustyn', who blessed the young man to go to Sarov. And the nun Elena, after life's persecution and sorrow, came to the Florovsky monastery a little later, where she spent decades of ascetic labor. Prepodobnaya Elena (Ekaterina Bakhteeva) was born in Zadonsk in the Voronezh province in 1756 into a rich and noble family of General Bakhteev. When she was 18 years old, she renounced all worldly blessings, secretly left her parental home and went to the Voronezh Convent, deciding to devote herself to the eternal service of the Lord. Ekaterina Bakhteeva received an excellent education, but how the general's family reacted to leaving the house of a rich and young heiress is not known. It is only known that the father searched for his daughter for a long time, until he found her in the Voronezh women's monastery. At first he categorically demanded that his daughter be returned to his father's house, personally talking with the abbess, but then, being a deeply religious person, he reconciled with her calling and went to Zadonsk, blessing his daughter. Pilgrims from different parts of Russia came to the nun Elena for advice, words of comfort, and requests for holy prayers, so great was her spiritual authority. Through the prayers of St. Elena many miracles happened, people got rid of poverty and serious illnesses, she helped everyone who sincerely prayed in life. In Optina pustyn', Elder Amvrosij was very famous and deeply respected. Amvrosij was born in the Tambov province in 1812 in a family of sexton. He always had poor health, several times in his life he was so seriously ill that he was at death. At the age of 17, Amvrosij went to the monastery (Kholostova, 2001).

Every day the elder received people who came to him, usually talking with them for 10-15 minutes. Being a subtle psychologist, he read in the soul of his interlocutor as in an open book, hinting to him at his weakness and making him think seriously about it. Intellectuals and aristocrats, military and merchants, townspeople, peasants came to meet with the old man. Lev Tolstoy, after a conversation with the elder Amvrosij, called him a holy man, having talked with him, it becomes easy and rejoicing in his soul, and the closeness of God is felt. Amvrosij, despite constant illnesses, the world perceived in bright colors. He believed that the triumph of evil over good was only temporary. A person cannot improve at the same time as social progress, since progress is manifested in the comforts of life and in external human affairs, and each person must go through moral improvement on his own, comparing it with the commandments of good. The church had great moral strength, thanks to Amvrosij and other spiritual ascetics. In 1911, pilgrimages from the Voronezh province were made to Belgorod, Kiev, the Trinity-Sergius Lavra, the Sarov Deserts, to Jerusalem and Mount Athos. According to official statistics, 20,704 people left the province on a pilgrimage annually, of which 14037 were women, and 6667 were men. Summarizing these data as a whole, using the example of 4 provinces of the Central Black Earth region: Voronezh, Tambov, Kursk and Orel, we note the following. At the beginning of the twentieth century, the number of pilgrims annually amounted to 1 million people, of which 800 thousand preferred the near pilgrimage, and 200 thousand chose distant shrines, of which up to 1 thousand Orthodox Christians undertook a foreign pilgrimage. The path to distant shrines could take from one month to several, especially if the pilgrims moved to Palestine through Odessa, on the way going to Kiev, and went back and forth only on foot. The maritime part of the pilgrimage route that moved to Jerusalem passed from the city of Odessa to the city of Jaffa and then back by sea. In the religious life of almost every Russian believer, an Orthodox pilgrimage was present. In the process of pilgrimage, the main thing during prayer is not the external performance of the rites, but the spiritual renewal and mood that occurs in the heart of every Orthodox Christian. In the process of studying the pilgrimage tradition, a large cultural and historical material is accumulated, which requires systematization. In the XIX - early XX centuries the main types of pilgrimage (Lebedeva, 2021).

Pilgrimages were made near the place of residence of the pilgrim; in his diocese, but not near the place of residence; to all-Russian holy places, sometimes remote from the place of residence of wanderers; overseas pilgrimages. The object of visiting pilgrims could be the relics of saints, miraculous icons, devotees of piety (elders and elders), holy sources, graves of ascetics. Over time, the main pilgrimage routes have been developed, which could depend on the time of the year and on the duration of the trip. The Russian Orthodox Church facilitated the pilgrimage, respecting people who visited Christian shrines, as in these places people learned about the spiritual traditions of monasteries, temples and their history, about saints and ascetics, whose life was connected with the shrines that included to the pilgrimage route, and about the features of worship (Shevtsov, 2012). Pilgrimage had a beneficial effect on the life of all believers, having performed which, they began to better understand themselves and their loved ones, and Christian sacraments were considered an integral part of their lives. Pilgrims realized that there is a mutual contact between the Russian Orthodox Church and the Russian state, and they are links in one chain that connects the past and future of the Great Russian people - and this is the meaning of pilgrimage as a fact of Russian history. Therefore, the materials of our study show that the Church in the XIX - early XX centuries was an influential spiritual and moral force. The merit of the Church consisted in the fact that it was actually the only institution conducting social work. In the XIX - early XX centuries. The church was an ally of the autocracy, pursuing a pro-government policy to disseminate loyal ideas in Russian society, which was expressed in exercising control over the education system, as well as the entire public life.

CONCLUSION

The development of the educational activity of the Orthodox Church in Russia and in the provinces of the Central Black Earth Region took place in several directions. The most important area was the translation activity of the Church. Conducting services and translating spiritual and moral literature made it possible to better assimilate the Orthodox faith. The translation activities of the clergy, along with the development of parish schools, created the conditions for the formation of a national intelligentsia. Thus, giving an objective assessment from the standpoint of historical science of the effectiveness of the Orthodox Church in the structure of public administration in the 19th and early 20th centuries, we can note certain objectively positive aspects.

The merit of the Church was the mass training of the population in literacy, the creation of a network of private and public public organizations for those in need of support, the monitoring of the spiritual and moral state of society, and the maintenance of stable neutral relations with representatives of other different faiths («inovercy»).

REFERENCES

Archive of the Russian Ethnographic Museum (AREM) F. 7. Op.1. D. 1140. Ethnographic description of the Oryol province. L. 21.

Belyakov, E. V. (2002). Deaconesses in the Russian Orthodox Church. *History (London)*, (9), 1–5.

Charitable institutions of the Russian Empire. (1990). Academic Press.

Kholostova, E. I. (2001). *Technologies of social work.* Academic Press.

Lebedeva, M. A., & Volkova, E. A. (2021). Socio-political movement in the Voronezh region in the middle of the XIX-th century. *State and Society in Modern Politics: Collection of Articles*, 8, 201–206.

Mitrofan, S. (1995). *Explanatory word. Materials for the life of the Martyr Grand Duchess Elizabeth. Letters, diaries, memoirs, documents.* Academic Press.

Shevtsov, V.V. (2012). Gubernskie vedomosti in the pre-revolutionary historiography of the periodical press. *Bulletin of Tomsk State University*, 414 - 421.

Zyryanov, P. N. (2002). *Russian monasteries and monasticism in the 19th - early 20th centuries.* M. Verbum.

Chapter 13

Church Land Tenure and Land Use

ABSTRACT

The practical life of monks has shown that their economic activity has a corrupting effect on the inner side of their lives. Only a few monasteries succeeded in organically incorporating agricultural and commercial activities into the routine of monastic life. The Orthodox Church in Russia owned three million hectares of land as property. A sign of the state's respect for millions of believing citizens and real material support for the Church was the transfer of land to the ownership of the temple. The land issue had a huge impact on the life of all the people of Russia and on its economy. In Russia, and in other countries of the world that are going through a time of change, the land issue is very important.

INTRODUCTION

In the XIX - early XX centuries the church played a significant role in the spiritual life of the people and in the economic relations of the country. In Russian historiography, much attention was paid to the spirituality of the Russian Orthodox Church.

In the 19th century, the issues of land ownership, land use, and the financial situation of the clergy were insufficiently disclosed. The question of the privileges of the clergy and their economic support, both financially and legally, by the state was not developed and was not considered.

DOI: 10.4018/978-1-6684-4915-8.ch013

An analysis of the socio-economic situation of the Russian Orthodox Church made it possible to reveal that the clergy were partially reoriented towards state salaries and moved away from traditional ways of providing. In the 19th century, the main sources of income for most of the parish clergy, at least the rural clergy, were still donations of agricultural products and parishioners' fees for services. During the 19th century, the government tried to improve the financial situation of the clergy, but it was not possible to completely transfer the priests to state salaries.

In imperial Russia, church land ownership was in difficult conditions. The life of the clergy, their material well-being and church activities depended on the amount of land, the quality of agricultural machinery. Data on the growth of church land ownership in the 19th - early 20th centuries are available only for individual spiritual subjects.

In his book «Land Ownership of Churches and Monasteries of the Russian Empire», historian I.A. Lyubinetsky cites information that 36 monasteries owned less than 100 acres of land; less than 50 acres - 16 monasteries. 44 monasteries had from 100 to 200 acres of land; 90 monasteries had from 200 to 1000 acres; from 1000 to 2000 acres - 12 monasteries; more than 10 thousand acres of land - 5 monasteries. In total, at that time, the monasteries of Russia owned 1 million acres of land.

In 1801, a law was issued on the initiative of the public figure N.S. Mordvinov, according to which persons of all classes and the clergy were allowed to acquire uninhabited lands. Thus, land ownership began to have a public character, which led to the emergence of a larger number of landowners.

The property rights of the Church, the allocation and management of land were given much attention in the "Code of Laws on the Conditions of People in the State" in 1835, 1842 and 1851. Lands on which churches were erected were recognized as inviolable property, and no one could have any claims on them (Article 446, vol. IX). In the event of the liquidation of the parish, lands and other lands were transferred to the church to which the parishioners of the liquidated parish were classified (Article 448, vol. IX). According to the Code of Laws, church lands were divided into manor lands, which were located under churches and houses of the clergy, vegetable gardens, orchards; and field fields, which included arable land (Art. 400 vol. IX).

For each church clerk («pricht»), according to the laws on land surveying, from 33 to 99 acres were allocated from the lands of the peasants. When surveying, they usually proceeded from the amount of land that was in use by the parishioners (Article 349 of the Code of Survey Laws).

«Pricht» — Cult ministers, clergy of some church. In the Russian Orthodox Church, «pricht» is the name of a group of persons serving at any one temple (parish): both clergy (priest and deacon) and clergy (psalmist, reader (cleric), church choir singer, etc.). The clergy at each church was formed according to the staff assigned to it, which was compiled by the spiritual consistory and the bishop at the request of members of the parish and if there were sufficient funds to support all members of the clergy. For the establishment of a new clergy, as well as for changes in its composition, the bishop each time requested the permission of the Holy Synod. The maintenance of the rural clergy was mainly provided by income from the "corrections" of the laity (shared among the members of the clergy according to the rules approved by the Synod), landed church property, sometimes ready-made premises in church houses, less often salaries.

The original right of the laity to elect members of the clergy, as a general one, was abolished, but the laity retained the right to declare to the diocesan bishop their desire to have a well-known person a member of the clergy of their church.

If each peasant accounted for less than 4 acres of land or there was no land at all, the parishioners were obliged to pay a reward in cash or food.

60 acres of land were assigned to the bishop's house, from 100 to 150 acres - to the monastery. Lands above the legal proportion, but already belonging to the churches, and henceforth remained their inviolable property. The lands that were allotted to churches from parishioners for the maintenance of clergy (clause 2 of article 400 vol. IX according to the edition of 1876) were not subject to alienation according to the Highest approval of the State Council of November 15, 1883. If the sale of the land was beneficial for the church, then exceptions to this rule were allowed, and the land could be sold.

Alienation of church lands could be carried out only with the Highest Decree of the State Council. The amount of money received from the sale of church lands was to be directed either to the purchase of other land, or to the purchase of government interest-bearing papers. The proceeds from these activities belonged to the Russian Orthodox Church. Restrictions were placed on the lease of church lands. This was allowed when the field lands were leased for no more than 1 year, and only under a written condition. Shops, houses, mills, fishing grounds could be leased out for no more than 12 years with the permission of the diocesan authorities.

The land property of the Russian Orthodox Church can be divided into monastic land and parish land. Monasteries were less in need of arable, forest holdings, meadow lands. The government paid more attention to those who voluntarily chose an ascetic lifestyle. However, the white clergy, who had large families, needed material assistance more (Kartashev, 2000).

Between 1836 and 1861 years 170 monasteries received more than 9,000 arable and meadow land and more than 16,000 acres of forest. During the second half of the 19th century, the monastic land ownership increased.

The works of the church historian V. Kilchevsky say that it is impossible to get a complete picture of the number of land plots owned by the monasteries. Sometimes estate lands, in addition to churches, houses, shops, included lands given over to cemeteries. Manor land at 62 monasteries was not listed in the documents at all.

Due to the poor quality of the soil, the poor development of the land, and the remoteness of the land from the monasteries, the monks received a very small income. If the land was remote from the monasteries, the monks leased such land, and they themselves rented nearby land from their neighbors. Forest areas also decreased, so most of the clergy had one arable share each. The plots were located in different places from each other and from the place of residence of the clergy at a distance of 20 to 40 miles. The clergy could not properly develop these lands, since the nature of their official duties required their daily presence in the Church.

In this regard, on April 17, 1822, a decree of the Holy Synod was issued, sent to the Voronezh Spiritual Consistory, where it was said that the clergy should be very attentive to their duties. Therefore, in order for the clergy to better observe the church charter, they should be released from work on the ground.

In Russia, a large number of churches owned small plots of land from 30 to 50 acres. A very small number of clergy owned plots of 100 acres of land.

In 1859, the Klirovaya Vedomosti at the Dmitrievskaya Church in the Tambov province stated that there was no hay and manor land, only arable land - 99 acres. If the land is divided equally, then for each acting clergyman there will be from 9 to 11 tithes for each family, and for peasants - 2 tithes for tax.

Tambov province had an agrarian regional feature. The townspeople made up only a few percent, and the peasant communities had large private land holdings with a traditional way of life and way of life. In the memoirs of the family of the Tambov priest, one can read that life in their house was very simple. The priest's hut differed from the peasant ("smoke") hut only in that it was "with a chimney", that is, the hut had a chimney. The father-priest himself plowed the land, mowed hay, harvested and threshed bread, and carried agricultural products for sale. Mother was engaged in a garden, livestock and poultry. The conversations of the father, mother and children were about the harvest, about the monetary profit of the parish and the arrival of the dean and the bishop.

In the 19th century, the growth of episcopal, church and monastic land ownership continued. During the reign of Alexander I and Nicholas II, monasteries and churches received several tens of thousands of acres from state lands.

A significant increase in the land ownership of churches and monasteries was combined with changes in the methods and forms of land management. Monasteries were often unable to cultivate their own lands on their own. With the large size of the monastic lands, the new conditions in the country's economy in the second quarter of the 19th century required the speedy restructuring of the economy of the monasteries on a new capitalist basis. However, churches and monasteries are beginning to gradually adapt to the new economic realities. If at the beginning of the 19th century the lands of the monasteries were cultivated by peasants specially assigned to the Orthodox monastery, then in the second half of the 19th century the monasteries were forced to switch to the use of hired labor.

In the event that the monastery was not able to pay for the work of hired workers, then this monastery preferred to lease its landed property for cash rent, but not for trading establishments. In addition to renting out their land, the monasteries cultivated their lands on their own, using the labor of hired workers. Hired workers were an invariable phenomenon in the life of monasteries in the 19th century.

When analyzing the use of hired labor by monasteries, it must be said that in the 19th century the supply of labor was greater than the demand. This determined the comparative cheapness of hired labor. The cost of harvesting and processing 1 acres of land by hired workers was 11.2-12.9 rubles for spring fields and 12.8-14.7 rubles for winter fields. Payment for daily work in the spring in different years ranged from 20 to 38 kopecks, and in the summer - from 33 to 60 kopecks per month.

Thus, churches and monasteries, possessing impressive material resources and a sufficient amount of land, could be the organizers of grain farms, which were characterized by a significant amount of plowing and the use of free labor (Veselovsky, 1886).

An example of a privately owned grain farm is the farm of a priest from the Fatezh district of the Kursk province N.A. Bulgakov, who, according to data for 1884, owned an estate of 70 acres of land, of which almost 3.5 acres (or 5%) were occupied by the estate, 63.5 acres (or 90.7%) were arable land, 3 acres (or 3%) were allocated to the meadow. N.A. Bulgakov was helped to manage a large farm by 5 hired field workers.

The most important reason for endowing churches with land was inflation. The salaries of clerics were increased. The government patronized the clergy, but state control over the church was very strict. The monasteries did not have the opportunity to independently manage their own economy.

In the middle of the 19th century, it was forbidden for monasteries to own land with or without people. It was impossible to increase the amount of land or sell it, strictly defined lands were placed at the disposal of the clergy. It was forbidden for the parish clergy to cultivate the land on their own "due to the inconsistency of this matter with the clergy", and therefore the parishioners cultivated the land. This caused the clergy to depend on the peasants, although, of course, the clergy were spared from worldly concerns unusual for them.

The clergy during the reign of Alexander I, with the personal permission of the emperor, could buy houses and lands. For the clergy of the Assumption Church of the Voronezh province in 1851, sub-church houses were built on public land. The land for use by the clergy was marked off on August 13, 1849, 33 tithes. The data on the land are in the plan of the boundary book, which is at the church.

According to the plan of M.M. Speransky, in order to improve the financial position of Russia in 1811, a Decree was issued on the sale of government land. In 1814, the sale of land was stopped. But since 1824, the clergy and the peasantry have not again begun to work on state lands.

The government was not able to provide churches, monasteries, archbishop's houses with lands because of their own Decrees call, so went to these measures. Sometimes disputed lands were assigned to churches. The Voronezh Ecclesiastical Consistory decided: on August 3, 1816, to transfer the case to the district court to resolve the controversial issue of land ownership between the priests of the Belolutskaya settlement of the Starobelsky district and the city of Ostrogozhsk. The court ruled: not to prevent the priest Jokim Efremov from crossing this land to people heading to the Elias Church («Il'inskaya tserkov'»).

The clergy could only bequeath or buy uninhabited lands. Lands inhabited by peasants could be in the possession of clerics if the clergy had noble rights.

In the 19th century, state control over the state and development of church land ownership became less rigid. The government paid great attention to the state of churches and temples destroyed in 1812, allocated them the necessary sums for restoration and exempted them from taxes.

Since 1820, with the permission of the emperor, monasteries were allowed to accept real estate by will. During the reign of Alexander I, the construction of monasteries resumed, as the financial situation of the clergy improved. Church historian I.K. Smolich noted that "in the first half of the 19th century, all monastic funds were spent on construction."

In 1823, the Borisoglebsk monastery monastery was officially opened, which was located not far from the Savin Monastery and was connected with the monastery both spiritually and economically and administratively. This monastery was founded by Abbess (igumen'ya) Evgenia (knyaginya Ye.N. Meshcherskaya). The abbess contributed 10,000 rubles, 3 acres of meadow land and 6 acres of arable land, especially in order to found a new monastery.

At the beginning of the 19th century, the allocation of land to parish churches continued - they gave 33 tithes each. The priests were not always satisfied with the land allotments allotted to them, as the hay land was maintained by economic peasants.

Economic peasants - in Russia in the second half of the 18th century, a category of state peasants, formed after Catherine II carried out a secularization reform in 1764 from former monastic and church peasants. The economic peasants were initially transferred to the management of the college of economy (which is why they were called economic). In 1786, after the abolition of this collegium, the economic peasants were transferred to the management of the state chambers. They had personal freedom.

Churches were endowed with allotments from state economic and private lands. If the amount of land was insufficient, the clergy received payments in cash or in kind from a private person.

In 1863, Archpriest V.A. Kuznetsov gave the house to the clergy of the Ascension Church in the city of Voronezh, which is at the Chugunovsky cemetery, with buildings belonging to it along Staro-Moskovskaya Street. Church real estate included 19 sazhens and one and a half arshins of land along Vasilievskaya Street, as well as 36 sazhens with the estate of the merchant brother Joseph Sinitsin.

If the clergy said that "they themselves own the land", then in this case they did not receive any monetary or in-kind payments either from the private owner of the land or from the treasury. Some members of the clergy were unhappy with this.

In 1835, the deacon of the Nikolaev church filed a petition "for his equalization in possession of church lands." This petition states that each of the clergy had their own part of the church land and could rent out their plot on their own, regardless of other members of the clergy. If you wanted to rent out the wasteland, the clergy advertised in the spiritual board. Tenants were required to fertilize the land so that it was capable of arable farming or haymaking.

Nicholas I, more than all other sovereigns, contributed to the growth of church land ownership. The number of church lands during his reign increased by 2-3 times. Emperor Nicholas I personally managed the affairs of the Church. He established new orders in church administration: a report on the state of the dioceses, a report on events that happened in churches, and so on.

In the Nikolaev era, the number of church parishes increased significantly. In 1840, there were about 34,049 churches, 9,305 chapels and prayer houses in the Russian Empire. By 1860 these numbers had risen to 37,657 churches and 12,486 chapels and houses of worship. The state, in turn, sought to somehow financially provide for the newly opened and already functioning old church parishes.

In 1829, the "Regulations on ways to improve the condition of the clergy" was published. The patronizing policy of Nicholas I in relation to the Church acquired a wide scope. The clergy were endowed with houses, monasteries, bishops' houses and churches - with land and lands. Pensions were assigned to the clergy, and monetary allowances for the maintenance of monasteries increased significantly. The parish clergy began to receive permanent auxiliary salaries, and the financial situation of rural parishes improved.

In the 1830s the government allocated lands to the monasteries on which it was possible to conduct a serious economy. Until that time, the government was not able to adequately support the clergy and the monasteries fell into decay. There was only one way out: to endow the monasteries with 100–150 acres of land for farming. The monks themselves or hired workers had to cultivate this land, and the land could also be leased. The land was taken away from the department of the Ministry of State Property.

Monasteries were endowed with lands and forests gradually. In 1835, the monasteries were endowed from state dachas from 100 to 150 acres, and in 1838 from 50 to 150 acres of land - from forest dachas.

In 1832, rural parishes began to be endowed with state forests.

From 1836 to 1841 25,000 acres of land (16,000 acres of forest and 9,000 acres of arable land and hayfields) were assigned to 170 monasteries (Maslov, 1995).

In the estate «Dolzhnik» of the Belogorsky Voskresensky Monastery in the Ostrogozhsky district of the Voronezh province, there were 93.2 acres of land: 7.2 acres of the estate, 83 acres of arable land and 3 acres of forest. The monastery had its own inventory: 4 wooden plows («sokhi»), 3 plows, 9 wooden and iron harrows and 1 horse thresher. Four hired workers constantly worked on the estate of the monastery.

The Sarov Uspensky male «pustyn'» was among the Tambov monasteries the largest owner of land (out of 460 acres of land, most of it was occupied by forests). The major owner of the land was the Orzhevsky Tisheninovsky convent, which had 284.7 acres of land.

Monasteries that did not have land received monetary compensation. Monetary compensation was based on the amount of income due to them land, as a result of which many monasteries acquired significant land.

At the request of Bishop Anthony II, in 1837, Countess Anna Orlova-Chesmenskaya donated 6,000 rubles and 5 acres of timber to the Voronezh Divnogorsky Monastery for a log house in the dachas in the village of Khrenovoye.

The Divnogorsky Monastery inherited the lands of the Korotoyaksky Ascension Monastery, and in the 19th century, this monastery became the owner of land plots from pious laity.

The monastery in the Korotoyaksky district owned 250 acres of the land of the Nagai dacha. However, the soil on the site was sandy, and 100 acres of this land did not give any income to the monastery. In the Korotoyaksky district, near the village of Nikolaevsky, the monastery owned a forest plot of 60 acres, but there were only 17 acres in the forest.

In the Nizhnedevitsky district, the monastery owned 150 acres of land, 186 acres of former state land, and 11 acres of meadows. These plots were in different places, which was inconvenient for the monastery. The former abbots tried to acquire land under the monastery, but their attempts were unsuccessful. In the 19th century, churches, monasteries, episcopal and synodal houses received appropriations from the treasury every year. Beginning in 1839, the state treasury issued sums of money in the amount of 158,000 silver rubles.

So, in the 19th century, monasteries and churches became large landowners. They owned a lot of land. Thanks to the decrees of Alexander I of 1805 and 1810, the Church acquired the status of a legal entity. From now on, the Church had the opportunity to accept uninhabited lands as a gift and according to a spiritual will, and she could also buy them, which had a positive effect on the position of monasteries and churches.

This period was the heyday of church life. Since 1838, individual plots began to be excluded from the forest department and transferred to the ownership of monasteries. The monasteries could use the forest for their own needs, the timber trade became possible in the second half of the 19th century. Monasteries economically used forest resources, and therefore it was beneficial for the state to put the protection of forests under the supervision of monasteries. The monasteries had almost no income from forest plots, and if there were any, the government recommended that the monasteries use these incomes for the needs of charity. In the case of the sale of the monastery forest, the money went to help poor clergy.

In 1838, a decree was issued, according to which it was ordered to separate plots from state forest dachas and give them to monasteries to reinforce their existence. At first, the monasteries were allowed to use only deadwood, then, with the "permission of the diocesan bishops, and so that the afforestation in the monastic plots was not depleted," the clergy could use the trees for their own needs.

Monasteries that did not have forests received forest material for repair and the construction of monastic buildings free of charge. Forest plots were not assigned to monasteries, which did not have the opportunity to protect them. Subsequent decrees confirmed the desire of the government to entrust the monasteries with the supervision of forests. The forests belonging to monasteries and churches were supposed to serve as a source of their permanent income.

In the pre-reform and post-reform times, monasteries were endowed mainly with forest plots. In the middle of the 19th century, the monasteries invested their capital in urban land ownership and had a large amount of arable land and forests. 2,360,251 tithes was the total area of the church land, of which 230,266 tithes were unsuitable wastelands.

On the basis of the Highest order of the sovereign in 1833, the forest plots were assigned to: the Borisoglebsky Anosin Monastery, the Savvino-Storozhevsky Monastery (a total of 19 monasteries), which was noted in the report of the chief prosecutor in 1842.

33 tithes of convenient land for the clergy remained the norm for parish churches. Churches were allotted 99 acres of land in the case when the peasants had 15 acres. Churches located on state lands had 99.66 or 49.5 acres each, depending on the amount of land owned by the peasants. According to the data for 1856, in the Voronezh province of church and monastery lands, there were 328.9 acres, with the number of clergy in 17398 people.

In 1856, in the Voronezh province, the average size of church land property was 51.8 tithes of land, which is 6.3 tithes less than in European Russia and 8.3 tithes less than the all-Russian average.

Tendencies in the development of church landownership were diverse.

First, there was an increase in the amount of church land in the Voronezh province. From 1877 to 1905, church land ownership in the Voronezh diocese increased from 419.8 acres of land to 474.3 acres.

Secondly, monastic land ownership developed most actively. In the Voronezh province, monastic land ownership from 1877 to 1905. increased from 307.2 acres in 1877 to 653.3 acres in 1905.

Thirdly, in the second half of the 19th century, new trends clearly manifested themselves in the development of church land ownership, expressed in the development of private land ownership of the clergy. The clergy gradually began to turn into a class of landowners.

In 1878, in the Voronezh province, there were only 58 clergy landowners who owned 163.2 acres, and the amount of private property was 14.5 acres. In 1905, private landowners from the Voronezh clergy owned 376 acres of land, the average size of private property was 29.6 acres.

In the second half of the 19th century, the peasant question in the Russian Empire escalated to the limit. It should be said that, being shackled by the "vice" of the state mechanism and being under the control of the chief prosecutor, the clergy for a long time did not have the opportunity to directly express their negative attitude towards many negative phenomena that were associated with serfdom.

Nevertheless, starting from the era of Peter I, individual clerics repeatedly called on the nobles to treat their serfs with a human touch. The church constantly supported the peasants with prayers, who suffered from the greed and arbitrariness of the landowners. Often rural priests acted as an "arbiter" in the preparation of charters that determined mutual obligations, land ownership, as well as the rights of peasant communities and landlords.

However, the most important role in the abolition of serfdom was played by the Moscow Metropolitan Philaret Drozdov. He was the largest Orthodox theologian in Russia. It is significant that back in 1853, Filaret, relying on the negative experience of the abolition of serfdom in Austria, in his message to Archimandrite Anthony Medvedev spoke about the inadmissibility of freeing peasants without a land allotment. And it is no coincidence that it was to him, having rejected 2 unsuccessful projects, that Alexander II entrusted the drafting of a manifesto on the liberation of the peasants. Fully understanding the enormous significance of this act, Filaret did everything necessary to make the text of the manifesto accessible and understandable to the common people. He also tried to make it meet the ideals of Orthodoxy.

The state strictly controlled the economic activities of the clergy. The government made sure that the clergy did not have land with personally dependent peasants. Churches had only 33 tithes on the landlord's land, 2 or 3 tithes were under vegetable gardens, and the rest of the land was meadow and forest land.

In the 1860s-1880s, the process of reform was experienced not only by the peasantry and the nobility, but also by the clergy. The state understood what a huge influence the clergy had on the parishioners in their parishes, and therefore the government could no longer tolerate the plight of the clergy. Increasing the role of the clergy in the life of society, improving the material well-being of the clergy - this is the main task of church reforms (Bogoslovskij, 1880).

This was facilitated by an increase in church parishes that received salaries, an increase in salaries, a reduction in unprofitable parishes, as well as the creation of parish guardianships. As historical data show, in the provinces of the Central Chernozem region, among the clergy, a layer of landowners gradually formed, who owned private land property.

So, in the Voronezh province, for example, according to data from 1884, the priest V.D. Protopopov owned private land property in the amount of 149.5 acres of land. The basis of the estate V.D. Protopopov was 116 acres of arable land, in addition to this, 8 acres were occupied by the estate, 5 acres - a flood meadow, 15.5 acres - a pasture, and 5 acres of land were unusable.

Unfortunately, the statistics do not reflect the presence of Protopopov's own inventory and working cattle. Little is said about his economic activity. We only note that 10 acres of land were fertilized annually. An interesting fact is that V.D. Protopopov rented 40 acres for money, at the same time he rented out 5 acres of hayfields and 28.5 acres of arable land for 1,500 rubles and a garden for 200 rubles for 3 years.

In the Voronezh province there were facts of economic cooperation between the clergy and representatives of the nobility. In the Voronezh district there was a joint estate "Bor" of the priest S.P. Karpov and Baron V.D. Shening.

According to the statistics of 1884, these representatives of the clergy and nobility owned 1,271.8 acres of land. The estate of Karpov and Shening consisted of the following lands:

- 15.8 acres of manor land (more than 1%),
- 150 acres of arable land (or 12%),

- 75 acres of water meadow (or 5.9%),
- 500 acres (or 40%) timber,
- 531.7 acres of wood forest (or 42%).

There is no information about the availability of their own working equipment and horses from the owners. Although there is data on the number of small cattle at 165 heads, as well as 5 dairy cows and 5 calves. 4 hired workers constantly worked on the farm. It is likely that this farm was focused mainly on the production of livestock products.

Since it was difficult for the clergy to combine their main work in the church with agricultural labor, they sometimes asked their parishioners to help in harvesting or processing the crop. And yet, most of the clergy managed their own households. For example, the clergy of the Nicholas Church in the village of Igumenki, according to the data of 1892, had at its disposal 33 acres of land, "little capable of arable farming." The clergy themselves cultivated the land, and did not receive any funds for the upkeep of the clergy. Therefore, the clergy led the poorest existence.

According to 4 provinces of the Central agricultural region (these included the Kursk and Voronezh provinces), in 1877 there lived 1167 landowners from the clergy, who owned 531.3 acres of land. In the Kursk province, according to information for 1877, there were 435 landowners from the clergy, they owned 299 acres of land, and 14 acres were owned by the clergy. In the Voronezh province there were 58 landowners who owned 163.3 acres of land, and the average size of property was 18.2 acres. In total, according to the Kursk and Voronezh provinces, there were 493 owners in them, or 42.2% of the total number of owners. The clergy of the post-reform period were mainly engaged in buying up landed property. In the Central Black Earth region, representatives of the clergy acted as buyers in 1131 transactions, and as sellers in 464. 261.8 acres of land were purchased and 698.9 acres were sold. The value of the acquired land property was 10,412 rubles, and the value of the property sold was 33,893 rubles. From 1871 to 1876, two cases of the sale of their own land by the clergy were recorded, the buyers, in all likelihood, were also persons of the clergy, and land was acquired 96.7 acres.

Thus, church and monastic land ownership in Russia in the XIX - early XX centuries. developed dynamically, aided by assistance from private individuals and the state. It should be noted that by the end of the 1870s, the monasteries of the Central Chernozem region were large land owners, which created great potential for the further development of the monastic economy in the Chernozem region.

By the end of the 19th century, two distinct development trends emerged in the development of church land ownership. First, the transformation of church land ownership and land use and its adaptation to the new bourgeois conditions of functioning began. On the all-estate land market, representatives of the Church acted primarily as buyers, and secondarily as sellers. Secondly, the dynamic growth of monastic land ownership began, the monastic economy was rebuilt on a capitalist basis. The church land not involved in its own economy was rented out. For example, the Kursk (Kurskaya) Blagoveshchenskaya Church (tserkov') rented 79 acres of land for 300 rubles a year to single-palaces from the village of Lomanova.

Thus, we can conclude that this clergy did not need workers at all, but rented out all the land.

Church land was rented in 10 out of 12 districts of the Voronezh province. If we analyze the county data on the lease of church lands, it should be noted that the largest number of plots of church property leased was registered in 1887 in Biryuchensky district (49 plots or 26% of the total). The second place was occupied by the Ostrogozhsky district (37 sites or 19%), the third place - Bobrovsky district (28 sites, or 14%), and the fourth - Valuysky district (27 sites, or 13%). The lowest figures for the lease of church land property were noted in Bogucharsky district - 8 plots or 4%, as well as in Nizhnedevitsky - 4% and Novokhopyorsky district - 1.5%.

The rent for 1 tithe of church land in the Voronezh province, according to the Central Statistical Committee of the Ministry of Internal Affairs, was 9 rubles 66 kopecks for 1 tithe of arable land and 6 rubles 33 kopecks for 1 tithe of meadow land.

By comparison, in the Oryol province, the rent for 1 tithe of arable land was 11 rubles 90 kopecks, and for 1 tithe of meadow land - 7 rubles 38 kopecks. In 1887, only 7 plots of monastery land were rented in the Voronezh province. The total area of monastic land leased was only 422 acres, or a little over 10% of the total amount of monastic lands in the Voronezh province. Monastic lands were rented in the Zadonsk district out of 458 acres of land owned by monasteries, a land plot of 50 acres of land was rented, which accounted for 11.3% of the total amount of leased monastic property. The average size of the monastic plot rented in the district was 50 acres, respectively. In the Korotoyak Uyezd, monasteries leased 372 acres, which accounted for 88.7% of the total leased land of monasteries.

In the Voronezh province there were landowners from the clergy, who leased their own estates in full force. Priest Semyon Fedorov at the village of Sitnikovo in the Ostrogozhsky district of the Voronezh province rented out his estate of 60 acres of arable land, and Kozlovskaya Matryona Semyonovna, the priest's widow, rented out her estate in full force near the village of Yurasovka. The size of the estate was 96.7 acres of land: 80 acres of arable land (or 83%), 4 acres of water meadows (or 4.2%) and 12.7 acres of forest and shrubs (or 13%) .

A similar situation was observed in the Kursk province. According to data for 1901, almost 20% of the total amount of monastic land and only 4.5% of the total amount of church land were leased in the Kursk province. The reason that hindered the development of the lease of church lands in Russia (and in particular in the Voronezh and Kursk provinces) was its unprofitability.

As church researcher T.G. Leontieva, it was difficult to lease the land divided among the members of the clergy into even strips of the best, average and worst land in the conditions of low market activity of the peasants, who were more concerned with the problems of elementary economic survival.

The development of the lease of church land was hindered by a significant lease fund of noble land. The limited opportunities for leasing land made the leasing of church lands unprofitable for the clergy themselves, so the degree of its development in the Voronezh province was rather low. The lease of monastic lands, in comparison with the lease of church lands, was more developed. In particular, in 1887, in the Voronezh province, 10% of the land was leased, and in Kursk, according to 1901 data, — 20% of the land.

However, for the monastic economy with its dynamically developing land ownership, the percentage of land leased was not high. A significant number of monastic lands were either simply not used in the economy, or used with inadequate efficiency. Based on the above statistics, we can draw the following conclusion: the lease of church and monastery lands in the Voronezh and Kursk provinces in the 19th and early 20th centuries was not sufficiently developed. Statistical data for 1887 for the Voronezh Governorate show that 8.7% of church lands and more than 10% of monastic lands were leased. The average size of church and monastic property in the provinces of the Central Chernozem region was 703.2 acres. In the Kursk province, the average size of church land property was 175.7 acres and was almost 4 times lower than the average for monasteries and churches in the Central Black Earth provinces. In the Voronezh province, the average size of the landed property of the Church was 365 acres and was more than 1.8 times less than the average for the provinces of the Central Chernozem Region. The price of monastic land, according to data for 1890, in the Kursk province was 786,408 rubles. In the Voronezh province, church land was estimated lower - only

543,585 rubles, and according to this indicator, the Voronezh province was inferior to both the Kursk and Oryol dioceses.

It can be noted that in no county of the Kursk province the size of the possessions of the clergy did not exceed 1000 acres. In 10 of the 15 counties, where 205 owners were registered, the size of the clergy's possessions did not exceed 400 acres. In 4 districts, the private property of the clergy did not exceed 200 tithes, in another four - the possessions of the clergy did not exceed 400 tithes.

For example, the Kazan Church in the village of Dvizhkovo, Kursk province, had an allotment of 46 acres, 16 of which were unusable, and the remaining 30 acres were in the use of the clergy themselves. The Dormition Church in the village of Avdotyevo had at its disposal 155 acres of land, which was cultivated by the clergy himself. The large size of the allotment of the above church is offset by the poor quality of the land. In the "Clear Statement" of this church, it is noted that the church land was partly "clay, and partly swampy." The Archangel'skaya Church in the village of Gosyukhino used 69 tithes of land, and the Voskresenskaya Church in the village of Polyanskoe owned 56 tithes. You can also note the Ascension Church in the village of Kozlovka, Voronezh province. The only document describing the Ascension Church is the Klirovye Vedomosti of 1911. The construction of the Ascension Church was completed in 1906, and in February 1907 services began. The parish owned 545 houses, in which 4277 people lived. A priest and a psalmist served in this parish. At the temple there were 2 acres of manor land, the houses were built at the expense of the parishioners. The church did not have arable land, instead the rural parishioners paid a parish of 440 rubles. By the beginning of the 20th century, there was an increase in church lands in the provinces of the Central Black Earth Region. The reason for the growth of church landownership was the number of parishes. After all, each newly opened church received a land allotment. The largest number of Churches had property ranging from 50 to 300 acres of land. In the Voronezh province, 9 out of 16 monasteries owned land, the size of which did not exceed 300 acres. The land area of more than 500 acres was managed by 5 monasteries-owners. Of these, the property of 4 ranged from 600 to 700 acres of land. Church income from agriculture amounted to 9,030,000 rubles, and monastic - 1,207,813 rubles. Church lands were valued at 116,195,000 rubles, and monastic lands - 26,595,000. Monastic landownership in the public consciousness did not cause protest, but this issue was viewed differently from the standpoint of the Church (Ershov, 2019) .

The practical life of monks has shown that their economic activity has a corrupting effect on the inner side of their lives. Only a few monasteries succeeded in organically incorporating agricultural and commercial activities into the routine of monastic life. The Orthodox Church in Russia owned 3 million hectares of land as property. A sign of the state's respect for millions of believing citizens and real material support for the Church was the transfer of land to the ownership of the temple. The land issue had a huge impact on the life of all the people of Russia and on its economy. In Russia, and in other countries of the world that are going through a time of change, the land issue is very important. The settlement of land relations affected many citizens, so the Church decided to take part in the discussion of this problem. From the beginning of the 19th century, a policy was pursued in Russia to return economic power to the Church as a religious organization. Emperor Alexander I by his Decrees of 1805 and 1810 made the first contribution to this process. The decrees of Alexander I played a huge role in strengthening the economic potential of the Russian Orthodox Church. State guardianship and assistance to the Church by the state continued in the 19th century until the 1890s.

CONCLUSION

The practice of allocating land to the clergy, which developed in pre-reform Russia, reduced the high social status of the clergy. Parish priests believed that their vocation was to serve God, and not to engage in peasant labor on earth. The clergy could not devote enough time to work on their own land, since most of the time the priests had to serve in the temple and perform all sorts of "requirements": weddings, baptisms, funerals. Therefore, the economy in the clergy was less efficient than the peasant economy. In the economic activity of the Churches and monasteries, two trends were observed: the development of the lease of monastic lands and the development of their own economy with the use of hired labor.

Churches and monasteries sought to create their own processing enterprises, such as mills, oil mills. Monastic farms were forced to switch to a capitalist basis for managing their economy. The reason for this transition was the lack of state funding for the Russian Orthodox Church and monasteries. The whole system of monastic life was closed, it had the opposite of everything "worldly", which did not contribute to the normal development and capitalization of the church and monastic economy, which was less efficient compared to the private economy.

REFERENCES

Anthony, St. (2003). *Glorified Saints. Saints, New Martyrs, Rev. Prince 1.* Academic Press.

Archive of the Russian Ethnographic Museum (AREM) F. 7. Op.1. D. 1140. Ethnographic description of the Oryol province. L. 21.

Bogoslovskij, N. G. (1860). *A practical look at the life of a priest. Father's letters to his son.* Academic Press.

Ershov, B., Novikov, Y. N., Voytovich, D., Ermilova, O., Dushkin, O., & Lubkin, Y. (2019). Physical culture in formation of spiritual education of young people in Russia. In *The European Proceedings of Social and Behavioural Sciences Complex. Research Institute named after Kh. I. Ibragimov.* Russian Academy of Sciences.

Ershov, B., Novikov, Y.N., Voytovich, D., Ermilova, O., Dushkin, O., & Lubkin, Y. (2019). Physical culture in formation of spiritual education of young people in Russia. *The European Proceedings of Social & Behavioural Sciences,* 3648-3653.

Ershov, B. A., & Lubkin, Y. Y. (2016). The activities of the Russian Orthodox Church in countering extremism and terrorism in modern Russia. Historical, philosophical, political and legal sciences, cultural studies and art history. *Questions of Theory and Practice, 11*(73), 97–99.

Ershov, B. A., Nebolsin, V. A., & Solovieva, S. R. (2020). Higher education in technical universities of Russia. *7th International Conference on Education and Social Sciences. Abstracts & Proceedings,* 55-58.

Kartashev, A. V. (2000). *Essays on the history of the Russian church* (Vol. M). Eksmo-Press.

Maslov, I. (1995). *The Prelate Tikhon of Zadonsky and his doctrine of salvation.* Boxwood.

Veselovsky, G. (1886). Historical sketch of the city of Voronezh. 1586-1886. Voronezh: Veselovsky Publishing House.

Chapter 14

Missionary Activity of the Church

ABSTRACT

In the provinces there were changes in the mentality and lifestyle of broad sections of society, which occurred under the influence of the "great reforms" and industrialization in Russia. The spread of education and the liberalization of social life created the conditions for spiritual emancipation and the destruction of traditional isolation, the spread of otkhodnichestvo, and the emergence of factories, and factories contributed to the spread of new religious ideas. Missionary work in the Russian Orthodox Church was internal and external: the internal carried out work directed against schismatics and sectarians, and the external was oriented towards foreigners inside Russia and outside it.

INTRODUCTION

In the XIX - early XX centuries Russian Orthodox missionary work spread throughout the vast Russian Empire. Russian missionaries did a lot of work with the small peoples of the North, the Far East and Siberia to convert them to Orthodoxy. During this historical period, the country was being modernized, and there was also a crisis of traditional values and the growth of sectarianism, which is consonant with the present. Missionary work in the Russian Orthodox Church was internal and external: the internal carried

DOI: 10.4018/978-1-6684-4915-8.ch014

out work directed against schismatics and sectarians; and the external was oriented towards foreigners inside Russia and outside it.

Before the revolution of 1917, the Voronezh province was the center of the old Russian sectarianism. The new sectarianism was fundamentally different from the old Russian sects, which arose spontaneously, did not have a dogmatic system, and were distinguished by mysticism. Such, for example, are «khlysty» that appeared in the Voronezh province at the beginning of the 19th century.

In 1803, a report was sent to the governor of Voronezh from the Bogucharsky district police officer, which states that the missionary Mikhail Granatovsky arrived in the Shiryaevo settlement of the Bogucharsky district, who turned to the volost foreman with a request to collect «khlysty» for a religious conversation. Khlysty gathered in the composition of 18-20 people in the premises of the zemstvo school. The purpose of the conversation was to strengthen the Orthodox faith and to explain to this sect their false doctrine. Riots began in the school building, which were provoked by representatives of the sect. The district police officer reported that the perpetrators were brought to justice. This was reported to the Kharkiv Judicial Chamber and the Ostrogozhsky District Court. Subbotniks, who stood apart and were the heirs of the Novgorod "heresy of the Judaizers", subsequently finally converted to Judaism. At the beginning of the 19th century, in the Voronezh province, they settled in the village of Ilyinka.

In 1890, in an article by M. Bylov, which was published in the Voronezh Diocesan Vedomosti, reports appeared about the Subbotniky sect. The article uses archival materials from the fund of the Voronezh Spiritual Consistory.

The peasants of the villages of Mechetki, Puzevo, Gvazda of Bobrovsky and Pavlovsky districts of the Voronezh province, interrogated in the consistory in 1802, described their "superstition" as follows: "do not worship holy icons; do not go to God's Church; not to confess and not to take communion, but to believe in God in the soul; read psalms; do not eat pork; to honor Saturday, but not to honor Sunday; Don't wear crosses."

The "Subbotniky" completely rejected Orthodoxy and Christianity and built their doctrine and life according to the Old Testament. They did not know Jewish prayers, and therefore, instead of prayers, they read those psalms that could be found in Orthodox books. Thus, a large and significant Jewish community was formed in Russia.

The Synod, local diocesan bishops paid special attention to subbotniks, so the Russian archives contain a lot of material about sectarians.

The funds of the Russian State Historical Archive contain one of these documents. The Ministry of Spiritual Affairs and Public Education conducted an investigation into the relationship of the Jew Leib Klodnya, a resident of the city of Pinsk, with Efim Lukyanchenkov, a subbotnik peasant from the Voronezh province. These people, interrogated by the St. Petersburg police in 1822, were suspected that L. Klodnya was teaching, and E. Lukyanchenkov was accepting the "Jewish teaching about faith." Numerous manuscripts containing translations of Jewish prayers and information about Jewish holidays fully confirmed the suspicions.

The main culprit, L. Klodnya, was sentenced to exile in Siberia under police supervision, and E. Lukyanchenkov had to be "confirmed" in Orthodoxy by the rector of the Kazan Cathedral in St. Petersburg. The Synod demanded that experienced clergymen be sent to the villages infected with "Jewishness", capable of leading hardened hearts to repentance, to meekness, humility and prudence.

Prince (knyaz') A. Golitsyn, the Minister of Spiritual Affairs and Public Education, also reported that Jews in the Voronezh province were spreading their teachings among the local population, for which Alexander I issued a decree "On the incontinence of Jews in the domestic service of Christians." Count V. Kochubey, the Minister of the Interior, in 1823 submitted to the Cabinet of Ministers a report on the "Subbotniky", of which there were about 20 thousand people in different regions of Russia, and on what measures were being taken to combat this sect (Ershov, 2017).

In 1825, at his suggestion, the Synod issued a decree against the spread of the Jewish subbotnik sect. According to this Decree, all distributors of heresy were immediately drafted into the army, and those unfit for military service were exiled to Siberia for a settlement; Jews were expelled from those counties in which the sect existed, and in the future they were not allowed to be there.

At the beginning of the 19th century, the Russian government made an attempt to get an idea of the extent of the spread of the "old faith" in the empire. In 1812, special commissions managed to collect relevant information on some Russian regions, among which was the Voronezh province. 8776 people were listed in the "schismatic statements" here. However, the data obtained concerned only those who openly admitted their falling away from the official religion. In addition, it was not possible to obtain more reliable information then, both because of the inefficient accounting system and the lack of clear criteria for who should be considered old-believers («starovery»).

An analysis of the results of the 1812 census shows that census takers often confused representatives of Russian sects with the old-believers.

A systematic collection of data on the number of old-believers was organized under Nicholas I. In 1827, the government received data on the number of "schismatics" in all Russian provinces. According to them, the old-believers lived in the Voronezh province - 11049. In the Oryol province there were: schismatics accepting the priesthood, 7033 people of different sexes; 644 people who do not accept the priesthood, of different sexes.

However, both this information and the data received by the government in the next quarter of a century could not be called reliable either. On the contrary, the tendency to underestimate the numbers clearly intensified, since the emperor wanted to see victory over the schism and the triumph of official Orthodoxy as one of the results of his reign. Both the police and the clergy were interested in concealing the true number of "schismatics", which resulted in, in the words of P.N. Milyukov, "a ridiculous contradiction between official figures and reality." This situation is very clearly characterized by the fact that the author of the "History of the Ministry of Internal Affairs" N.V. Varadinov, citing in his book information on the number of old-believers in the Russian provinces for 1839 and 1841, does not even try to sum up the overall result, arguing that the statistics are completely unreliable.

Official data for the Oryol province during the entire 19th century consistently point to a figure equal to approximately 7,000 old-believers of different classes and sexes. It is likely that this information is inaccurate, however, at the same time, it cannot be said that the true number of explicit old-believers in the province was undoubtedly greater.

Considering these factors, the total number of old-believers in the Oryol province during the reign of Nicholas I was approximately 2 times larger, but the most possible today is the number of 10-11 thousand people of both sexes of various classes. It is currently not possible to establish the number of "secret" old-believers. More true figures could only be presented by the clergy. However, the documents sent by them to the spiritual consistory have not been preserved today. The materials of the Oryol province show that the fundamental mass of cases on schismatics in the 19th century falls on the era of the reign of Nicholas I. At the same time, the maximum number of Emperor's Decrees prohibiting the activities of the old-believers was also noted. Later it turned out that there were much more bespopovtsy in the province.

In 1860, followers of Novopomortsy, Fedoseevtsy, Filippovtsy lived in 75 densely populated areas of the Oryol province. Therefore, the local administration: the governor, police chief, police chiefs, and other officials unintentionally contributed to the spread of the old-believers, concealing from the Ministry of Internal Affairs the true number of "Old Orthodox".

During the reign of Nicholas I, the old-believers were constantly subjected to persecution of their faith in all its manifestations. While issuing several laws each year aimed at eliminating the old-believers, the government, however, could not achieve their strict implementation on the ground. On the example of the Oryol province, it can be said that the local administration played a significant role in the general religious policy of the central government. That is why the peak of the persecution of schismatics in the provinces of the Russian Empire during the reign of Nicholas I falls on different years. This is due, first of all, to the more or less loyal attitude of the governors towards the old-believers. Thus, most of the laws that limited the rights of schismatics were adopted in the 1830s. However, in the Oryol province, these laws began to be applied only in the 1840s.

If one statesman considered "humble suggestions" to be the main thing in his work and acted cautiously, fearing to harm the common cause with rigidity and perseverance, then another, carried out the same decisions and laws of the central government, immediately punishing the "guilty" of "spreading the split" and demanded the same from his subordinates.

Every year, submitting reports to the capital on the number of old-believers in the province, the governor of the Oryol province reported to the Ministry of the Interior about the same number of schismatics. At the same time, this figure was compiled by artificially reducing the number of old-believers in one village and increasing it in another.

During the first quarter of the 19th century, the number of bespopovtsy in the province continued to grow at the expense of landless and destitute peasants. This is indicated by cases of declining people to the old-believers. First in one, then in another county of the province, the peasants gradually turned into priesthood with complete families, and sometimes even entire villages, as happened in the villages of Bolshaya Kolchevka, Rechitsa, Kolchevsky Vyselki.

Only in the late XIX - early XX centuries. from Orel to the old-believers' settlements of the province began to send special fellow-religious clergy for missionary purposes. Here, priests held services in Orthodox churches, read prayers from church books.

On February 21, 1871, an Orthodox missionary society was founded in the diocese of the Oryol province, which took care of maintaining among the inhabitants of the Oryol diocese sympathy for the sacred tasks of domestic missions and to attract donations in sufficient quantities to satisfy the needs and requirements of these missions. However, in the Oryol diocese, missionary activity did not reach a large scale, since the national and confessional composition of the population was homogeneous.

In 1853, the Decree "On bringing to the notice of the current situation of the schism" was issued, in which the provincial authorities were instructed to reorganize the system of registration of the old-believers in order to "bring to the exact knowledge of the current situation of the schism." The result of the expanded campaign was the intensification of the collection of information about the Old Believers in the Russian regions, as well as a slight increase in statistical figures reflecting the number of "zealots of antiquity". In the Voronezh province, the required statistics appeared only in 1857. According to the reports submitted, in 1857 there were 935,012 old-believers in the Voronezh province.

Such persecution of the old-believers, which was under Nicholas I, ceased under Alexander II. At that time, their number ranged from 8 to 12 million people. Liberal press in 1850-1860 proposed to legalize the "schism", considering the persecution of the old-believers as illegal if they do not violate the laws of the state. The liberals believed that repressive measures against schismatics lead in practice to the opposite results: the persecuted become hardened, conflicts arise, and these measures are ineffective, since brute force cannot be used against the faith of ideas and doctrine.

In the second half of the 19th century, the need for a deep study of the schism and the need for knowledgeable missionaries prompted the Holy Synod to establish missionary departments in the academies and seminaries. Their successive discovery began in 1855. These departments were formed from students of the highest course, as well as from students who had completed the course, but had not yet received a position. The course of lectures of these departments included:

1. the history of the schism - its appearance and spread,
2. a review of books and manuscripts honored by schismatics, as well as those written in his refutation,
3. apologetics of the Orthodox Church, i.e. refutation of schismatic doctrines,
4. pastoral pedagogy, explaining to students how they should behave with schismatics.

At the end of the course, students were sent to places inhabited by schismatics.

In 1858, in a report to Alexander II, Minister of the Interior S.S. Lanskoy for the first time officially raised the question of legalizing the split. However, it was not until 1864 that a committee was formed to revise the secession law. According to the "Rules", approved by the emperor in the same year, most of the old-believers' interpretations and consents were legalized, they were given the right to freely conduct their worship and travel abroad. Old-believer's metric records acquired legal force. The old-believers were allowed to organize their own literacy schools, hold public positions and perform icon painting for their own needs. However, these rights did not extend to whips, eunuchs, runners, wanderers who did not recognize church and secular authority (Perevozchikova, 2017).

In the Voronezh province, among the population were landowners who did not consider themselves Old Believers, but did not recognize the Orthodox Church either. In this regard, we can refer to the correspondence with district police officers on religious issues, which contains a message from Bishop Anastassy of Voronezh and Zadonsk to the office of the Voronezh Governor about the allocation of material resources to the priest of the settlement of Elenovka, Bogucharsky district, Pavel Ageev, and funds to the parochial school located in this freedom. These funds are necessary for the struggle of the priest P. Ageev with the corrupting influence of the landowner Vladimir Chertkov, a follower of the teachings of Leo Tolstoy (1828-1910).

Archival documents say that the landowner V. Chertkov ridicules the clergy, rejects the church, did not take the oath of allegiance to the emperor, and does not fulfill the duties assigned to him when communicating with parishioners. In view of such a dangerous situation, it is highly desirable to protect the clergy from any material dependence on the parishioners, in order, on the one hand, to attract the best forces to the composition of the clergy, and on the other hand, to give the clergy the opportunity for greater religious and moral influence on the parishioners.

In this regard, in 1898, the decision of the Holy Synod was adopted that the clergy of this parish were allocated a state salary in the amount of 550 rubles, in addition, a salary of 300 rubles for the deacon and 200 rubles for the psalmist was established.

Old Belief («staroveriye»), being an oppressed religious denomination, according to the logic of the highest authorities, should have been steadily reduced. However, in practice this did not happen. Therefore, the information that was submitted from the field at the request of various higher authorities and on which statistics were based, and in the second half of the 19th century, was often greatly distorted downward. First of all, this applies to parish priests who are responsible for collecting initial information. The growth in the number of old-believers in their parishes could become the basis for accusations of "condoning the schism" and a severe reprimand from the church authorities. Therefore, they, and after them the deans of church districts, most often wrote that "the schism in the territory under their jurisdiction is not growing numerically," giving information from last year or close to them. In addition, only those "zealots of antiquity" were officially recognized as old-believers, over whom no sacraments were performed by the dominant church. The old-believers, baptized in the parish church or married there, in order to legalize marriage, were considered "Orthodox" according to church books. This situation, taking into account the old-believers, characteristic of many provinces of the empire, led to the preservation in Russia of a large number of "unrecorded" old-believers.

In one of the documents of the Voronezh missionaries of 1903, for example, it is said that "in addition to officially registered schismatics, there are many secret ones within the diocese, who, although they are listed as Orthodox, think and live in a schismatic way." Usually the "religious authority" of the old-believers was supported by their way of life. The authorities, which until 1905 struggled with the split, nevertheless recognized the "reliability" of the old-believers, their hard work, sobriety and obedience to all government orders, as stated in the archival materials of the Voronezh province.

In the second half of the 19th century, historians, publicists, and public figures began to pay attention to the fundamental differences in the way of life of the Old Believers and the official Orthodox subjects of the empire. Schism researchers in the 1880s wrote that the predecessors paid attention only to the difference in the rituals of the old-believers and official Orthodoxy, and did not want to see that the worldview of the old-believers was built on other principles, compared to Orthodoxy.

According to the materials of the Russian State Historical Archive for 1850-1860, "the peasants who lived next to the old-believers considered the "schismatic faith" to be holy, truly Christian, and only in this faith one can be saved, and that this faith is worldly" . Orthodox peasants said: "We believe in Christ, but we are worldly, vain people ... Christians are those who pray according to the old faith, not in our way, but we have no time."

In 1878, one of the peasants of the Voronezh province, in response to an "anti-schismatic" speech, told an Orthodox missionary that "if it weren't for the old-believers, we wouldn't even go to church. And when you look at the old-believers, you become ashamed of yourself.

On the one hand, thanks to the Old Believers, Orthodox traditions were preserved in the villages of the Voronezh province, and on the other hand, religious "zealots of antiquity" irritated the Orthodox Church, which took measures for more scrupulous spiritual familiarization of parishioners.

In 1906, an appeal was published in the Voronezh province to spread the Orthodox faith among non-believers. The appeal said that many pagans live inside Russia in the Volga region, in the Caucasus, in the Crimea. In Moscow, at the suggestion of Bishop Innokenty, an Orthodox Missionary Society was formed, which helped preach Christianity in distant Siberian lands. Thus, in particular, according to the latest report of the Orthodox Missionary Society, about 2,000 people were converted to Christianity. Bishop Innokenty sent a petition to all the dioceses of the Russian Empire for a donation of funds for the spread of the Orthodox faith. The petition was sent to the Voronezh Spiritual Consistory, which decided to establish a plate collection in all churches of the Voronezh province.

One of the Voronezh missionaries in the second half of the 19th century was Archpriest Nikolai Fomich Okolovich, who was born on May 4, 1863 in the village of Uzhlyatin, Vitebsk district, Vitebsk province, in the family of a psalm reader. In 1877 he graduated from the theological school in Vitebsk, and in 1883 from the Vitebsk Theological Seminary in the first category. From 1883 to 1887, N. F. Okolovich studied at the Theological Academy in Moscow and graduated from it with a degree in theology.

From 1907 to 1912 N.F. Okolovich becomes the rector of the theological seminary in the city of Voronezh and is the editor-in-chief of Diocesan Gazette.

In 1911, in Voronezh, under the leadership of Archpriest N.F. Okolovich, missionary and pedagogical courses were organized for the clergy and teachers of parochial schools.

Archpriest N.F. Okolovich was chairman of the Voronezh Diocesan Missionary Council from October 14, 1908 until his departure from Voronezh. As the Voronezh diocesan missionary Lev Zakharovich Kuntsevich assures, the missionary council under the leadership of Archpriest N.F. Okolovich functioned productively. Many regretted the departure of the missionary leader from Voronezh, who was sympathetic and cordial, and he was able to unite the members of the council into one family who worked in the name of a common cause.

The period of the 19th century, according to church historians, was controversial, but against the background of unfavorable trends, one can single out the widespread development of the missionary and translation activities of the Orthodox Church. The missionary and translation activity of the Orthodox Church was the main sign of the reign of Metropolitan Philaret Drozdov, when theological education became as fundamental as secular education, and a productive dialogue emerged between the two educational systems. In the era of Filaret, significant changes took place in the relations between secular science and the Orthodox Church, which made these relations constructive and purposeful. At this time, new works of Orthodox missionaries, archimandrites Pallady Kafarov, Gury Karpov, Makariy Glukharev, Avvakum the Honest, appeared, who combined theology with folklore, ethnography, linguistics, and natural science.

However, along with the successes of Orthodox missionary work, difficulties arise in the educational activities of the Church during this period, which are due to the loss of Orthodox worldview foundations by society; the spread of ideas hostile to Christianity; the activation of sects whose activities were directed against the policy of the Russian bureaucracy. Against the missionaries Archimandrites Macarius Glukharev and Iakinf Bichurin, as well as other prominent biblical translators who independently engaged in the interpretation and translation of the Holy Scriptures, the synodal bureaucracy used repression, which interfered with the dialogue between the Church and secular science. But this dialogue was not interrupted, the largest scientific works belonging to theology and linguistics helped to overcome the emerging problems.

In 1869, Kazan published the "Grammar of the Altai language", the authors of which were a young hieromonk who served in the Altai Spiritual Mission, the future Metropolitan of Moscow Macarius Nevsky, and orientalist N.I. Ilminsky is a teacher at Kazan University and the Kazan Theological Academy.

The content of this work was unusual, as evidenced by the proximity of these names on the cover of the book. This book was intended not only for missionaries and the church reader, but also for secular science, because the future metropolitan was one of the first to get acquainted with the people of Altai, mysterious to Europeans. "Grammar of the Altai language" summarized the experience of the dialogue between secular science and the Church, and this dialogue led to new frontiers.

Representatives of pre-Soviet historiography F.M. Starikov, V.N. Shishonko, M.V. Tolstoy also explored the missionary activities of the Church. M.V. Tolstoy believed that missionary work encountered difficulties because of the savagery and stubbornness of the pagans; he put on the "holy" fathers of the Church the halo of martyrdom. V.N. Shishonko said that the policy of the Church was not always peaceful, but in the 19th century the clergy excluded violence from means and methods. F.M. Starikov noted that the "foreigners" formally accepted Orthodoxy and only for the sake of the state policy of Orthodoxy, but in fact they preserved the faith of the fathers.

Usually the missionary activity of the Russian Orthodox Church was consecrated, giving a description of sectarian or old-believer movements, positively evaluating the missionary activity of the clergy. Scientific works of P.S. Smirnov and A. Rozhdestvensky were devoted to the analysis of the sectarian movement and the fight against it.

It should be noted that the missionary activity of the Church was well organized in the Tambov province. For the first time, Bishop Feofilakt Shiryaev became interested in this issue at the general diocesan level, setting himself the task of "curbing sectarianism and schism in the diocese", starting with collecting information about sectarian teachings, their location and number, which was important, and this accumulated information helped Bishop Feofilakt Shiryaev publish a manual for the clergy, which gave advice on how to deal with the Molokans.

Vladyka Theophylact waged a real war with the Molokans and Dukhobors, who at that time were quite numerous in the diocese. He collected information about the sectarians and found out that they settled mainly in four districts of the diocese. In these counties, Vladyka ordered 35 of the most capable priests to carry out missionary work, and to help in this matter, he demanded additional salaries from the treasury.

Bishop Theophylact in the fight against schismatics and sectarians, in addition to pastoral influence, turned to the government for help. He demanded the eviction of the Dukhobors and Molokans from the diocese, as a result of which the sectarians were evicted from some villages to the Taurida province and the Caucasus. We can note Bishop Nikolai Dobrokhotov, who tried to bring the lost into the Church with the help of persuasion and preaching, as a result of which the dissatisfied Tambov governor Bulgakov, accusing the bishop of inaction and indulgence to sectarians, complained about the bishop to the Synod.

But the real executor of the decision of the Synod on the organization of missionary brotherhoods in the dioceses of the Russian Empire was considered Bishop Pallady Raev. Prior to the opening of the Brotherhood, a missionary society already existed in Tambov, which was engaged in raising funds for missionary activities in Russia.

On October 24, 1874, Bishop Pallady informed the Tambov governor N.M. Garting that in order to fight against schismatics and Mohammedans, he decided to organize a missionary brotherhood, and the draft charter of the Brotherhood was to be drawn up by Archpriest G.V. Khitrov. The ceremonial opening of the Brotherhood took place in the bishop's house on May 11, 1875, the new institution became known as the Tambov Kazan-Mother of God Missionary Brotherhood. The charter, approved on May 5, 1875, defined the tasks of the Brotherhood, which were supposed to help the conversion of Mohammedans to Orthodoxy; attract sectarians and Old Believers to Orthodoxy; assist new converts in spiritual and moral education and the improvement of religious morality.

For this, agents were appointed to collect information, missionaries, libraries and schools were opened. The missionary society received membership dues and donations on subscription lists, half of these contributions were used by the activities of this Brotherhood. Any person could join the Brotherhood, there were no restrictions on gender and estate. Members were active, the contribution of which was annually not less than 3 rubles; and employees whose annual contribution was less than 3 rubles. At the general meeting, once a year, a Council was elected to manage the current affairs of the Brotherhood.

In 1885, the Brotherhood consisted of 50 associates, 85 temporary active, 16 permanent and 8 honorary members. In 1898, the Brotherhood held the first missionary congress, which was attended by the Voronezh missionary T.S. Rozhdestvensky and the representative of the Chief Prosecutor V.M. Skvortsov, a famous missionary and Orthodox publicist. At the congress, it was decided to divide the entire diocese into 7 missionary districts, increase the number of diocesan missionaries, open reading rooms and libraries, reduce prices for paintings and brochures, and hold missionary meetings annually.

The funds that were collected for the activities of the Brotherhood made it possible to send missionaries to the city of Tambov, as well as to the Tambov district, Elatomsky district, Spassky district, Shatsky district. Edinoverie parishes were created in the village of Pokas, Elatomsk district, in the village of Kirillovo, Spassky district, in the village of Lakhmytovka, Kirsanov district, the number of co-religionists in 1910 was more than 3,000 people.

Thus, it can be noted that the activity of the Brotherhood was positive. But the result of this activity is difficult to determine. The main thing was that the number of non-Orthodox in the diocese did not increase, and in 1911, according to the report of the Tambov governor, it was approximately 19,000 people, which, with a population of three million people in the province, was negligible, and this is the merit of the Brotherhood.

The Kursk Diocesan Brotherhood of St. Theodosius of the Caves was established in 1891, it was located in the building of the seminary. The main tasks of the Brotherhood were "the establishment and dissemination among the people of religious and moral education in the spirit of the Orthodox

Church", "the weakening of the schism, the conversion of schismatics to Orthodoxy and protection from the harmful influence of the schism of the Orthodox population of the Kursk diocese."

From the reporting information of the Brotherhood it is clear that in order to achieve its goal, the Brotherhood was active. In the cities and villages of the province, Sunday and festive readings of religious content were constantly organized by representatives of the Brotherhood, and local parish priests who graduated from seminaries also acted as lecturers. The Brotherhood distributed "anti-schismatic" literature, organized public disputes with the Old Believers, and an "anti-schismatic" library was created to debate the schism. Every year the Brotherhood spent about 10,000 rubles to fight the schism.

Members of the Brotherhood and diocesan missionaries, fighting the schism, tried to make the schismatics recognize the authority of the local clergy, and at least occasionally visited the parish church. Sometimes, mainly in villages where sectarians or old-believers were in the minority, this was possible.

In 1892, the Bishop of Kursk reported to the Synod that in the village of Chernaya Olkha, Sudzhansky district, thanks to missionaries and the local priest S. Titov, the number of schismatics had decreased over the past few years from 350 to 158 people.

In 1908, the Brotherhood of the Mother of God of the Sign was formed with a missionary orientation. This Brotherhood organized and coordinated the fight against the old-believers. Diocesan missionaries were now required to follow the instructions of his Council.

According to the instructions of the new Brotherhood, missionary circles began to be organized in the localities, acting constantly, these circles included the priests of this district. The priests had to keep track of the number of schismatics, their "strength" and influence on the Orthodox, and take measures to weaken this influence - deliver missionary sermons, visit the homes of "doubting" parishioners, distribute "anti-schismatic" and anti-sectarian literature, which was supplied by the Znamensko-Mother of God Brotherhood («Znamensko-Bogorodichnoye Bratstvo»).

Since 1907, in order to prepare such missionaries for polemics with the Old Believers, the Brotherhood began to create missionary courses for the clergy in different places of the diocese (Belgorod, Glinskaya Pustyn', Kursk, Rylsk). Since 1908, the Brotherhood began to publish small magazines - "Missionary Leaflets" and distribute them free of charge to the people. These magazines published church stories that raised the authority of the church in the eyes of the parishioners, and cited examples of "ignorance", "false superstitions" and "pride" of schismatics. The Missionary Leaflets published reports of the missionaries on the work done, and recommendations were given "how to dissuade the schismatics of their lies." Also, ordinary parishioners began to be attracted to this work, for this, in the areas "infected with schism", the Brotherhood began to organize circles of "zealots of Orthodoxy", which were supposed to help the pastor in the religious and moral improvement of the village (Ershov, 2017).

To organize such a circle, the local clergyman had to bring all literate, sober and pious parishioners closer to him, teach them the teachings of the Orthodox faith, and also conduct anti-schismatic and anti-sectarian conversations by reading the Missionary Leaflets. It was believed that after such preparation, the laity would be able to become a counterbalance to the "dissident teachers" and influence the "misguided" fellow villagers.

In the Kursk province in the village of Nizhnie Derevenki, Lgovsky district, half of the local population was made up of Old Believers-beglopopovtsy. The local priest I. Serokurov attracted 44 people from the "laity" and from members of the clergy of two local churches to the circle. In 1907, members of the circle held 19 religious and moral interviews and readings, and they also went to the houses of the old-believers. In the premises of the rural society of sobriety there was a missionary library, where polemics were conducted daily between members of the circle and the old-believers, the most discussed topics were Nikon's book correction, the legality of fleeing clergy, and signification. As a result, in 1908, 12 Old Believers were persuaded to join official Orthodoxy.

By the beginning of the 20th century, according to the census, 98.7% of the population professed Orthodoxy in the Kursk province, however, there were religious sects of old-believers and renovationists, but these currents did not have much influence on the Orthodox population of the province, since the pastors fought against perversions of faith and apostasy.

In the Oryol province at the end of the 19th century, brotherhoods and church-educational scientific societies were also opened. In memory of the Hieromartyr (Svyashchennomuchenik) Kuksha, a Brotherhood is established in Mtsensk. On March 2, 1887, the Oryol Orthodox Petropavlovskoye Brotherhood was created at the Peter and Paul Cathedral. Since 1899, the Oryol department of the Orthodox Imperial Palestinian Society began its work.

At the beginning of the twentieth century, the activities of the laity, priests, church hierarchs - Orthodox missionaries - led to a positive result: the theological defense of Orthodoxy in polemics with sectarians deepened. In school theology, the influence of Western rationalism is overcome; educational spiritual literature is published for a wide range of readers; parochial schools are organized; parish life revives in the sphere of social service of the church.

In 1896-1900 the Voronezh missionary Rozhdestvensky, corresponding with parish priests and collecting data on sectarianism, published about ten "Open Letters" in Diocesan Gazette, where he demanded a merciless fight against sectarianism and use the "state sword" for this fight.

At the same time, the creative and scientific intelligentsia changed their attitude towards Orthodoxy, a phenomenon known in the history of culture as the "Russian religious renaissance", which influenced the intellectual life of Western Europe.

Russian religious thinkers discovered the spiritual and religious meaning of works of F.M. Dostoevsky, N.A. Berdyaev, S.N. Bulgakov. The Russian Empire was a multi-confessional power, there were four religions of world significance in it: Christianity with the dominant position of Orthodoxy, Judaism, Buddhism, Islam.

An important component of the development of religious dissent in the XIX - early XX centuries. in the provinces there were changes in the mentality and lifestyle of broad sections of society, which occurred under the influence of the "great reforms" and industrialization in Russia. The spread of education and the liberalization of social life created the conditions for spiritual emancipation ("emancipation"), and the destruction of traditional isolation, the spread of otkhodnichestvo, the emergence of factories and factories contributed to the spread of new religious ideas. Under these conditions, the church needed thoughtful and effective measures aimed at strengthening the religious faith among the parishioners, maintaining influence on the minds of the broad masses, as well as its own missionary activities to combat the growth of sectarianism.

The ratio of religious and cultural communities was also reflected in the Voronezh province, which at that time was a classic Russian province. In 1911 there were 27 Orthodox parishes in Voronezh; 2 synagogues; 2 Catholic churches, Lithuanian and Polish; a Baptist prayer house and a Lutheran church. There were no confessional conflicts in the Voronezh province. Each denomination had its own cultural and historical type, and the numerical ratio of religious communities reflected the national composition of the urban population.

Svyatitel' Feofan Zatvornik, when he spoke about religious tolerance, showed the attitude of the Orthodox faith towards sectarians, heterodoxy and heterodoxy. From a spiritual point of view, religious tolerance does not mean indifference in religion. Svyatitel' Feofan Zatvornik believed that religious tolerance honors the one holy faith, takes care of its glory and purity, elevates the faith, but also gives place to other faiths.

In addition, it can be noted that in the 19th century in the Voronezh province, the position of the Orthodox faith was gradually strengthened. So, in the confession sheets of the Zadonsk district of the Voronezh province, the village of Kozino at the Church of the Epiphany in 1883-1886 there were residents of the Orthodox confession, the military who confessed and took communion - 100, merchants, petty bourgeois, shop workers - 27, peasants - 582 people.

In the second half of the XIX - early XX centuries. in the missionary territories, an intra-church movement began to develop dynamically, advocating the unification of missionary activity with school, educational and enlightenment work among the common people.

Thus, before the 1917 revolution, Orthodoxy was widespread outside the Russian Empire, which helped to strengthen the cultural and political positions of Russia on the world stage. Orthodoxy in Russia was the official state religion, which was strengthened by the missionary activities of the Russian Orthodox Church.

In the 19th century, on the territory of the Russian Empire, the missionary activity of the Russian Orthodox Church was aimed at combating the Old Believers and sectarianism; to conduct sermons among lamaists, Muslims and shamanists. Under the Holy Synod, a special body was created - the Missionary Council, which directs this activity.

In 1865, the Orthodox Missionary Society was formed, attracting the general public to assist Russian missionaries. The main task of the Orthodox mission in the second half of the 19th century, according to the reports of diocesan committees, was "preservation of Christians in the herd of foreigners."

Since 1869, the missionary activity of the Russian Church has also been carried out in Japan. In 1880 a missionary diocese was organized there, which in 1900 had 25,230 believers, 152 catechists, 28 priests, and 231 congregations.

On December 16, 1875, Alexander II issued a decree on the opening of a collection of donations throughout Russia in favor of the Orthodox Japanese Mission. This was due to the following circumstances.

Firstly, the Japanese were missionaries from different areas, and those of them who needed material assistance were supported by the Orthodox Japanese Mission from 3 to 6 months.

Secondly, there were 12 disciples at the mission who were being prepared to preach the «word of God».

Thirdly, a school was founded for Christian children at the mission, where there were 60 students.

In addition, the mission needs funds for the secondary publication of spiritual books. To meet all these needs, the head of the Japan Ecclesiastical Mission, Archimandrite Nikolai, petitions to allocate 4,800 rubles annually to the mission. This Decree was sent to all the provinces of the Russian Empire, including the provinces of the Central Chernozem Region.

The Voronezh Spiritual Consistory decided to announce the collection of donations for the needs of the Orthodox Spiritual Mission in Japan so that all the donations were delivered to the Voronezh Spiritual Consistory within a year. This decree was signed by Archpriest Evlampiy Svyatozarov.

In church circles in the 1880s a system of internal mission is being formed, providing spiritual influence on people who have departed from the state religion. The creation of this system contributed to the emergence of new professional missionaries from the category of clergy, who did not conduct parish services, but "admonished the lost" and engaged in anti-schismatic rhetoric.

A significant role in the formation of the ideological foundations of the internal mission was played by the adopted in 1888 and 1908. Holy Synod "Rules on the organization of the mission", as well as the decisions of the All-Russian missionary congresses held from 1887 to 1910.

An analysis of the relevant archival documents led to the conclusion that a characteristic feature of church work with those who "fell away from Orthodoxy" before 1905 was the combination of actual missionary methods with policemen; after the announcement of religious freedoms, emphasis was placed on propaganda activities (public lectures, disputes with old-believers and sectarians, the distribution of "anti-schismatic" literature, the creation of circles of "zealots of Orthodoxy").

It should be noted that in the XIX - early XX centuries. the intensification of the missionary activity of the Orthodox Church was associated with the political views of the tsarist government, which tried to strengthen and expand the foundations of Orthodoxy in Russia, which were an integral part of the official ideology, although this view was one-sided. The Orthodox faith could not spread without the enthusiasm of Russian Orthodox missionaries and the donations of the laity.

In 1910, an appeal was published to all the inhabitants of Russia that a society had been formed in Moscow with the goal of helping preachers of the faith and promoting the spread of Orthodoxy outside the country. It was a missionary society. It consisted of 11,000 representatives of the Orthodox faith and spent 250,000 rubles annually. The proclamation said that people should help this society as much as possible. This requires a fixed three-ruble annual fee. And those people who are not able to do this, let them donate as much as they can. And with such small donations great "works of God" («Bozh'i dela») were accomplished.

In the XIX - early XX centuries Russian Orthodox Church faced problems that were caused by modernization in the state and society, expressed in the weakening of the role of religion among the masses; in the destruction of the patriarchal way of life; in the growth of sectarianism and atheistic sentiments (Ershov, 2018).

At the end of the XIXth century, the Orthodox Church was able to create a significant system of religious education and missionary work, capable of preserving the Orthodox traditions of the population in the provinces of the Central Black Earth Region.

CONCLUSION

In conclusion, it should be said that on the one hand, the XIX - early XX centuries were the heyday of Russian Orthodox missionary work on the territory of the Russian state and beyond. On the other hand, the activities of Orthodox missionaries did not always achieve the necessary results, sometimes the number of baptized people for one or another period of time was calculated in units. However, the importance of Russian missionary work in the development of intercultural relations between Russia and various countries of the world was enormous. As a result of the translation activities of Russian missionaries, the Holy Scriptures and other spiritual literature were translated into Kalmyk, Finnish, Japanese, Chinese and other languages. In the countries of the East and in other regions of the world, Orthodox churches were built, which were beautiful examples of Russian architecture and architecture.

REFERENCES

Ashmarov, I. A., & Ershov, B. A. (2019). Nekotorye aspekty vzaimodejstviya cerkvi i svetskoj vlasti v Rossii v XIX - nachale XX v. In Shestnadcatye Damianovskie chteniya: Russkaya pravoslavnaya cerkov' i obshchestvo v istorii Rossii i Kurskogo kraya. Materialy Vserossijskoj (nacional'noj) nauchno-prakticheskoj konferencii.

Ashmarov, I. A., & Ershov, B. A. (2019). Rol' cerkvi v ekonomicheskoj zhizni obshchestva XIX - nachala XX veka. In Pravoslavie i obshchestvo: grani vzaimodejstviya. Sbornik statej III Mezhdunarodnoj nauchno-prakticheskoj konferencii v ramkah IX Zabajkal'skih Rozhdestvenskih obrazovatel'nyh chtenij, regional'nogo etapa XXVIII Mezhdunarodnyh Rozhdestvenskih obrazovatel'nyh chtenij.

Ershov, B. A., & Ashmarov, I. A. (2018). Interaction Of The Orthodox Church And The State In Russia At The Present Stage. *Vestnik Èkonomiceskoj Teorii,* (2), 19–24.

Ershov, B.A., Ashmarov, I.A., & Danilchenko, S.L. (2018). *The Development Of Russian Church Architecture In The 1990s-2017: The State And Prospects.* Stat'ya v otkrytom arhive N° 1.

Ershov, B.A., Ashmarov, I.A., Drobyshev, A.V., Zhdanova, T.A., & Buravlev, I.A. (2017). Property And Land Relations Of Russian Orthodox Church And State In Russia. *The European Proceedings of Social & Behavioural Sciences,* 324-331.

Perevozchikova, L.S., Ershov, B.A., Ashmarov, I.A., & Volkova, E.A. (2017). Role of Russian Orthodox Church in Life of Peasants in Russia in XIX - the Beginning of the XXth Centuries. *Bylye Gody, 43*(1), 121-128.

Chapter 15
Orthodox Posts in the Life of the Russian Province

ABSTRACT

In the 19th century, the financial position of the parish clergy in the countryside was not much higher than that of wealthy peasants, and in the city, it was comparable to the position of the lower part of the bureaucracy and the bulk of the townspeople (with the exception of the clergy of cathedrals and, of course, the court clergy). At this time, the practice (not formally legalized by any civil code or church canon) of the actual inheritance of church parishes was established, when the diocesan bishop, when the parish priest retired, secured, at the request of the latter, a place for his son or son-in-law.

INTRODUCTION

In the 19th century, Russia continued to be a powerful power with distinctive traditions in many areas of life. Largely, this was facilitated by the fact that the Russian Orthodox Church remained state and dominant. The emperor could not profess any other faith than the Orthodox, but at the same time, there was freedom of religion. The holders of the royal throne sought to preserve the faith of their ancestors, including within the framework of the well-known thesis "Orthodoxy - autocracy - nationality."

During the reign of Alexander III (1881-1894), many temples were built in the traditional style, he took special care of educating his subjects in the spirit of Orthodoxy, which was formalized by legislative acts.

DOI: 10.4018/978-1-6684-4915-8.ch015

It can be said that the 19th century was characterized by a certain strengthening of faith, despite the departure from the faith of representatives of the liberal and revolutionary-democratic trend, to the spread of socialist ideas, often leading to atheism. That is why until the beginning of the 20th century those religious concepts were preserved, without which love for the Fatherland is unthinkable.

Numerous observations of contemporaries, fiction and popular literature, diaries of travelers, memoirs, materials published in scientific publications, as well as unpublished, but deposited in the archives, indicate that in the 19th century. fasting was observed according to church regulations.

From archival sources, handwritten materials of the Russian Geographical Society and the Ethnographic Bureau of Prince V.N. Tenishev, created in St. Petersburg in the 19th century. They are answers to various questions from programs that were sent throughout Russia in order to collect ethnographic information about the inhabitants of the empire. They contain a lot of information about how the Russian people behaved and how they ate during fasting days. It can be said without exaggeration that the entire system of public nutrition was based on the alternation of fasting and meat-eater.

As in previous centuries, the spiritual experience of domestic ascetics of piety, who came from different social strata of the population, to a large extent contributed to the preservation of the tradition of fasting in the life of the Russian provinces.

According to one of the sermons of St. Ioann Zlatoust, the meaning of fasting lies not only in the infringement of one's own desires, but also in the cultivation of sacrifice through service to others, through feasible donations for the needs of the suffering.

The saint Ioann Zlatoust advises before Lent to calculate how much money is spent on food with meat, and then during Lent - on food without meat, and give the difference to those in need. And fasting appears before us in a new aspect - it turns out that we are not required to change our diet at all, not to transfer our cash costs from meat and milk to beans and nuts. It is necessary not only to save this money in order to spend it later, but again for yourself. For the sake of God, we need something valuable, which we ourselves would gladly use, to tear it away from us forever, to give it to someone else. This is the most effective exercise for cultivating love for God and the people around you.

Another key sign of proper fasting is the independent personal desire of a person to bring such a sacrifice to God. When a "believing" family member limits food to his household without their desire and consent, it turns out not to be a fast, but a forced hunger strike. The spiritual benefit of such a practice would be questionable. Also, true fasting should be invisible to those around you: "…when you fast, anoint your head and wash your face, so that you may appear fasting not before people, but before your Father who is in secret; and your Father, who sees in secret, will reward you openly" (Matthew 6:17). This approach will make it easy to avoid many obstacles in fasting.

Often the reason for not fasting is fear of lack of experience or secular prejudice. The main perplexed question is "what then is there?" solved once and for all by the first book on lean cuisine or a similar query on the Internet. The prejudice about starvation due to insufficiently high-calorie food (this also includes belief in essential amino acids) is refuted by the fact of the existence of vegetarians who, in principle, do not eat meat at all. By the way, along with eggs, caviar and fish. And not only do they feel surprisingly great, they also tease those who eat meat. But before the appearance of potatoes in Russia, when cucumbers, cabbage, turnips and lentils were the central products of the lean diet, fasting was indeed a feat, especially in the countryside, with its usual physical exertion.

The Monk Serafim Sarovskiy, being on obedience in the Sarovskiy monastery, from a young age kept fasts. Subsequently, sharing his rich spiritual experience, he advised the monks: "Sitting at the meal, do not look and do not judge who eats how much, abstain at dinner. On Wednesday and Friday, if you can, eat once a day." (Perevozchikova, 2017).

Serafim Sarovskiy, often in solitude, did not eat any food on Wednesday and Friday, and on other days of the week, he took it only once, combining abstinence and fasting with prayer.

Carrying feats in his deserted cell, the monk ate dry and stale bread, which he took from the monastery for a whole week on Sundays, and vegetables that he grew in a small garden - potatoes, beets, onions and grass, called "snot".

During the first week of Great Lent, he usually did not eat at all until Communion of the Holy Mysteries on Saturday. Sometime later, the abstinence and fasting of St. Seraphim reached the highest level. Completely ceasing to take bread from the monastery, he lived for more than two and a half years without any maintenance, eating only goatweed grass.

Many discussions about fasting were left by the inhabitants of the famous Optina pustyn', including Hieroschemamonk Amvrosiy. In correspondence with spiritual children, he repeatedly reminded of the essence of fasting: "The Holy Fathers, moved by the Holy Spirit, established fasts, both for our spiritual and bodily benefit. The expectation of the holiday for those who do not fast does not bring such joy as those who prepare themselves for fasting - but not only bodily, but also spiritual".

Saint Righteous Ioann Kronshtadtskiy, summarizing his personal pastoral experience, reminded: "It is necessary for a Christian to fast in order to clarify the mind and excite and develop feelings, and move the will to good activity. We overshadow and suppress these three abilities most of all by overeating, drunkenness and worldly cares, and through that we fall away from the source of life - God and fall into corruption and vanity, perverting and defiling the image of God in ourselves. what a lofty flight all the fasters and ascetics had! They, like eagles, soared in the heavens..."

"The Shepherd of Truth" - this is how contemporaries called Ioann Kronshtadtskiy: even being seriously ill, he did not follow the prescriptions of doctors who advised him to maintain strength with fast food. His authority among the believers, for whom he was an example, was very great.

Such a case was indicative. In the summer of 1896, many residents of the Totemsky district who suffered from dysentery were advised by a local paramedic to eat milk and eggs, but since this time was on a post, all the peasants resolutely refused to do so. "The saints often fasted," they said, "and lived for a long time. But Jesus Christ did not eat anything for forty days." Abstinence from fast food was facilitated by the story of Father John of Kronstadt, who neglected the advice of doctors. "If God has not crossed the century, then you will always come to life, and if God orders to die, then nothing can be done against God," the peasants believed, based on the experience of a famous Christian ascetic.

The Monk Siluan Afonskiy, a native of the peasants of the Tambov province, throughout his life repeated the ascetic experience of the Church Fathers - famous ascetics, piety. In forgiveness, the elder saw the way to salvation and never made concessions. "However," he said, "it is possible to fast a lot, pray a lot and do a lot of good, but if we are conceited at the same time, we will be like a tambourine that rattles, but is empty inside".

The number of examples of forgiveness by well-known ascetics can be greatly multiplied; in general, they represented the clearest example of piety for a Russian person who was accustomed to going on a pilgrimage, which means adopting the spiritual experience of ascetics. And although the monastic fast differs from the fast of the laity, in observing the fasts, the laity strove to imitate the monks, since monastic life in Russia has always been revered.

The guide for Christian believers was the church charter, or "Typicon", containing instructions regarding the order of services and meals during fasting in relation to worldly life. Of great importance were the sermons addressed to believers by famous priests, in which they explained the meaning of fasting. Believers were required to confess and take communion at least once a year. It is interesting that people who were supposed to appear in court as witnesses, but did not go to confession for three years, the opposing side had the right to reject.

Of course, there were big differences in how residents of large cities, especially St. Petersburg and Moscow, and small, provincial towns ate on the days of fasting. Among rich and poor citizens, the difference became even sharper.

In the cities, with the beginning of the post, all kinds of spectacles were forbidden. First of all, this concerned urban theatrical performances, balls and masquerades: they were cancelled. Bathhouses and shops that sold meat and other modest products were also closed, except for those selling basic necessities; court proceedings were suspended.

In the 1830-40s of in St. Petersburg during Great Lent, not only in Russian, but also in German restaurants, Lenten dishes were served. In the "Stroganov" tavern on Nevsky Prospekt, the food on the first and Holy weeks was no different from the monastery: they prepared only dishes from mushrooms, peas and jelly. They drank tea with raisins and honey, cooked sbiten.

Moscow "the first throne" in comparison with St. Petersburg retained the customs of their ancestors for a longer time. According to the recollections of many Muscovites, they began to prepare for Lent ahead of time.

The famous writer I.S. Shmelev, who came from a merchant family, described in his book "Leto Gospodne" («Summer of the God») how they were preparing for Lent in their parents' house: they lit "lenten" lamps - simple, not colored glass, hung pictures of secular content, changed clothes and even dishes for more modest ones. Cabbage, cucumbers, mushrooms were salted ahead of time: "In the hall there were bowls with yellow pickles, with dill umbrellas stuck in them and with chopped cabbage, sour, slightly sprinkled with anise - such a delight. I grab pinches - how crunchy! And I give myself a word do not go fast during the whole fast. Why go fast, which destroys the soul, if everything is delicious without that?

Many names of dishes that I.S. Shmelev, were forgotten, they were characteristic of the prosperous urban population. In addition, the choice of Lenten dishes in the city was much wider than in the countryside.

In Moscow, starting from the first Lenten Monday, there was a lively trade taking into account the needs of the Lenten table. Mushroom rows stretched in an uninterrupted line from Ustyinsky to Moskvoretsky bridge, and sometimes further - to Kamenny bridge. Here, all those who did not have time to stock up on lean products replenished their edible stocks (State Archive of the Tambov Region, 1907).

I.S. Shmelev, P.I. Bogatyrev, I.A. Belousov wrote about mushroom auctions. Writer N.D. Teleshov recalled: "There were a lot of products here! And radish, and potatoes, and all kinds of vegetables. Long threads and garlands hung on the walls of the tents and on shafts raised up above the sledges dried mushrooms of various qualities - white and yellow, as well as cheap dark boats. Here are baskets of cranberries, and vats of fragrant honey - linden and buckwheat - you can't count everything!

In other cities, fasting was observed no less strictly. I.S. Aksakov, who traveled a lot around Russia on business, wrote the following to his relatives from Kaluga in 1847: "Thank God, this is Great Lent! there are whole crowds of goblers quietly going to church ... ".

The first Monday after Forgiveness Sunday is popularly called Clean Monday. On this day, people were "cleansed" from the past Maslenitsa, in temples and houses everyone congratulated each other on the upcoming fast.

On Saturday of the first week - the day of the Great Martyr Theodore Tiron - lenten pancakes were baked everywhere. This custom was observed not only in remote provinces, but also in both capitals, however, mainly among the middle class and merchants.

You can learn about how residents of other cities fasted from the answers of correspondents of the Russian Geographical Society. In Voznesensky Posad, Vladimir province, on fast days, in addition to bread and "gray" cabbage soup, they ate boiled peas, steamed turnips ("bushma"), and drank kvass.

In the Knyazhnin of the Nizhny Novgorod province, millet and barley porridge and potatoes were more often eaten; in Pudozh - oatmeal pancakes with mushrooms and kvass, by the way, kvass was made here not only from bread, but also from dried turnips, it was called "repitsa"; they also ate radishes, rutabagas, potatoes, and fish.

Residents of Galich, Kostroma province, also ate cabbage soup, porridge, mushrooms, but did not use turnips and beets. The townspeople of Verkhovazhsky Posad, Vologda Province, ate the same as the local peasants: lean cabbage soup with the addition of cereals, various kinds of stews, sea fish, often salted and dry (cod, halibut, fresh herring, saithe), mushrooms, berries, vegetables, mainly - onions, potatoes, radishes, cabbage, rutabaga, and carrots, beans, pumpkin, lettuce, parsley, dill, poppy seeds, horseradish - in small quantities, pies made from rye, oatmeal, barley and wheat, rarely from grain flour. From liquid dishes - potatoes with kvass, «onion vzvarets» - sauce; turnips here were not only steamed, but also fried.

A festive dinner on fast days consisted of a variety of dishes from sea and river fish, barley porridge with hemp oil and jelly with honey. Stocks of products that were used during fasts were partially replenished in local shops or at county fairs and fairs.

The presence of a garden helped to diversify the table during fasts. For example, in Rostov the Great, almost every city dweller had gardens: here, more than in other cities, they ate vegetables, especially potatoes, they ate them cold, boiled, baked and fried. In Menzelinsk, Ufa province, they also ate a lot of vegetables. In Lenotaevsk, Astrakhan province, they ate a lot of fish. In Salt Zaimishche of the same province, as in the center of Russia, they ate mainly cabbage soup and porridge. In Fatezh, Kursk province, "cold potatoes and beets" were distributed during Lent. In Yadrin, Kazan province, on fast days, in addition to the usual cabbage soup and porridge, sauerkraut, potatoes and beets, they prepared "permeni" - dumplings with white cabbage, as well as baked pumpkin. If a holiday fell on a fast, they ate fish soup, stew with potatoes and carrots, pies with potatoes, carrots, cabbage, fish and onions, fried potatoes, mushrooms or fish. In the 19th century potatoes are widespread.

In rural areas, as the responses of the correspondents of the Tenishevsky bureau showed, fasts were observed strictly.

The nature of the food of the peasants during the fasts largely depended on the level of development of their economy, which, in turn, was determined by natural, climatic and social conditions. In the north, in the absence of a choice, dishes were prepared from cereals, mainly from oats, in the south, vegetables and fruits diversified the lean diet. In those cases when settlements were located along rivers, near lakes or on the sea coast, their inhabitants ate a lot of fish. Fairs made up for the lack of certain products in a particular locality. It is no coincidence that specific auctions, auctions and bazaars («torgi, torzhki i bazary») were timed to the posts. In particular, posts made it possible to profitably sell meat and dairy products.

They prepared for the fasts in advance, the products were distributed for the whole year - taking into account all multi-day and one-day fasts. This accounting contributed to the rational management of the economy. Obviously, the ability to diversify lenten food directly depended on the level of prosperity: it was easier for rich and middle-income peasants to do this, the poor had to limit themselves to a minimum set of products.

In Central Russia, the main food on fasting days was bread, water, cabbage soup, soups, stews with the addition of cabbage, potatoes, peas, beans or lentils, cereals, boiled and fried mushrooms with the addition of a small amount of sunflower, linseed or hemp oil, jelly, vegetables, steamed turnip, pumpkin, cranberries, cranberries, raisins, honey.

The most plentiful and varied table was in autumn and winter, when after the harvest of the last harvest there were sufficient food supplies. His lack began to be felt in the spring. At this time, the diet of a poor family was reduced to a minimum: rye bread, water, kvass, pickles, potatoes, cereals. It became quite scarce in the summer, when stocks were depleted.

In the central non-chernozem provinces of Russia, for example, in the Melenkovsky district of the Vladimir province, the daily diet included cabbage soup with cabbage, potatoes, beets, boiled peas, radish, stews, oatmeal with kvass. For the winter they salted cucumbers, mushrooms, cabbage, soaked apples. In the Shuya district, on the days when it was possible, they ate fish; it was brought from the Urals, the Don and the Volga. In Yuryevsky uyezd, where families of average prosperity prevailed, the order of cooking changed from day to day. Common cheesecakes made from rye flour with cottage cheese ("tubolki") were replaced with pancakes made from buckwheat or barley flour during fasting. Crushed horseradish was used as seasoning (it was eaten with kvass), less often - garlic.

In the Tver province they ate bread, cereals, peas, and radishes. If fasting fell on holidays, then instead of bread they baked pies made from rye flour, mushrooms with vegetable oil. If there were guests these days, then no exceptions were allowed, however, the guests themselves fasted. For example, when a midwife, according to tradition, cooked "babin" porridge after christening, they ate it without milk and butter.

Residents of the Molozhsky district of the Yaroslavl province - "sitskari" - during the fasting period ate rye pie, or "sitnik", small pies made from batter - "fresh", or "kulyabysh", radish, saffron milk caps, serukhs and other dried mushrooms, cabbage soup with onions and butter "in crumbs", sometimes with "snapshots" (small dried fish); pea dishes; millet or wheat porridge (buckwheat porridge was not liked here); potatoes with vegetable oil. If fasting fell on holidays, then they would certainly prepare wheat "springs" - cookies in vegetable oil ("otherwise there would be no holiday"); fresh fish, and if it was not, then salted. They rarely ate stellate sturgeon, more often they made fish soup from fresh pike, but in general they caught little fish.

Unlike neighboring provinces, gardening here was insignificant and barely satisfied the small needs of the peasants, although radishes, carrots, and beets were grown in sufficient quantities. Little cabbage was planted, more often bought in Mologa. For the lack of wild sorrel - "sour", prepared oatmeal stew.

During fasting, not every housewife agreed to sell a glass of milk for fear of sinning. The pot in which fast food was cooked was never used to prepare lean meals. Those who did not observe the fasts were spoken of as apostates: "There he is - and he eats beef during the fasts."

In the Lukoyanovsky district of the Nizhny Novgorod province, cabbage soup was cooked from "black" (not white) cabbage without any seasoning. Not everyone and not always ate buckwheat porridge: most of the villagers ate it only on Sundays and other holidays. Wealthy peasants sometimes ate peas, potatoes (there was little grown here), cucumbers and radishes, but this was already considered a luxurious table. Onions, radishes, carrots, beans, beets, cabbage, cucumbers were planted here in small quantities. On holidays, food was not much different from everyday food: the same empty cabbage soup, bread and water. Kvass was rarely drunk in these places.

In a completely different way, Russian peasants held posts on the right bank of the Volga River. The main food here was "sieve" white ("sitnyy", "reshetnyy") bread, not as black and sour as in the steppe provinces; they ate it only with cabbage soup («shchi»). A rare housewife did not bake daily sieve and unleavened wheat cakes mixed with vegetable oil - "kokurok": they were baked in ashes. In addition, they ate pea jelly.

A significant place in the diet of the inhabitants of the northern provinces, for example, the Arkhangelsk province, was occupied by turnips and radishes. Turnips were eaten in different forms, they were added to kvass, called "turnips". On fasting days, they prepared grated radish with finely chopped onions, salt, kvass and vegetable oil, and to beat off bitterness, they mixed it with grated swede. For the White Sea coast-dwellers of the same province, fish was their daily bread, which distinguished their diet from the diet of the inhabitants of other northern provinces with an agricultural way of life.

In the Vologda province, almost everywhere the main dish was "molos" - lean cabbage soup with barley or oatmeal, hence their name "grain". Shchi was eaten hot and cold. In the lakeside regions, soup on fasting days was cooked with dried fish - "smelt". In addition to cabbage soup, various soups were prepared. The simplest of bread, crumbled into water with vegetable oil, was called "tyurya", "murik".

Numerous lenten dishes were prepared from various cereals, especially from oats. During processing, oats were ground into groats ("zaspa"), groats and oatmeal. Porridge was cooked from oatmeal. Oatmeal was kneaded with kvass, sometimes crushed lingonberries were added.

Cabbage was used almost everywhere in sauerkraut. Fresh cabbage was dried and eaten in winter with kvass and vegetable oil. Turnips and rutabaga were widespread horticultural crops, which accounted for most of the annual food supply. Soup was cooked from them; a dish of boiled beets was called "rosol", and from fresh turnips steamed in the oven - "parenitsa". There were quite a lot of vegetable dishes: "liver" - turnips or turnips baked in ashes, eaten with vegetable oil; "carrot" - carrots baked with different cereals; "bryukovnitsa" - the same from rutabagas. From the steamed turnip they made a cold sweet dish - "kislukha". Onions, lingonberries or finely chopped beets, carrots, rutabaga, also steamed in the oven, were added to it. Radishes were eaten with kvass. Peas were consumed steamed in the oven, porridge, jelly were cooked from pea flour, bread was baked. Mushrooms and berries prepared for the future were a special delicacy. Dried mushrooms were used for stews: "golomudka" was prepared from porcini or saffron mushrooms; from dry mushrooms boiled with oatmeal - "lip". Lingonberries, cranberries were usually soaked for the winter.

The greatest sin was considered not only the use of fast food, but even touching it, which was usually accompanied by lamentations: "Oh, what have I done?" During field work (haymaking, harvesting, threshing, etc.), as well as help, if they fell on fast days, food was prepared without the use of fast foods, while the pomochan was generously treated: the lenten meal was, as a rule, plentiful and tasty.

"Today," they said, "only we peasants can fast, and scientists and noble fasts will not observe them - they can't live a day without tea and beef." (Ershov, 2018).

In the southern provinces, on fast days they cooked mainly cabbage soup with cabbage, more often borscht, potato dishes, ate a lot of vegetables and fruits.

In the Ryazan province, since autumn, sour cabbage was harvested for future use, adding pickled cucumbers, onions, caraway seeds and other spices to it - for smell. During the winter fast they ate coarser food than during the summer fasts. Breakfast, lunch and dinner consisted of kvass with sauerkraut and potatoes, often with radishes or cabbage (wholly fermented), cabbage soup with vegetable oil, sometimes stew and buckwheat or millet porridge with butter. In the summer fasting time, they ate radish with kvass, kvass with cucumbers and fish, mainly salted pike perch, potatoes, boiled beets, stew and porridge with hemp oil.

Residents of the Voronezh province ate sauerkraut with kvass, onions and pickles during Lent; grated radish with salted kvass or cut into pieces; potatoes with cucumbers and kvass; boiled peas or boiled and crushed with kvass, and sometimes with vegetable oil; ate porridge with kvass; and among wealthy peasants, porridge was served with hemp oil. Shchi was prepared mainly from sauerkraut or sauerkraut (beetroot). Sometimes they ate raw ("malted") dough and steamed with viburnum berries: this dish was called "kulaga". They cooked "straw" from oatmeal, they ate it with hemp oil or kvass. The Russians, moving to the vast Siberian lands, adapted to the new conditions of life, but preserved the traditions of their native places. In Siberia, there were especially many immigrants from the provinces of the European part of Russia.

The peasants of Eastern Siberia in the summer, when food was scarcer, gathered wild garlic along the wooded slopes - a plant from the onion family with edible, garlic-smelling leaves, which were crushed and eaten with kvass, a little salt. The table was supplemented by last year's stocks of potatoes and radishes. On holidays, if they were fasting and if it was possible to eat fish, they baked pies with fish, boiled "shcherba" (the local name for fish soup), fried "tel" (boneless fish, chopped and mixed with flour) in oil, made dumplings with fish. They also cooked wheat, pea and berry (mainly from sea buckthorn) kissels, baked pancakes, pancakes, "pryazhenniki" - pies with minced meat, fried in hemp or cedar oil.

Residents of the steppe region of Eastern Siberia ate millet or barley porridge with hemp or camelina oil (from the seeds of the oily plant "saffron milk cap"), as well as with fish oil; cabbage soup ("shti") from chopped cabbage with barley groats. They also ate a variety of vegetable dishes: "potato" (potato stew); boiled peas, "repnitsa" with poppy seeds (turnip stew), turnip or carrot pareniki with wort ("wort" - a sweetish broth on flour and malt, was used as gravy); "carrot" (carrot soup); radish, cabbage, sauerkraut. Among everyday dishes were kulaga and thick kvass. In this case, kulaga was a mixture of rye flour and malt, brewed with boiling water, steamed and aged in the cold; among lenten dishes, it was considered a delicacy. Lenten festive table, as a rule, was distinguished by a set of fish and flour dishes. Information about the food of the peasants of the Kainsky district coincides with the description of that of the inhabitants of the neighboring Tara district, Minusinsk and Ishim districts.

Residents of the Altai Territory ate wild or garden green onions during Lent, salted and mixed with kvass, grouts, cereals, boiled potatoes, cereal cabbage soup, talkers, tyurya from bread crumble with kvass and water. Mushrooms, cucumbers and cabbage were salted for future use. A local specialty was boiled noodles made from rye dough. Peas were used a lot: more than a dozen dishes were prepared from it. On a holiday, when it was allowed by the charter, they fried fish, baked pies, cooked «shcherba» («ukha») from fresh fish, and boiled stews with dried fish. They flavored any food with linseed, hemp, camelina and cedar oil.

The daily life of an Orthodox monk consisted of a cyclical alternation of prayer, work, meals and rest, arranged in a certain order. Much depended on the church calendar and the peculiarities of the monastic charter associated with it.

The daily routine in the cenobitic monastery was something like this. At 2-3 o'clock in the morning - matins (if there was no all-night vigil), after it it was possible to rest a little, then at 6-7 o'clock - early liturgy. Then obediences (works) began, and part of the brethren from 8–9 o'clock participated in the late liturgy. At 10-11 o'clock - lunch, after which obediences were again due. Around 5:00 pm - Vespers, then dinner and a rule: a certain set of prayers, including prayers for the future, reading a commemoration book listing the living and the dead, an individual cell rule. After that (about 22 hours) it was possible to go to sleep. On the eve of Sundays and major feasts, instead of Vespers and Matins, a long all-night vigil was served, which began at 18 and ended around 23-24. The beginning of each type of divine service was announced by the ringing of bells - the gospel.

It was worship that set the rhythm of everyday life. In cenobitic monasteries, in contrast to parish churches, it was long, unhurried, and strict. Its different parts fell at different times of the day and were separated by breaks (while in parish churches, for convenience, matins were combined with vespers and served in the evening). New trends slowly penetrated the cenobitic monasteries, for example, partes singing that came from Europe (poly-voiced, in parts, reminiscent of a concert). Here the ancient Znamenny singing was in use (monophonic, its melody was recorded with special signs - hooks).

Writer Lydia Veselitskaya-Mikulich recalled: "I liked the sense of proportion that is reflected in everything in Optina. All three churches were very simple on the outside and fairly decorated on the inside. There was no overwhelming splendor and flashy wealth in them, the singers did not flaunt the performance of refined compositions, the deacons did not shake the vaults of the temple with deafening roars. Everything bore the imprint of caring for the inside, and not about the outside.

The longest type of church service was the so-called. "all-night vigil".

The writer and traveler Andrey Muravyov said: "In the course of one month, I saw several such all-night vigils in three desert monasteries: on the White Banks, in the Holy Mountains and here, in Optina pustyn', and not a single one seemed tiring to me, despite its duration: this came partly from the deep attention of the clergy, from the clear reading and pleasant singing of the faces according to their ancient desert tunes, partly from the very variety with which the experienced fathers wisely decided to perform these long services, in fact, in order to sacred rites and alternate reading and singing reverently maintain the attention of the worshipers.

Often it was the peculiarities of worship that most of all attracted pilgrims to such cloisters. As for the monastics, everyone was supposed to come to church services, except for those engaged in special obediences that required constant presence (for example, cooking). And it was supposed to be at the very beginning. The monks and novices in the temple stood apart from the laity.

In one of the temples, a round-the-clock reading of the Psalter was performed (the inhabitants changed each other every few hours) with the commemoration of the deceased brothers and benefactors, whose names were recorded in special books - synodics.

In the skete, the monastics read the daily prayer rule in their cells, services were performed less often, and on some holidays the skete attended services in the monastery and stayed there for a meal.

It was customary to cleanse one's conscience and take communion in monasteries four or six times a year during many days of fasting (in the world - once or twice a year). In the 19th century, this norm was so accustomed to that more frequent communion attracted everyone's attention and raised questions.

In addition, each monk had his own cell rule, which consisted of daily reading of the Gospel and the Apostle, a certain number of prayers, bows, etc. guardian and 50 to all the saints. Elder Barsanuphius instructed his disciples: "Hold on to the five hundred like a pillar, there is great power in it."

In addition, each monk had his own cell rule, which consisted of daily reading of the Gospel and the Apostle, a certain number of prayers, prostrations, etc.

In Optina pustyn' they practiced the so-called «pyatisotnitsu»: every day they recited 300 Jesus prayers, 100 to the Mother of God, 50 to the guardian angel and 50 to all the saints. Elder Barsanuphius instructed his disciples: "Hold on to the «pyatisotnitsa» (five hundred prayers) like a pillar, there is great power in it."

In the 19th century, in some monasteries, the ancient practice of the Jesus Prayer ("Lord Jesus Christ, Son of God, have mercy on me a sinner") was revived, which had to be done as continuously as possible. Incessant prayer, in essence, meant constant remembrance of God, which was the strongest weapon against sinful thoughts. All monks were called to this work, and there were various teachings on this subject. The popularity of this practice was promoted by the artistic book "Frank Stories of a Wanderer to His Spiritual

Father", which became a kind of bestseller. However, the Jesus Prayer was never widely adopted.

In a cenobitic monastery, food was the same for everyone, not excluding the abbot, and everyone was supposed to eat together in the refectory. Eating in his cell was allowed only in case of illness.

The meal was considered a continuation of worship. This was emphasized by a number of details. For example, after the liturgy, an ancient rite of panagia could be performed: the brethren, breaking up in pairs, walked from the church to the refectory with prayers, and in front they carried a panagia - a prosphora, from which a particle in honor of the Mother of God was taken out at the liturgy. At the end of the meal, the monks ate particles of this prosphora.

In the refectory room, a lectern was placed, behind which stood a successive (changing) monk: while everyone was eating, he read the interpretation of the Gospel, the lives of the saints or patristic teachings related to the current day of the church calendar. The "Rules of outward behavior for novice monks" states:

"Staying at the meal for refreshment with food should be, as it were, a continuation of the divine service. The brethren, while nourishing the body with prudent contentment with the food offered, must at the same time nourish the soul with the word of God, which is read during the meal. For this, deep silence is observed in the meal. If you need to say something, then it is said very quietly and briefly, so as not to interfere with hearing the reading.

The very preparation of food was also connected with the spiritual life: the cook took a blessing from the abbot, and the stove was kindled with fire taken from the inextinguishable lamp from the temple.

Against the backdrop of a traditional, sustainable monastic meal, the most noticeable phenomenon was the rapid spread of tea. In Russia in the 19th century, it became a national drink and quickly penetrated the monasteries. However, in conservative cenobitic cloisters and in sketes, tea was perceived as a delicacy, pampering, an "stimulant" that should be limited. At the common meal, the main drink was the traditional kvass. And they drank tea in cells from samovars: they were at the rector's, and at the elder's, and in hotels. Sugar was used as a snack, sometimes a sweet roll or even cream served as an addition to tea.

In some monasteries, tea and sugar were distributed to all the brethren on a monthly basis. It also happened that the abbot or elder periodically gathered everyone at his place and gave tea to drink. In Optina Hermitage, it was customary to drink no more than three cups of tea a day. And when one cunning monk got himself a bigger cup, the elder personally for him limited the number of daily cups to two. Ascetics who were especially strict with themselves refused tea on principle or repented of being addicted to it as a serious sin. The most authoritative Metropolitan Filaret (Drozdov) issued the following resolution on this subject: "The use of tea is a whim that should not have been in monasteries. But if it has already been admitted due to weakness, then the treat of the brethren at the rector on a holiday is more befitting to the hostel than the distribution of sugar and tea to the cells.

The highest manifestation of the vow of obedience was the submission of one's will to the elder. In the 19th century, eldership was established in very few monasteries, but those centers where it existed differed markedly in spirit. The elder was the informal spiritual leader of the community, he received the revelation of thoughts from the brethren and instructed them in the spiritual life. The disciple was obliged to give the elder full confidence, open his whole soul to him and betray his will to him. And the elder, relying on his rich spiritual experience, guided not only his actions, but also his words and thoughts, helping to fight with passions and temptations.

At the same time, the elder was not an official, he was not appointed or dismissed, he was not obliged to report to his superiors. He could carry the position of confessor or some other. Formally, the elder did not belong to the monastic leadership, but his authority had a different, charismatic dimension, and even the abbot could consult with him, render him obedience.

When the skete existed, the elders, as a rule, were placed in it. For monks, it was supposed to come to the revelation of thoughts daily in the evenings or at least weekly. During the conversation with the elder, it was customary to kneel.

In the 19th century, the traditional type of pilgrim-prayer collided with a new type of secular traveler who could also visit a monastery, but rather for the sake of curiosity, breathe fresh air, look at ancient architecture, and talk with interesting people. But on the whole, the number of visitors to the monasteries grew steadily over the course of the century. A particularly large influx was observed on the patronal feasts of local churches.

The main attribute that made the monastery extremely popular was eldership, the most striking feature of which in this era was its connection with the outside world. Crowds of pilgrims from the surrounding counties and distant cities could rush to the most revered elders. It was an all-class meeting - from monks of other monasteries and ordinary peasants to famous writers, philosophers and members of the imperial family.

The holy elders especially supported female monasticism, which then began to develop rapidly. The formation of the Diveevo community cannot be imagined without Father Seraphim of Sarovsky, and the formation of the Shamorda community without Ambrose of Optinsky. Both of them later became large monasteries.

Outside visitors were received by the elders all day long, with breaks for divine services. If the elder was in the skete, the men went straight inside and waited for their turn in the hallway. Women, for whom the entrance to the skete was forbidden, the elder received at the holy gates. In addition, he had extensive correspondence with spiritual children.

Pilgrims lived in hotels, fed free of charge. Men could eat at the fraternal refectory or at the hotel, women - only at the hotel. The pilgrims attended divine services, went to talk to the elders, to the holy spring, ordered the commemoration of their living and deceased loved ones. If a pilgrim went to church (prepared for communion), he was supposed to fast for three days, attend all services and, of course, confess.

Lent consisted of 40 days (Fourteen days); two holidays (Lazarus Saturday and Palm Sunday), as well as Holy Week - a total of 48 days. It is called Great not only because of its duration (it is longer than all the others), but also because of the great significance of this post in the life of a Christian.

In addition to 7 weeks of fasting itself, the charter prescribes another 3 preparatory weeks for it. They begin with the Sunday of the publican and the Pharisee. From the beginning of the 3rd week until its end, there is no longer any meat at the meal, it will appear only at breaking the fast during the Easter meal. The whole week is also called Cheese, or Shrovetide, because the main food during it are dairy products, fish, eggs, cheese.

3 weeks before Lent, on Sunday, when the gospel text of the parable of the publican and the Pharisee is read at the liturgy, the Lenten Triodion, a book of liturgical texts that defines the features of worship during Great Lent, begins to be used in the service.

On Sunday, which is called the Week of the Publican and the Pharisee, at Matins they sing a special prayer of repentance from the 50th Psalm: "Open the doors of repentance to me..." This is the beginning of preparation for fasting. The singing of the prayer of repentance continues at Matins on Sundays (Weeks) of the 2nd, 3rd, 4th and 5th weeks of Great Lent inclusive.

The Week of the Prodigal Son is the second preparation week. On Sunday, at the liturgy, the Gospel is read with the parable of the prodigal son. At Matins, a new penitential hymn sounds: "On the rivers of Babylon ..." (Psalm 136).

The Week of the Last Judgment is the third preparatory week. On Sunday the Gospel of the Last Judgment is read. This Sunday is also called meat-fare, as it is the last day of the meat-eater. From Monday to Easter meat can not be eaten.

On the eve of meat-fare Sunday - Ecumenical (meat-fat) parental Saturday. On this day, the memory of all the departed Orthodox Christians is celebrated.

The week following this Sunday is called «Maslenitsa».

Week of remembrance of Adam's exile - Forgiveness Sunday. On this Sunday, the gospel passage is read about the forgiveness of offenses and fasting. Adam's exile is mentioned in many liturgical texts. In the evening, everyone gathers in the temple for the rite of forgiveness. The service is already sentry, the vestment is black, bows and penitential singing. At the end of the service, a sermon is read about forgiveness of offenses, about fasting, and a prayer with a blessing for Great Lent. The clergy, starting with the eldest, ask the people and each other for forgiveness. Then everyone approaches the priests in turn, bows, asks for forgiveness and forgives them all their sins and insults, while kissing the cross and the Gospel as a sign of the sincerity of what is being said. Parishioners ask for forgiveness from each other. Such forgiveness of mutual insults is an indispensable condition for the purification of the heart and the successful celebration of Great Lent.

Lent was distinguished from the rest of the year by special services.

Firstly, on Monday, Tuesday and Thursday, the Divine Liturgy is not served (except for a few holidays), on Wednesday and Friday the Liturgy of the Presanctified Gifts is served, and on Sundays the Liturgy of Basil the Great.

Secondly, in worship the volume of texts read from the Psalter increases, singing becomes much less.

Thirdly, the prayer of St. Ephraim the Syrian is read with 16 bows, waist and earthly. Special prayers with bows and kneeling are added to the divine service.

All these differences determine the special spiritual atmosphere of fasting, which is not characteristic of the whole year. Orthodox more often than always visit the temple, so as not to miss special services.

Orthodox religious traditions are based on four main dogmas - immutable truths taken on faith and determining the life of the church and all adherents of the Orthodox faith.

The first dogma is that Father, Son and Holy Spirit are not three gods, but three masks of one deity, radiating universal Love.

Second, Jesus Christ is God in human form and flesh. When people turn to God in a prayer of thanksgiving and ask to forgive all voluntary and involuntary sins, then God hears and understands all those who pray, since he himself felt all human physical and mental suffering.

The third is faith in the coming resurrection. Christ, after being crucified on the cross, conquered death and resurrected. Orthodox Christians believe that they can be resurrected in the flesh and enter into eternal life after the second coming of Christ.

The fourth dogma is faith in the church. It is possible to get closer to the Almighty only through the church; attending church services among Christians is considered a sign that God resides in a person's heart.

The most important holiday for Orthodox Christians is Easter. It was established in honor of the Resurrection of Jesus Christ, the date of the holiday is calculated according to the lunisolar calendar, on the first Sunday after the spring full moon.

In Orthodoxy, there is a close connection between church and home life, and most of the family traditions prescribed in church canons are observed today. The father is considered the head of the family. The wife and children see in him the image of Christ, the protector, comforter and educator. The mother is responsible for the upbringing of children and serves as an example of morality and virtue for them.

One of the oldest and most strictly observed Orthodox traditions (customs) is the tradition of baptizing children, which serves as evidence of a person's becoming on the path of approaching God. The rite of baptism is performed by a priest. The child is dipped into the water of the holy font three times, accompanying the ritual with the reading of prayers, then a pectoral cross is put on the neck of the baptized baby as a sign that he has become a member of the Orthodox Church, and can take part in all church rites.

Traditional rituals of the Orthodox are also inherent in marriage. This is matchmaking, bride-to-be, conspiracy, bachelorette and bachelor parties, weddings, wedding feasts and the wedding night. Each of the rites is important and has a special meaning.

Matchmaking, bride and groom - this is the acquaintance and negotiations of the families of the bride and groom, the assessment of their moral and material merits. The stage ends with an agreement that consolidates the decision to create a wedding union.

In the 19th century, simple believing people still kept their original piety, their way of life inherited from their ancestors and churchly consecrated. Before the reforms of the 1860s, not much had changed in the religious and moral type of the devout Russian peasant, in the make-up of his soul, compared to pre-Petrine times.

But the reforms - peasant, zemstvo, military and judicial - shook the stable peasant life. Universal conscription introduced by the military reform, freedom of movement, which previously made it difficult for serfs, the proletarianization of the rural poor, which intensified after the abolition of serfdom, the resettlement of ruined peasants in cities and factory towns, pulled people out of the way of life that had been established for centuries, introduced disunity into the peasant environment. New life circumstances became a temptation for many, led to religious cooling, and in exceptional cases to the loss of faith.

In the 1860s, zemstvo elementary schools for peasant children began to open in Russia. But the teachers in them were not always people of Orthodox beliefs. The curricula of zemstvo schools devoted little time to studying the Law of God, and therefore the people did not particularly sympathize with these schools. And there were still very few parochial schools, first introduced under Alexander I. In addition, the level of general education in them lagged behind the zemstvo schools. This situation in the field of public education caused concern among the clergy and the highest church authorities. The Holy Synod believed that public schools should have a close relationship with the Church, so that knowledge of literacy would give the people access to church books, so that literate peasant children could participate in Divine services and read soul-saving books to their parents at home.

In the second half of the 19th century, cases of falling away from the Orthodox Church into sectarianism multiplied among the people. The shepherds were seriously alarmed by the spread of drunkenness, first among the urban poor, and then in the countryside, which posed a formidable danger to the physical and moral health of the nation.

In the late 1850s, on the initiative of the parish clergy and under their leadership, sobriety societies began to be established. And in the circles of the radical intelligentsia, temperance societies were viewed as a fruitless philanthropic undertaking. Meanwhile, tens of thousands of drunk people, joining societies and taking a vow of complete abstinence from alcohol, really became teetotalers, and thus saved not only life, but also the soul. At the beginning of the 19th century, the number of members of these societies approached 500,000 people.

At the beginning of the XX century. in the Russian Orthodox Church there were: more than 100 bishops, over 50 thousand (54,923 in 1914) parish churches, about 100 thousand (117,915 in 1914) white clergy, including priests, deacons and clerks, about 1,000 (953 in 1914) monasteries, over 90 thousand (94,629 in 1914) monastics, including novices and novices. The number of churches during the last reign (of Emperor Nicholas II) increased by 10 thousand, amounting to 57 thousand by 1917, and the number of monasteries by more than 250 (by 1917 there were 1025). According to the statistics of the All-Russian population census of 1897, persons of the Orthodox confession made up 67% of the country's population. The total number of Orthodox believers by 1914 was estimated at 98,363,874 people (Minzaripov, 2019).

During the reign of Emperor Nicholas II, more saints were glorified than in all previous reigns. On the personal initiative of the Sovereign, St. Seraphim of Sarov was canonized. His canonization was the beginning of the glorification of many Russian saints. Among them are St. Joasaph of Belgorod, the Holy Blessed Princess Anna of Kashinskaya, Hieromartyr Hermogenes, Patriarch of Moscow and All Russia, St. John of Tobolsk, St. Euphrosyne of Polotsk. Many churches and monasteries were built at the same time.

The clergy was considered a privileged, honorary class in Russia in all periods of its history. The Orthodox clergy was divided into black (all monastics) and white, and the latter included both the clergy proper (protopresbyters and archpriests, presbyters, priests, protodeacons and subdeacons, as well as clerks in the rank of psalmists), and clergy (sextonaries, deacons, etc.). d.). Since the black clergy, as monks who had renounced the world, could not have property, had no offspring, or terminated all civil ties with children, parents and all relatives, and persons of the upper classes entering monasticism could not enjoy any class privileges, to speak of the clergy as class group is possible, primarily in relation to the white clergy.

In the XVIII - XIX centuries. the financial position of the parish clergy in the countryside was not much higher than that of wealthy peasants, and in the city it was comparable to the position of the lower part of the bureaucracy and the bulk of the townspeople (with the exception of the clergy of cathedrals and, of course, the court clergy). At this time, the practice (not formally legalized by any civil code or church canon) of the actual inheritance of church parishes was established, when the diocesan bishop, when the parish priest retired, secured, at the request of the latter, a place for his son or son-in-law.

As a result, the applicant could most often get a church parish by marrying the daughter of a priest, for which even lists of brides were kept in the spiritual consistories and recommendations were given to those who wished. At the same time, the principle of the need for spiritual education to occupy a clergy position, enshrined in the Spiritual Regulations, was finally established.

From the very beginning, the clergy were free from state taxes, first of all, from the poll tax, recruitment (from the moment it was established and until the introduction of universal military service), and from 1874 - military service and from military billeting. The freedom of clergy (priests and deacons) from corporal punishment was proclaimed as early as 1747.

Persons of the clergy were deprived of the right to own serfs (before secularization, this right was exercised corporately by monasteries, bishops' houses, and even some churches), but priests who transferred to the clergy from the nobility and also received orders were recognized this right. The clergy could own uninhabited lands and houses. When owning houses for clerics, there was one restriction: it was impossible to place taverns and drinking establishments in these houses. Clerics could not engage in contracts and deliveries and act as guarantors for them. In general, persons of the clergy were forbidden to engage in "uncharacteristic" commercial trades, entailing their inclusion in the trading category (ie, registration in guilds and workshops). This prohibition went along the same lines as the prohibition for the clergy to visit "games", play cards, etc.

Belonging to the clergy was assimilated at birth and upon entry into the ranks of the white clergy from other classes. In principle, the law permitted entry into the clergy to persons of all estates, except for serfs who did not receive a leave of absence from their owners, but persons of taxable estates could join the ranks of the clergy only if the local diocesan authorities certified that there were not enough clergy to fill the corresponding position, with "approving behavior and in the presence of a certificate of discharge from a peasant or urban society.

The transition to the white clergy of persons of the nobility until the beginning of the 20th century. for Russia was uncharacteristic, but this practice was quite common in Ukraine. The children of the clergy inherited their class affiliation and were not supposed to choose their own kind of life upon reaching adulthood, but those who remained with their fathers until the age of 15 without being sent to theological schools and appropriate training or expelled from theological schools for dullness and laziness were excluded from the spiritual rank and had to choose their own kind of life, i.e. to be assigned to any community of the taxable class - petty-bourgeois or peasant - or to sign up as a merchant. The children of clergy who voluntarily evaded the clergy had to choose their own way of life. For the "superfluous" children of the clergy, so-called "analysis" was periodically arranged, in which the children of the clergy, who were not recorded anywhere and were not identified anywhere, were given into soldiers. This practice finally ceased only by the 1860s.

The children of the clergy had the right (and initially this right meant an obligation) to receive education in theological schools. Graduates of theological seminaries and theological academies might wish to choose a secular career for themselves. To do this, they had to resign from the spiritual department. Those born in the clergy upon entering the civil service enjoyed the same rights as the children of personal nobles, but this applied only to clergy children. When entering - voluntarily or by analysis - into the military service, the children of the clergy who graduated from the secondary department of the seminary and were not dismissed from the seminary for vices, enjoyed the rights of volunteers. But for persons who voluntarily resigned from the priesthood and wished to enter the civil service, such entry was prohibited for priests for 10 years after the removal of the dignity, and for deacons - 6 years.

In practice, the most common option for changing the class affiliation for children of the clergy in the XVIII - early XIX centuries. there was entry into the civil service as a clerk until reaching the first class rank, and later - to universities and other educational institutions. The prohibition in 1884 for graduates of seminaries to enter universities significantly limited this path of class and social mobility of the clergy. At the same time, the greater openness of ecclesiastical educational institutions (according to the charters of 1867 and 1884) for people of all classes, as well as the formal prohibition of the inheritance of parishes, contributed to greater openness of the clergy.

The wives of the clergy adopted their class affiliation and retained it after the death of their husbands (until the second marriage). Persons belonging to the Orthodox clergy were subject to the court of the spiritual department.

Evidence of belonging to the clergy was metrical certificates, clerical statements compiled in consistories, as well as protege letters.

The clergy did not have a special corporate estate organization, except for the beginnings of such an organization in the form of diocesan congresses and attempts to introduce in the 1860s and early 1880s. the election of the deans. Inherited at birth, belonging to the clergy was preserved upon reaching the age of majority only upon admission to a clergy position.

Belonging to the clergy could be combined with inborn or received (for example, by order) rights of nobility and honorary citizenship. In general, the relations of confessions developed in four planes: religious, political (sometimes even military-political), economic, cultural. The nature of the relationship, namely, confrontation, tolerant coexistence or cooperation, of different confessions with each other was dictated by a number of closely intertwined, mutually determining factors rooted both in the creeds themselves and in the external environment of their existence. Dogmatic, canonical (church organizational), ritual, missionary activity, moral authority of religious organizations, the political orientation of their activities, etc., affected here.

To a large extent, the possibility of interaction between the Russian Orthodox Church and other confessions in the XIX century. determined by the influence of the noted factors, as well as by the fact that orthodox Orthodoxy was finally integrated into the system of the state apparatus of power, having received de jure the status of the dominant official religion.

It was very difficult for the Russian Orthodox Church to contact the old-believers. In addition to ideological differences, the fact that the old-believers, being divided into numerous sects, often at enmity with each other, brought up intolerance towards dissidents in their adherents. [2]Each old-believer sect considered its [2]faith[2] to be the only true one and, accordingly, looked at other sects as [2]apostates[2].

Russian Orthodox Church pursued the old-believers as the main competitor in the struggle for minds and influence on believers. No wonder "seduction into schism" was considered as a criminal offense. In this, the views of the Russian Orthodox Church and the government coincided, because: "Nicholas I considered the "transition into schism" dangerous not only in religious, but also in political terms, because religious "dissidence" ... prepared minds for the realization of the possibility of disobedience to the authorities, developed freethinking." To weaken the influence of the Old Believers, in relation to its moderate part, the experience of liquidating the Greek Catholic Church was used.

Since 1800, there has been a unity of faith, a kind of union between the Russian Orthodox Church and the old-believers of the priestly sense, when the Old Believers received the priesthood from the Orthodox Church, they could legally open their churches, observe the old rites, and print books based on samples not subjected to correction during Nikon's reform. In organizational terms, the parishes of the same faith were subordinate to the corresponding Orthodox-Orthodox bishop. Thus, through common faith, part of the old-believers integrated with the Russian Orthodox Church and the opposition moment was neutralized to some extent. At the All-Russian Local Council of the Russian Orthodox Church in 1917–1918, which restored the patriarchate and elected the holy Patriarch Tikhon, much attention was paid to the reform of the parish community and many other problems that confronted the Church in connection with the normalization of the entire structure of church life. But all these labors and decisions of the Council were essentially swept away by the hurricane of persecution that overtook the Church. The time for church reforms was lost, and again only the path of personal achievement remained, indicated by the ancient and new saints, martyrs. The persecution of the Church began immediately after the October Revolution of 1917. At first, it had the character of a massacre against clerics who "fell under the arm". Then, under the leadership of L.D. Trotsky, V.I. Lenin and the Politburo, all-Russian campaigns are being carried out to open the relics and seize church valuables, grandiose trials of the Moscow and Petrograd clergy (similarly in many other areas), then a course was taken for the complete liquidation of the Church by all means. Splits, all kinds of provocations, mass arrests, torture, executions. According to our data, by the beginning of the Great Patriotic War in 1941, all Orthodox monasteries, all church educational institutions were closed, and 90% of all Orthodox churches were also closed. The authors of this book have often seen abandoned Russian Orthodox churches. Some churches were built in the 19th century, but even more ancient structures built in the 17th-18th centuries have been preserved on the territory of Russia. And no one is following them. All these symbols of divine power make a frightening impression, because once upon a time prayers were offered up in these very walls, and today the wind is walking here and spreading dust from collapsing walls around. Each of the dilapidated temples once received parishioners under its arches, and now their only visitors are only travelers, photographers and lovers of ancient antiquity.

We can see one of these abandoned churches in the historic village with the euphonious name «Argamach-Palna». It is located in the Lipetsk region, 13 kilometers from Yelets, and we drove here purposefully to visit the Argamach archaeological park. In this place there is a beautiful tract, which is located in this picturesque place, which is worth a visit. Even at the entrance to the Argamach-Palna village, from afar we can see the high bell tower of the church, and then the dilapidated red brick church itself, which rises above the ancient village. This Russian Orthodox church was abandoned and today the church is in a deplorable state. The church can be viewed from all sides, but it is not possible to look inside, since the door is tightly closed, and all the windows of the building are walled up with stones.

In these photos we can see the Church of the Nativity of the Blessed Virgin (tserkov' Rozhdestva Presvyatoy Bogoroditsy), which was built in 1844. There is no detailed information on the Internet about this church, since there are hundreds, if not thousands, of such churches in Russia (Ashmarov, 2019).

According to local residents, this church is not completely abandoned. There are even some paintings on the walls of the temple. And from time to time there are church services. However, this is very doubtful, because it is dangerous to be inside such an emergency building. Yes, and everything around here is overgrown with weeds, I can't imagine how you can get inside through such thickets. We know that this stone Orthodox church was built at the expense of ordinary parishioners. And after the revolution of 1917, like most churches, this church was closed. During the Great Patriotic War, the front line passed through Yelets, and a hospital was located in the building of the former parish school. There is simply no information about the future fate of the temple on the network. And at present, the Church of the Nativity of the Blessed Virgin (tserkov' Rozhdestva Presvyatoy Bogoroditsy) continues to collapse and overgrow with wild thickets. And it stands, useless to anyone, frightening passers-by with a bare frame left over from the spire that once crowned the high bell tower. We are very sorry, but this church is not alone. How many more such abandoned structures in Russia are in a deplorable state and simply dream of reconstruction. Each of these forgotten churches can tell its own story, in such places a person always experiences excitement and sadness, seeing how the treasures of the unique Russian church architecture perish. The historical tragedy of the growing secular state persecution of the church served to radically change the Russian Orthodox Church, its spiritual purification and subsequent later revival. True, most of the laity of little faith renounced their faith and departed from the church. Even part of the clergy, under the threat of physical violence, went into the so-called "renovationism." It cannot be said that those who remained in the "Tikhonov" church were a monolithic mass, but the spiritual and church level of the "Tikhonites" was already completely different. Almost immediately or very quickly, most of the external organizational issues disappeared, the administrative and economic activities of the Russian Patriarch, bishops, deans, rectors lost their scale along with the loss of freedom, state support, communications, land, buildings, etc. It was difficult to remain within the framework of the Orthodox Church in this difficult time of the dominance of the Soviet state in all spheres of society, all the more so based on reverence and love for Christian rites, on the habit of Orthodox church traditions.

CONCLUSION

In conclusion, it should be said that on the one hand, the XIX - early XX centuries were the heyday of Russian Orthodox missionary work on the territory of the Russian state and beyond. On the other hand, the activities of Orthodox missionaries did not always achieve the necessary results, sometimes the number of baptized people for one or another period of time was calculated in units. However, the importance of Russian missionary work in the development of intercultural relations between Russia and various countries of the world was enormous. As a result of the translation activities of Russian missionaries, the Holy Scriptures and other spiritual literature were translated into Kalmyk, Finnish, Japanese, Chinese and other languages. In the countries of the East and in other regions of the world, Orthodox churches were built, which were beautiful examples of Russian architecture and architecture.

Charles Darwin, despite his seemingly anti-divine theory of the origin of man, himself believed in God. He represented him as the supreme being who determines the laws of the entire universe. However, over time, his faith was rather weakened after the death of his own daughter.

REFERENCES

Ashmarov, I. A., & Ershov, B. A. (2019) Nekotorye aspekty vzaimodejstviya cerkvi i svetskoj vlasti v Rossii v XIX - nachale XX v. In Shestnadcatye Damianovskie chteniya: Russkaya pravoslavnaya cerkov' i obshchestvo v istorii Rossii i Kurskogo kraya. Materialy Vserossijskoj (nacional'noj) nauchno-prakticheskoj konferencii.

Ashmarov, I. A., & Ershov, B. A. (2019). Rol' cerkvi v ekonomicheskoj zhizni obshchestva XIX - nachala XX veka. In Pravoslavie i obshchestvo: grani vzaimodejstviya. Sbornik statej III Mezhdunarodnoj nauchno-prakticheskoj konferencii v ramkah IX Zabajkal'skih Rozhdestvenskih obrazovatel'nyh chtenij, regional'nogo etapa XXVIII Mezhdunarodnyh Rozhdestvenskih obrazovatel'nyh chtenij.

Maslova, M. V. (2018). Russia's humanitarian security in the context of modern strategic instability. *Fundamental Aspects of Mental Health, 1,* 51–56.

Medynskiy, E.N. (1925-1930). *The history of pedagogy in connection with the economic development of society.* Academic Press.

Minzaripov, R. G., Fursova, V. V., & Makhambetova, M. A. (2019). Material status University teachers in the context of social well-being. *Kazan Socio-Humanitarian Bulletin, 5,* 9–14.

Perevozchikova, L.S., Ershov, B.A., Ashmarov, I.A., & Volkova, E.A. (2017). Role of Russian Orthodox Church in Life of Peasants in Russia in XIX - the Beginning of the XXth Centuries. *Bylye Gody, 43*(1), 121-128.

Conclusion

The history of the Russian Orthodox Church in the Central Black Earth provinces in the undertaken research developed during the contradictory period of the 1801-1917s, when the clergy experienced the direct impact of social changes and gradually merged into the public life of the Russian state. In the 19th century, relations between the Church and state power in Russia were based on the principles of cooperation, but, despite the emperors' careful attention to the needs of the clergy, the state often impeded the development of church life. Restrictions were introduced into the canonization of saints, which led to the fact that during the entire synodal period, before the reign of Emperor Nicholas II, four saints and not a single reverend were glorified. The need for church ceremonies for all public servants was a difficult side in the church life of the 19th century. Along with official duties, confession and communion became an annual state duty, and the clergy was obliged to observe their performance.

State policy was complex and controversial with respect to the Russian Orthodox Church in the 19th century, as evidenced by its socio-economic situation. Nicholas I contributed most to the growth of church ownership. The number of church lands during his reign increased by 2-3 times. In the provinces of the Central Black Earth Region, small owners constituted the bulk of the landowners from the clergy, methods and forms, the management of which depended on the size of possessions. In the second half of the 19th century, monastic land ownership began to develop more intensively.

It should be noted that with the abolition of serfdom, the attribution system for providing monasteries was abolished, using the labor of state peasants who had to work for the monastery for 25 years. In exchange for peasants, monasteries began to receive money from the state, as well as various donations of land and money, monasteries could buy land or receive it for debts. As a result, in the XIX - early XX centuries monastic land ownership began to grow.

In the 19th century, Russian society and the Orthodox Church were not a single organism. The wealth of individual church people and churches could be contrasted with the poverty of a large number of clergy. Deacons and clerks within the same province were a less well-to-do part of the clergy, except for those who served in the cathedrals. Where parishes were crowded and the population was more affluent, deacons and clerks were provided much better than priests in the provinces or from poor areas of the country, and the level of prices had to be taken into account. The clergy departed from traditional means of support and reoriented to official salaries, while continuing to get involved in the bureaucratic apparatus. The more affluent clergy, in material terms, did not differ from the nobility in terms of their income. At the level of the most well-to-do officials, financially, there were priors, protopresbyters, bishops of prosperous monasteries and cathedrals. The government, discussing the problems of the financial situation of the Russian Orthodox Church, tried in various ways to solve them. In the period under review, the Church already had significant material resources, but they were insufficient, so efforts to increase them did not stop.

In the XIX century, the boundaries of the Russian Orthodox Church expanded, and the number of dioceses increased, their number was 68 with 71 vicars. During this period, a rather significant evolution took place in the clergy in the sphere of various internal and general quantitative characteristics. The number of clergy has changed; the relations between its strata have begun to be redistributed: protopresbyters and bishops, rectors of monasteries, monks - priestniks, deacons, hierodeacon, hieromonks, and monks. By increasing the number of higher strata, archpriests and priests, and reducing the number of clergy, the internal monolithic nature of the white clergy has grown. At the same time, the number of pastors in relation to the Orthodox population gradually decreased.

The crisis in Russian Orthodoxy was an indicator of the state of tension and generated public thoughts about the fate of the Orthodox Church. Looking at the history of the Russian Orthodox Church in a sufficiently large period of time, we see that the Church changed under the influence of the changes that took place in Russia in the 19th and early 20th centuries. However, these changes were small in comparison with the radical changes taking place with the country and population, which led to a drop in the authority of the clergy and the Church, which were unable to respond correctly to the requests of the time and parishioners. The bans of official and synodal authorities to address social and political issues in the sermons had a negative impact on relations between parish clergy and parishioners. Therefore, those parishioners who first sought answers to urgent questions of interest to their spiritual fathers, without receiving the necessary explanations, continued to search other preachers in other places.

The conflict between the government and society was deepened due to the lack of church independence, which generated mutual distrust and was regarded as a sign of impending catastrophe. Intense ideological struggle, which also affected the Church, was generated by unstable modernization and the choice of ways of social development. The Russian clergy believed that spiritual development should take place on the basis of Christian principles of renewal. Contradictions between secular and church norms were resolved through the adoption of case-law by the Senate. In general, the Church maintained the leading role of Orthodoxy in society.

The monograph discloses the socio-cultural interaction of the state, the Church as a social institution, society and personality, which manifested itself in the regulatory role of the Church and consisted in the fact that the Church offered the highest system of moral values that are vital to man. Having a stable position in the state and remaining open to the individual, the Church provided an opportunity to form a constructive worldview and provided the conditions for the positive orientation of the individual.

In the XIX - early XX centuries Russian Orthodoxy grew up among the laity and clergy of thinking and creatively gifted theologians. The Russian Orthodox Church strictly assessed the ideas of her predecessors and formed a unified teaching in all sections and directions of theology. The educational activity of the spiritual ascetics of the Central Black Earth region was of particular importance in the development of Orthodoxy, and much attention was paid to it in this study. Such spiritual ascetics include Tikhon Zadonsky, bishop of Voronezh and Yelets, who led the Voronezh Theological School; Saint Anthony of Smirnitsky; Bishop of Tambov and Shatsky Theofil Raev; Bishop of Tambov and Shatsky, Makarii Bulgakov. All of them contributed to the development of enlightenment of the clergy and theological schools.

The sphere of education made it possible for the clergy of the provinces of the Central Black Earth Region to use their forces in the struggle for the younger generation. The educational activities of the theological seminaries contributed to the publication of books, magazines and newspapers, and then influenced the development of the regional educational environment. The professional field of clergy was the spread of Christian culture. Domestic spiritual education was fully formed in the first half of the 19th century. At this time, the theological school was often subjected to reform due to changes in the spiritual, educational and church policies, which led to the centralized management of educational institutions and the division of the educational field throughout the country into four educational districts, which headed the theological academies. The academies have become cultural, educational, scientific, methodological and theological centers. Between academies, seminaries and colleges vertically established strict continuity.

Until 1867, that is, before the establishment of the charter of theological schools, two periods can be defined in Russian spiritual education. The most successful period for the development of the system of spiritual education was from 1808 to 1839, when the quality of education increased, the material base of the spiritual school expanded, funding improved, theological academies became leading centers of theological science. The second period lasted from 1830 to the 1860s. That was the time when a spiritual education was fully formed in Russia, and theological schools became independent in the material and educational process from the local diocesan authority. In the first half of the 19th century, the formation of a general education began in the provinces of the Central Chernozem Region, where spiritual education was of systemic importance. At first, the provincial secular school was staffed with cadres of theological school, and then there was a mutual influence of secular and spiritual educational institutions. There were more theological schools in the provinces of the Central Black Earth Region than secular schools during this period, and the graduates of theological schools had great prospects, since spiritual education provided the opportunity for continuous education, but still lost to secular education.

Spiritual education contributed to the emergence in the province of a wider circle of educated and literate people. Highly educated cadres of the theological school had a powerful impact on the formation of the educational, cultural and moral environment. The contradictions in church-state relations were led by the shortcomings of the educational institutions, but the rapid rise of theological science in the mid-19th century made it possible to give a positive assessment to the achievements of the theological school of this period.

Revealing the family life of priests, we noted that in the XIX - early XX centuries the number of priest families has not changed. Compared to the nobility, priests were less prone to Europeanization. In the families of the clergy, the role of women and children is also increasing. The fragmentation of the patriarchal family was facilitated by the practice of appointing to places in the parishes, which increased the status of its younger members. Starting from adolescence, children of rural clergy lived separately, as they received education leaving their parents' homes, and only occasionally returned home.

In the families of clergy, a certain isolation remained. The gender roles of parents in spiritual families influenced marital strength, and then were assimilated and reproduced by children.

Analysis of the practical activities of various classes, namely, nobles and peasants, generalizations and conclusions contained in the study suggest that at the beginning of the 19th century the destruction of estate ownership rights deepened, and the social heterogeneity of society began to gradually increase. The interaction of nobles and peasants with the Church in the provinces of the Central Black Earth Region in the 19th and early 20th centuries. It was aimed at serving the Fatherland, the Church and the people and was blessed by Christian shrines. The largest number of literate people was the nobility, but it did not seek to transfer to the clergy. Due to the small number of theological schools, the study of sacred books, rites, and church services took place in a practical way. The main support of the autocracy were the nobles. Nobles and representatives of the black clergy had a privileged legal status, although the nobility had broader privileges and rights. Part of the clergy, having a sufficient level of education, understood the importance of their ministry and tried to achieve the position of the nobility, but its provision and small incomes served as an obstacle to this.

The clergy investigated the historical phenomena of the religious life of the region, realizing in their works the principles of the Church Orthodox worldview, while observing strict scientific conscientiousness. The press took part in the discussion of the problems of life and the spiritual activities of clergy.

In the XIX - early XX centuries the clergy was a nationwide leader, capable of leading the movement of society forward on the basis of the gospel. And therefore, the clergy, which was interconnected with society, played a large role in the history of the Church and the state. Parish clergy had a great influence on the people and were in close contact with them. In addition to religious duties, in the late XIX - early XX centuries the clergy also performed significant state functions. The Church had legislative powers to register acts of civil status, administer justice on a variety of issues, and its powers in the field of upbringing and education were expanded, which turned the Church into a public law institution.

At the end of the nineteenth century in Russia there was a need to adapt Orthodoxy to a new period in the development of society, which was associated with the development of capitalism, the growth of social tension and social polarization, the emergence of new ideas of radicalism. Throughout history, maintaining the Orthodox dogma, the Russian Orthodox Church has taken an active political position. In rare cases, the Church was contrary to the state, since its position was based on Byzantism. The limits and forms of the social mission of the clergy were expanding - not only as a connector of the heterogeneous parts of the "world" into a single whole, but also as a carrier of Christian love, a source of trust in society. Religious awakening was manifested in the restoration of the national consciousness of the people and historical memory. It meant a moral, spiritual and cultural renewal of the country's life. The church, uniting the spiritual forces of the nation, often saved the state, and during the period of stability never acted as an opposition and did not aspire to political domination.

The Russian Orthodox Church associated its history with the history of the Russian state, thanks to which the church could influence the political processes in the country. The relationship between the state and the Russian Orthodox Church that developed in the 19th century did not always meet Russia's needs. It can be argued that with respect for religion, some government officials acquired political dividends, but did not recognize religion as a fundamental area of public life. The state, subjugating the Church to itself, destroyed the spiritual dependence on the secular, which led to the elimination of moral principles in society and to internal discord. There was a merging of the Russian Orthodox Church and the state, which was recognized by the clergy themselves. The guardianship of the Church by secular authorities prompted religious leaders to the idea of the need for church reforms.

Interacting, civil and church authorities in the XIX - early XX centuries in the provinces of the Central Black Earth Region, they should take into account the opinions and the possibility of interference in decision-making by the spiritual and secular authorities, while observing mutual interests. The deanery of the parish churches, personally appointed by the bishop from the most experienced and active clergy and having great oversight rights over the various parties of the churches and clergy of their district, were the main business partners of the church organization with the county administration. Thus, in the province, the religious component was controversial. The county clergy in the provinces of the Central Black Earth Region were inferior to the civil authorities in adapting the diocesan authorities to local conditions. The clergy was bound by canon and hierarchy and had no right to independently resolve issues in their area of competence. However, ordinary priests and deans had a great influence on all social groups due to the state status of Orthodoxy and due to the religiosity of the population. Therefore, in a number of aspects, religious life in the province was politicized, but Orthodoxy also played a big role in the political life of the region. The only option for the interaction of the Church and the state in the XIX - early XX centuries on the path to the development of absolutism was the existence of only one source of power - the state.

State and public figures, entrepreneurs, officials and ordinary trustees in the study period were morally and materially interested in church charity. The outward activity of philanthropists was rooted in the nature of the pastoral ministry of the clergy and Christian morality. The church made many efforts to provide pensions for the clergy and their families.

Almshouses were organized in the dioceses of the Central Black Earth Region, in which the elderly representatives of the clergy and their families found refuge. A personal example of the clergy and their explanation that the tasks of charity are in line with Christian doctrine have attracted a large number of parishioners to active work for the development of the spirituality of society. However, the Church was not limited to only one educational work. The charity of individual churches and clergy, which was aimed at the dissemination of education, financial donations, and the search for cultural monuments located in the area belonging to the Church, was of great importance. Temples, monasteries and monasteries collected information about those in need and provided targeted assistance.

One of the main disadvantages of charity was the lack of necessary interaction in the work of religious and state organizations. Assistance was not always systemic due to historical conditions: a small amount of funds and many tasks that required resolution, insufficient perfection of legal laws, and vast territory. At the beginning of the 20th century, there was no sufficient state legislative system of social support for society.

Nevertheless, in the controversial historical period, the Church played a significant role in the development of social charity. In modern Russia, based on past experience of the Russian Orthodox Church, charity is being revived, which should be addressed to a specific person, his problems, prospects and development. The presence of charitable dwellings, such as the central community of charity, speak of the high level of the establishment of the public activity of the Russian Orthodox Church in the 19th and early 20th centuries.

In the XIX - early XX centuries in Russia, charitable and medical assistance to the population was provided by 30 thousand state, private and public institutions, among which the communities of charity sisters took their rightful place. In addition to providing high-quality and affordable medical care to the poor, the mercy center performed a major social function, it was necessary to keep the room open.

Their existence was mainly ensured by donations from philanthropists, and therefore the financial situation of the sisters of mercy was not stable. The leadership of the communities for the full functioning of their institutions was constantly looking for new sources of funds. The sovereigns and members of the Imperial family provided material assistance to the communities of charity sisters, thereby setting an example that inspired many Russian people. Representatives of the nobility and wealthy merchant families, who donated their capital to them, also patronized the communities of sisters of mercy. Social and cultural trends of that time contributed to the development of communities of nurses, the education of women, the participation of women in public life, Russia's accession to the conventions of the International Red Cross Society. But these factors also had a negative side, since under their influence the main positions of various public charitable organizations, including the activities of the communities of sisters of mercy, changed. But the idea of Christian service to others continued to play a major role.

In the 19th century, interest in pilgrimage increased. Thousands of pilgrims who worshiped icons, relics and other church relics visited the monasteries. Prayer books of the Russian Church and simple monks of the cloisters also attracted believers of all classes. However, among the pilgrims there were mainly petty bourgeois and peasants, who made up 80% of the population of Russia. The attitude to the pilgrims and wanderers was respectful; customs of hospitality («strannopriimstvo») were widespread.

The monograph shows that the Russian Orthodox Church, thanks to thinking forces and social upsurge, became an influential social force, emerging from a state of stillness and spiritual detachment from worldly concerns. Social, administrative and economic structures as a result of the relationship between the Church and the Russian state, in the minds of people merged with the Orthodox faith, therefore, the protection of these structures was perceived by the population as defending the faith. In the processes of development of Russian society, the clergy in the XIX - early XX centuries. Assisting in spiritual improvement was considered its main task.

Practical recommendations, substantiated in the monograph, will help to solve problems in state-church relations. These recommendations include the following ideas.

1. The training of professional personnel in the field of religion is able to prevent the penetration of socially dangerous sentiments into educational institutions; therefore, the strengthening of cooperation between the government and the Church in the educational sphere has been justified.

2. A more vigorous interaction between the state and the church is needed, aimed at eliminating the negative trends in the propaganda of cruelty, terrorism, immoral behavior in the media.

3. In order to preserve objects of cultural heritage, it is possible to propose the creation of joint commissions of the Russian Orthodox Church and the state to attract philanthropists, and the state can provide the latter with tax or other benefits.

4. The guarantee of the stable development of a multi-confessional Russian state at the present time may not only be a change in the colors of religion, but also the preservation of freedom of thought, as a fundamental principle of concern. Today, the role of the Church in the rejuvenation of society is, first of all, in support of the general human standards of peace, the ideals of peace, community and love.

Thus, it can be noted that the Orthodox Church in the provinces of the Central Black Earth Region, despite all the difficulties: financial, political, social, managed to determine the main directions of religious education of the population, charity, and missionary work. Of course, the state was interested in church politics, but secular authorities tried to preserve their own interests in this policy.

Appendix

Figure 1. Abandoned and forgotten Orthodox Church of the Nativity of the Blessed Virgin («tserkov' Rozhdestva Presvyatoy Bogoroditsy») in the Lipetsk region, Russia

Figure 2. Orthodox church — tserkov' Rozhdestva Presvyatoy Bogoroditsy

Figure 3. Orthodox church — tserkov' Rozhdestva Presvyatoy Bogoroditsy

Figure 4. Orthodox church — tserkov' Rozhdestva Presvyatoy Bogoroditsy

Figure 5. Orthodox church — tserkov' Rozhdestva Presvyatoy Bogoroditsy

Figure 6. Orthodox church — tserkov' Rozhdestva Presvyatoy Bogoroditsy

Figure 7. Orthodox church — tserkov' Rozhdestva Presvyatoy Bogoroditsy

Table 1. Church hierarchy of the Russian Orthodox Church

Hierarchical Degrees of Church Ministers	White (Married) Clergy	Black (Monastic) Clergy
III Episcopate (Bishopric or «Arkhiyereystvo»)	-	The Patriarch Metropolitan Archbishop Bishop
II Presbytery (Priesthood or «Iereystvo»)	Protopresbyter Archpriest Priest (Presbyter)	Archimandrite Hegumen Hieromonk
I Diaconate	Protodeacon Deacon	Archdeacon Hierodeacon

Figure 8.

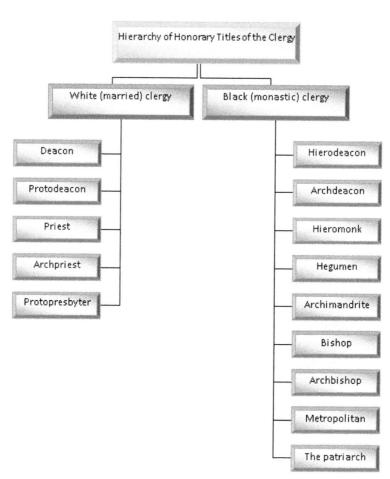

Figure 9. Saint Mitrofan, Bishop of Voronezh (1623–1703)

Figure 10. Theophan the Recluse (Feofan Zatvornik), Bishop of Tambov and Shatsky (1815–1894)

Figure 11. "Miropomazaniye". Artist Ekaterina Kononova (Voronezh State Institute of Arts).

Compilation of References

Afanasyev, V. V. (2008). *Optinsky were: Essays and stories from the history of the Vvedensky Optina desert*. Siberian Invertebrate.

Akin'shin, A. N. (2003). *Temples of Voronezh*. Kvarta Publishing House.

Anderson, L. W., & Krathwohl, D. (2001). *A taxonomy for learning, teaching, and assessing: A revision of Bloom's Taxonomy of Educational Objectives*. Longman.

Anthony, St. (2003). *Glorified Saints. Saints, New Martyrs, Rev. Prince 1*. Academic Press.

Apanasenok, A. V. (2010). *The formation and functioning of the Old Believer communities of the Central Black Earth region of Russia: The last third of the XVII - The beginning of the XX century*. Dr. East. Sciences.

Archive of the Russian Ethnographic Museum (AREM) F. 7. Op. 1. D. 1140. Ethnographic description of the Oryol province L. 16ob, 20-21ob.

Archive of the Russian Ethnographic Museum (AREM) F. 7. Op.1. D. 1140. Ethnographic description of the Oryol province. L. 21.

Ashmarov, I. A., & Ershov, B. A. (2019) Nekotorye aspekty vzaimodejstviya cerkvi i svetskoj vlasti v Rossii v XIX - nachale XX v. In Shestnadcatye Damianovskie chteniya: Russkaya pravoslavnaya cerkov' i obshchestvo v istorii Rossii i Kurskogo kraya. Materialy Vserossijskoj (nacional'noj) nauchno-prakticheskoj konferencii.

Ashmarov, I. A., & Ershov, B. A. (2019). Nekotorye aspekty vzaimodejstviya cerkvi i svetskoj vlasti v Rossii v XIX - nachale XX v. In Shestnadcatye Damianovskie chteniya: Russkaya pravoslavnaya cerkov' i obshchestvo v istorii Rossii i Kurskogo kraya. Materialy Vserossijskoj (nacional'noj) nauchno-prakticheskoj konferencii.

Ashmarov, I. A., & Ershov, B. A. (2019). Rol' cerkvi v ekonomicheskoj zhizni obshchestva XIX - nachala XX veka. In Pravoslavie i obshchestvo: grani vzaimodejstviya. Sbornik statej III Mezhdunarodnoj nauchno-prakticheskoj konferencii v ramkah IX Zabajkal'skih Rozhdestvenskih obrazovatel'nyh chtenij, regional'nogo etapa XXVIII Mezhdunarodnyh Rozhdestvenskih obrazovatel'nyh chtenij.

Ashmarov, I.A., Ershov, B.A., Bulavin, R.V., Shkarubo, S.N., & Danilchenko, S.L. (2020). The Material and Financial Situation of the Russian Orthodox Church in the XIX - Early XX Centuries. *Smart Innovation, Systems and Technologies*, 149-158.

Askochensky, V. I. (1900). In and. In *Russian Biographical Dictionary*. Academic Press.

Aydın, Z., & Yıldız, S. (2014). Using wikis to promote collaborative EFL writing. *Language Learning & Technology, 18*(1), 160–180.

Belyakov, E. V. (2002). Deaconesses in the Russian Orthodox Church. *History (London)*, (9), 1–5.

Benzin, V. M. (1906). *Parish charity in Russia after 1864. Labor Assistance 2*. Academic Press.

Blokhina, N. N. (1997). Moscow communities of sisters of mercy. Experimental curriculum of a special course for pedagogical secondary and higher educational institutions. *Moscow City Teachers' Seminary Scientific Collection*, 195–206.

Blokhin, V. F. (2009). "Gubernskie vedomosti" as a mirror of the Russian province (XIX - early XX century). *Bulletin of the Russian State University, 17*, 20–31.

Bogoslovskij, N. G. (1860). *A practical look at the life of a priest. Father's letters to his son*. Academic Press.

Bolkhovitinov, E. A. (1800). *Historical, geographical and economic description of the Voronezh province*. Voronezh.

Bunakov, N. (1907). *Rural school and public life*. Academic Press.

Charitable institutions of the Russian Empire. (1990). Academic Press.

Dmitrievsky, A. A. (2008). *The Imperial Orthodox Palestinian Society and its activities over the past quarter century: 1882–1907*. Publishing House of Oleg Abyshko.

Dobronravov, N. (1904). Patient care in ancient Christianity and in Russia. *Moscow Church Gazette*, (2), 14–18.

Dudzinskaya, E. A. (1983). Slavophiles in the social struggle. Academic Press.

Efremov, L. V. (1874). The Life of Matrena Naumovna Popova, the first organizer of the strange house of the Zadonsky monastery. Academic Press.

Ershov, B. A. (2011). Church charitable societies and institutions of the Voronezh province in the 19th century. *Bulletin of the Tambov University. Series: Humanities, 1*(93), 276-282.

Ershov, B. A., & Drobyshev, A.V. (2017). The emergence and role of church charitable institutions in the provinces of the Central Chernozem region in the XIX-early XX centuries. *History: Facts and symbols, 2*(11), 103-109.

Ershov, B., Novikov, Y.N., Voytovich, D., Ermilova, O., Dushkin, O., & Lubkin, Y. (2019). Physical culture in formation of spiritual education of young people in Russia. *The European Proceedings of Social & Behavioural Sciences,* 3648-3653.

Ershov, B.A., Ashmarov, I.A., & Danilchenko, S.L. (2018). *The Development Of Russian Church Architecture In The 1990s-2017: The State And Prospects.* Stat'ya v otkrytom arhive № 1.

Ershov, B.A., Ashmarov, I.A., Drobyshev, A.V., Zhdanova, T.A., & Buravlev, I.A. (2017). Property And Land Relations Of Russian Orthodox Church And State In Russia. *The European Proceedings of Social & Behavioural Sciences,* 324-331.

Ershov, B. A., & Ashmarov, I. A. (2018). Interaction Of The Orthodox Church And The State In Russia At The Present Stage. *Bulletin Social-Economic and Humanitarian Research, 2,* 19–24.

Ershov, B. A., & Ashmarov, I. A. (2018). Interaction Of The Orthodox Church And The State In Russia At The Present Stage. *Vestnik Èkonomiceskoj Teorii,* (2), 19–24.

Ershov, B. A., & Lubkin, Y. Y. (2016). The activities of the Russian Orthodox Church in countering extremism and terrorism in modern Russia. Historical, philosophical, political and legal sciences, cultural studies and art history. *Questions of Theory and Practice, 11*(73), 97–99.

Ershov, B. A., Nebolsin, V. A., & Solovieva, S. R. (2020). Higher education in technical universities of Russia. *7th International Conference on Education and Social Sciences. Abstracts & Proceedings,* 55-58.

Ershov, B. A., Perepelitsyn, A., Glazkov, E., Volkov, I., & Volkov, S. (2019). Church and state in Russia: management issues. *5th International Conference on Advances in Education and Social Sciences. Abstracts & Proceedings,* 26-29.

Ershov, B. A., Zhdanova, T. A., Kashirsky, S. N., & Monko, T. (2020). Education in the university as an important factor in the socialization of students in Russia. *6th International Conference on Advances in Education. Abstracts & Proceedings,* 517-520.

Ershov, B., Novikov, Y. N., Voytovich, D., Ermilova, O., Dushkin, O., & Lubkin, Y. (2019). Physical culture in formation of spiritual education of young people in Russia. In *The European Proceedings of Social and Behavioural Sciences Complex. Research Institute named after Kh. I. Ibragimov.* Russian Academy of Sciences.

Extract from the journal of the Special Department of the Scientific Committee of the Ministry of Education on December 4, 1879 on the teaching of the Law of God in public schools. 143 p.

Fedorov, V. A. (2005). Theological education in the Russian Orthodox Church in the 19th century. *Pedagogy,* (5), 67–83.

Frieze, G. L. (1991). Church, religion and political culture at sunset of old Russia. *History of the USSR,* (2), 107–115.

GAKO (State Archives of Kursk Region) F. 20. Op. 2. D. 174.L. 7.

GAOO (State Archive of the Oryol Region) F. 580. Op. 1. D. 2063 L. 7-8ob.

GATO (State Archive of the Tambov Region) F. 181. Op. 1. D. 1683. L. 430.

GAVO (State Archive of the Voronezh Region) F. I-84. Op. 2. D 47.L. 225.

Index of temple festivals in the Voronezh diocese. (1885). *Voronezh, 4.*

Kalinin, M. I. (1975). *About youth: Selected speeches and articles.* Young Guard.

Karpova, V. V. (2015). Everyday life of participants of student labor detachments in Russia (1915-1916). *Bulletin of the Tomsk State University. Leningrad State high fur boots named after A. S. Pushkin,* (2), 48–55.

Kartashev, A. V. (2000). *Essays on the history of the Russian church* (Vol. M). Eksmo-Press.

Kartashov, A. V. (1959). Essays on the history of the Russian Church. Academic Press.

Khavin, B. N. (1979). *All about the Olympic Games.* Physical Culture and Sport.

Kholostova, E. I. (2001). *Technologies of social work.* Academic Press.

Klyuchevsky, V. O. (2000). Orthodoxy in Russia. M. 310 p. Personal archive. Certificate N°. 7118. Personal archive. Certificate N°. 10104.

Klyuchevsky, V. O. (1908). *The course of Russian history. Part 2.* Academic Press.

Kolupaev, A. A. (2019). Organization of assistance to refugees during the First World War (on the example of the Kursk province). *Izvestiya Yugo-Zapadnogo gosudarstvennogo universiteta. Series. History and Law, 9*(6), 201–208.

Korf, M. A. (1906). *The nobility and its estate management for the century XVIII-XIX centuries.* Academic Press.

Kovrigina, V. A. (2000). Health care. In Essays on Russian culture of the XIX century: Vol. 2. Power and culture. Academic Press.

Kozyrev, E. E. (2015). Charity of the Royal family during the First World War. *Church and Medicine, 1*(13), 101-104.

Kuchenkova, V. A. (1993). Shrines of the Tambov diocese. Department of Moscow.

Kuhn, L. (1982). *Universal history of physical culture and sports.* Raduga.

Kulabukhov, V. S. (2005). *Evolution of the social status of the Orthodox clergy. Evolution of the class structure of the society of the Central Black Soil in the post-reform period (on the example of the Kursk province).* Academic Press.

Kursk region: An anthology of social work. (2001). Publishing House of MGSU Soyuz.

Lapotnikov, V. A. (1998). *History of nursing in Russia.* Academic Press.

Lapotnikov, V. A. (1998). *History of nursing in Russia.* Academic Press.

Lebedeva, M. A., & Volkova, E. A. (2021). Socio-political movement in the Voronezh region in the middle of the XIX-th century. *State and Society in Modern Politics: Collection of Articles, 8,* 201–206.

Lisichkin, V. M. (1984). Ideology and politics of modern Russian Orthodoxy. Academic Press.

Lisovoy, N. N. (2009). *Mission in Jerusalem*. St. Petersburg: Publishing House of Oleg Abyshko.

Listova, T. A. (2001). National Orthodox rite of creation of a family. *Orthodox life of Russian peasants of the 19th - 20th centuries: Results of ethnographic research*, 31–35.

Litvinov, V. V. (1911). Temples and limits dedicated to St. Tikhon Zadonsky. *Voronezh Antiquity, 10*, 19–25.

Lykoshina, P. I. (1901). *Charity Russia. History of state, public and private charity*. Academic Press.

Marru, A. I. (2003). *History of education in antiquity*. Academic Press.

Maslova, M. V. (2018). Russia's humanitarian security in the context of modern strategic instability. *Fundamental Aspects of Mental Health, 1*, 51–56.

Maslov, I. (1995). *The Prelate Tikhon of Zadonsky and his doctrine of salvation*. Boxwood.

Medynskiy, E.N. (1925-1930). *The history of pedagogy in connection with the economic development of society*. Academic Press.

Metropolitan Lemeshevsky Manuel. (2003). *Russian Orthodox hierarchs 992-1892, 2*, 87–88.

Milyukov, P. N. (1896). *Essays on the history of Russian culture: Part 2. Church and school (faith, creativity, education)*. Academic Press.

Minzaripov, R. G., Fursova, V. V., & Makhambetova, M. A. (2019). Material status University teachers in the context of social well-being. *Kazan Socio-Humanitarian Bulletin, 5*, 9–14.

Mitrofan, S. (1995). *Explanatory word. Materials for the life of the Martyr Grand Duchess Elizabeth. Letters, diaries, memoirs, documents*. Academic Press.

Nikolsky, P. V. (1899). Historical note on the state of the Voronezh Theological Seminary for the last 25 years. *Voronezh Diocesan Sheets, 10*, 426–440.

Oryol diocesan sheets. (1873). N°. 4. 200–207.

Oswalt, J. (1993). Clergy and parish life reform. 1861-1865. *Voprosy istorii, 11-12*, 140–149.

Perevozchikova, L.S., Ershov, B.A., Ashmarov, I.A., & Volkova, E.A. (2017). Role of Russian Orthodox Church in Life of Peasants in Russia in XIX - the Beginning of the XXth Centuries. *Bylye Gody, 43*(1), 121-128.

Polikarpov, F. (1907). Historical and Statistical Description of Churches and Parishes of the Nizhnedevitsky County of Voronezh Province. *Voronezh Antiquity*, (6), 12–15.

Pospelovsky, D. V. (1995). Russian Orthodox Church in the XX century. Academic Press.

Pospelovsky, D. V. (1996). *The Orthodox Church in the History of Russia*. Biblical and Theological Institute of St. Andrew.

Posternak, A. V. (2003). History of the Sisters of Charity communities. *Charity in Russia. Historical and social studies,* 312-320.

RGIA (Russian State Historical Archive) F. 796. Op. 442. D. 1420.L. 26.

RGIA (Russian State Historical Archive) F. 797. Op. 31. D.18a. Art. 3.

Rybakova, S. N. (2009). *Russian monasteries and temples. Traveling to holy places.* Astrel.

Sambikin, D. I. (1882). Assumption Church in the city of Voronezh. *Voronezh Diocesan Sheets, 19,* 623–632.

Selivanov, V. V. (1987). Year of the Russian farmer. *Letters from the village. Essays on the peasantry in Russia in the second half of the XIX century,* 104-108.

Shevtsov, V.V. (2012). Gubernskie vedomosti in the pre-revolutionary historiography of the periodical press. *Bulletin of Tomsk State University,* 414 - 421.

Shmeleva, M. N. (1999). *Public life of the middle of the XIX - beginning XX centuries.* Ecsmo.

Smolich, I. K. (1996). History of the Russian Church. 1700–1917. Publishing House of the Transfiguration of the Valaam Monastery.

Surova, L. V. (2008). Way to heaven. *Pilgrimage to the holy places.* Edition of the Church of St. John Chrysostom of the Moscow Diocese.

Tarasova, V. A. (2005). The Higher Theological School in Russia in the late XIX - early XX centuries. In *History of Imperial Orthodox Theological Academies.* New Chronograph.

The Code of Laws of the Russian Empire. (1912). St. Petersburg: Russian Book Partnership "The Worker". Collection of information on public charity. SPb. 1880–1886. T. 1-7. Archive Raven. spirit. Consistory, Cases Divnogor. Monastery, N°. 450.

The Holy Righteous John of Kronstadt. (1997). The Soul-Christian. *The Ladder.*

The memorial book of the Voronezh province for 1878-1879. (n.d.). Voronezh: Publishing House of the lips. Stat. Committee.

The memorial book of the Voronezh province. (1899). Printing house of Voronezh Lips.

Titlinov, B. V. (1924). *Church during the revolution.* Publishing House "Past".

Tvardovskaya, V. A. (1978) The ideology of the post-reform autocracy. Academic Press.

Tvardovskaya, V. A. (1978). The ideology of the post-reform autocracy. Academic Press.

Vargunin, N. A. (1897). The results of the activity of zemstvos in the field of public education. *Russian Wealth, 9,* 56–69.

Veselovsky, G. (1886). Historical sketch of the city of Voronezh. 1586-1886. Voronezh: Veselovsky Publishing House.

Veselovsky, G. M. (1867). *The city of Ostrogozhsk, Voronezh province and its county.* Voronezh: Type. Governorate. Board.

Veselovsky, G. M. (1876). *Cities of the Voronezh province, their history and current state, with a brief outline of the entire Voronezh province.* Voronezh: Veselovsky Publishing House.

Vvedensky, S. (1905). *Materials on the history of the Voronezh diocese.* Academic Press.

Weinberg, L. B. (1886). Voronezh jubilee collection in memory of the 300th anniversary of the city of Voronezh. Voronezh: Voronezh. Governorate. Stat. Committee.

Zlatoverkhovnikov, N. I. (1902). Monuments of antiquity and new time of Kursk province. Academic Press.

Znamensky, P. V. (1873). Parish clergy in Russia since the time of Peter. Academic Press.

Zyryanov, P. N. (2002). *Russian monasteries and monasticism in the 19th - early 20th centuries.* M. Verbum.

About the Authors

Bogdan Anatolyevich Ershov was born on June 18, 1982 in the city of Voronezh. In 1999 he entered the Voronezh State Pedagogical University at the full-time department of the Faculty of History, which he graduated in 2004 with a degree in History with an additional degree in Social Pedagogy. In November 2007 he defended his Ph.D. thesis on the topic: "Church of the Russian province in the XIX century (on the materials of the Voronezh province)", specialty 07.00.02 - Domestic history in the dissertation council created on the basis of the Voronezh State Pedagogical University. In 2012 he defended his doctoral dissertation on the topic "The Russian Orthodox Church in the system of state relations in the 19th - early 20th centuries. (based on materials from the Central Chernozem provinces) "in the specialty" Domestic history ". On April 15, 2013, the Presidium of the Higher Attestation Commission awarded the degree of Doctor of Historical Sciences. In 2013 he was awarded the academic title of Associate Professor. In 2014, he was awarded a diploma and a medal of the Russian Academy of Sciences as a winner in a competition in the field of history for young scientists of Russia for the monograph "The Russian Orthodox Church in the structure of government in the 19th - early 20th centuries." In 2017, he was awarded the academic title of Corresponding Member of the Russian Academy of Natural Sciences. In May 2020, following the results of elections to the full members of RAE, he was elected Academician of the Russian Academy of Natural Sciences. In 2020 Ershov B.A. underwent professional retraining at the Metropolitan Training Center (Moscow), in accordance with which he received a diploma with the qualification of a Specialist in the field of national and religious relations. Under the leadership of B.A. Ershov prepared two candidates of historical sciences. In 2020, the IGI Global publishing house (Pennsylvania, USA) published the monograph "Political, Economic and Social Factors Affecting the Development of Russian Statehood: New Research and Opportunities." The volume of the monograph is 155 pages.

Ershov B.A. published more than 200 scientific and educational-methodical works, of which 43 scientific articles were published in journals included in the list of the Higher Attestation Commission, 20 articles were published in publications included in the international databases Web of Science and Scopus. The Hirsch index in the RSCI is 19. Ershov B.A. is the editor-in-chief of the scientific online journal *Bulletin Social-Economic and Humanitarian Research*. The journal is included in the authoritative international citation bases: ERIH PLUS, EBSCOhost, EconBiz, Ulrich's Periodicals Directory, RSCI, Revistas científicas electrónicas IBT-CCG UNAM - Biblioteca, Biblioteca Virtual de Biotecnología Library, para las Congress Eric- Resources Online Catalog, WorldCat, The Online Books Page (University of Pennsylvania). Ershov B.A. is the editor-in-chief of the scientific online journal Agrarian History. The journal is included in the international database AGRIS, CAB Abstracts, GeoRef. Currently Ershov B.A. works as a professor at the Voronezh State Technical University at the Department of Philosophy, Sociology and History. The area of scientific interest is the history of the Russian Orthodox Church.

Igor Ashmarov was born on November 18, 1975 in Russia in the urban-type settlement (rgt.) Dobrinka, Lipetsk region. In 1992 he graduated from the Dobrinsky secondary school No. 1 with a gold medal. In 1992 he entered, and in 1997 he graduated from the Voronezh State University ("VSU"), Faculty of History; specialization Department of archeology and history of the ancient world (special group with in-depth study of the English language). Qualification: Historian. History teacher with the right to teach English. Graduated from foreign language courses (English) of the Language Center of Voronezh State University. In 1999-2003, he continued his studies as an applicant for the degree of candidate of sciences at the Voronezh State University ("VSU"), Faculty of Economics, Department of General Economic Theory (preparation and defense of a Ph.D. thesis in economic theory). PhD thesis topic: "Economic institutions of the labor market" (code of the Higher Attestation Commission of the Russian Federation: 08.00.01, supervisor - Doctor of Economics, Professor L.P. Kiyan. Place of defense - Voronezh, Voronezh State University (VSU)). In 2009 he received a certificate of associate professor in the Department of Economic Theory (Voronezh, Voronezh State Technical University (VSTU)). In 2011-2013, he passed retraining at the Voronezh State Technical University (VSTU), obtaining a qualification under the program "Teacher of Higher Education" (1080 hours). In 2018, he underwent professional retraining at the Capital Training Center (Moscow), obtaining a qualification under the program "Teacher, teacher of the basics of life safety. Teaching the basics of life safety in an educational organization (600 hours). In 2019, he completed professional retraining at the Capital Training Center (Moscow), obtaining a qualification under the program "Economist-analyst: An effective system of work in the production and economic activities of an organization" (600 hours). In 2020, he completed professional retraining at the Infourok training center (Smolensk), obtaining a qualification under the program "Management of creative, theater and concert organizations" (600 hours). In 2021, he completed professional retraining at the Capital Training Center (Moscow), obtaining qualifications under the programs "Teacher-psychologist" (600 hours), "Political scientist" (600 hours), "Head of the organization" (600 hours), " Tourism manager" in the direction of "Medical tourism" (600 hours). In 2021, he underwent professional retraining at the Institute of Contemporary Education (Voronezh), obtaining the qualification of an English teacher under the program Theory and Practice of Teaching a Foreign Language (English) in Higher Education (1280 hours). Awarded medal "For Achievement in the Education of Youth" No. 276 (2017) from the Russian Academy of Natural Sciences (RAE). Currently he works at the Voronezh State Institute of Arts (VGII) at the Department of Humanities and Social and Economic Disciplines. Experience of scientific and pedagogical work - 28 years, including teaching experience in higher educational institutions - 25 years. Repeatedly took part and took first place in the All-Russian Olympiad for the development of the national economy of Russia, held by the Youth Union of Economists and Financiers (MSEF) of the Russian Federation. Has a Letter of Acknowledgment from the Department of Education, Science and Youth Policy of the Voronezh Region (department order No. 157M dated December 8, 2009). Research interests: History: specialty 07.00.02 Domestic history (the history of the Great Patriotic War, the history of the Russian Orthodox Church); Economics: specialties 08.00.01 - economic theory, 08.01.05 - finance and credit. The number of scientific publications on elibrary.ru is 219. The Hirsch index for all publications is 13. Personal and professional qualities: during his scientific and pedagogical work, he has established himself as a knowledgeable, proactive, demanding employee of himself and others, a good organizer, responsible, sociable worker, respected among the team. Has the ability to learn quickly and improve the level of his education and qualifications. Currently lives and works in the city of Voronezh, Voronezh region, Russia. Has a driver's license.

Index

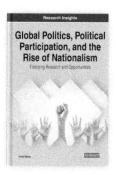

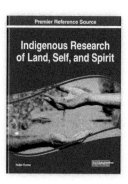

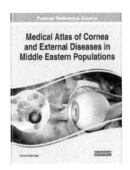

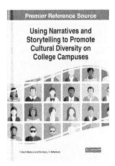

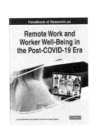

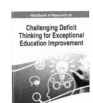

Lightning Source UK Ltd.
Milton Keynes UK
UKHW050728240622
404913UK00006B/448

9 781668 449165